How Will the Heart Endure

Photograph of Elizabeth Bowen, taken by Alfred A. Knopf in Regent's Park, London, 1946. (Courtesy of Mrs. Alfred A. Knopf.)

How Will the Heart Endure

Elizabeth Bowen and the Landscape of War

Heather Bryant Jordan

Ann Arbor

THE UNIVERSITY OF MICHIGAN PRESS

Copyright © by the University of Michigan 1992
All rights reserved
Published in the United States of America by
The University of Michigan Press
Manufactured in the United States of America

1995 1994 1993 1992   4 3 2 1

Library of Congress Cataloging-in-Publication Data

Jordan, Heather Bryant, 1959–
    How will the heart endure? : Elizabeth Bowen and the landscape of war / Heather Bryant Jordan.
       p.   cm.
    Includes bibliographical references and index.
    ISBN 0-472-10218-4 (alk. paper)
     1. Bowen, Elizabeth, 1899–1973—Criticism and interpretation.
2. Ireland—History—Civil War, 1922–1923—Literature and the war.
3. World War, 1914–1918—Literature and the war. 4. World War, 1939–1945—Literature and the war. 5. Ireland in literature.
6. War in literature.   I. Title.
PR6003.06757Z674   1992
823'.912—dc20   92-173
                                                                  CIP

For my parents

Literature is like landscape: its foreground,
the present, packed with moving figures,
sometimes too close to be judged; its
background, the past, showing these mountain
ranges which are the classics—but even
these seem to change, seem more or less
distant, higher or lower, as mountains do, in
the varying, changing lights of our own day.
—Cyril Connolly

War in the air, war of attrition, tank war,
war of propaganda, war of defence in depth,
war of movement, people's war, total war,
indivisible war, war infinite, war
incomprehensible, war of essence without
accidents, or attributes, metaphysical war,
war in time—space, war eternal.
—Evelyn Waugh

You play against a sickness past your cure.
How will the hands be strong? How will the heart endure?
—Robert Lowell

Preface

I first saw a copy of *Bowen's Court* on my mother's bedside table when I was fifteen years old. The image on the dust jacket of the classical gray stone facade of a house rising up out of the misty Irish landscape immediately captured my attention. Many years later, while I was reading for a doctoral examination, I rediscovered Elizabeth Bowen. It seemed to me then that her work expressed salient but contradictory responses to literary modernism and to contemporary events, particularly the two world wars. Sydney Warren, a young woman in residence in Bowen's first novel, *The Hotel*, appears to take many opposing ideas from the books she reads. Poised self-consciously on the verge of becoming "modern," she admits to a slight "degeneracy" in reading Hardy's *Jude the Obscure* before lunch.

Bowen embodied many paradoxes that are of interest to me: She avowed allegiance to the British literary inheritance, yet she also insisted on her membership in what she called the Anglo-Irish "race"; she loved her "Big House," the large Georgian house traditionally built by the Anglo-Irish on Irish soil; she wrote as a woman but denied that she was a feminist in any kind of political or social sense; she claimed not to be a historian, but she often discussed historical events in fiction and in essays. While I saw obvious intonations of the English novel in her work—a concern with the intricacies of social exchanges, a belief in class distinctions, and a focus on London and the English countryside—I began to discern more of the Irish tradition in her writing. This orientation manifested itself in her love of ghosts, in the unexpected twist at the end of a short story, in her sense of humor, her attachment to the soil, her love of word play—all made evident in her calling as a teller of tales.

It became increasingly obvious to me that Bowen was not simply recording through her fiction a brittle scene composed of tea parties and calling cards; she did not only portray the limited view that Peter de Vries's parody suggests: "Youth comes to an end in the afternoon. Middle Age arrives in the evening with the first book one rereads, but youth draws to a close in the afternoon, particularly a Friday afternoon in autumn."[1] Rather, her work conveys an alert awareness of each of the eras through which she lived, a sharp understanding of the history that she saw unfold.

While not a political writer in the familiar sense of the word, she created novels, short stories, essays, and autobiographical works in a war-torn world that saw successively the Great War, the guerilla war known as the Troubles in Ireland (1919–21), the Irish Civil War (1922–23), and finally the Second World War. Bowen's participation in these battles—as a resident of a Big House occupied during "the Troubled Times," as a nurse in Dublin in the First World War, and as both an air raid warden and an employee of the Ministry of Information in London during the Second World War—sharpened her consciousness of and involvement in present-day events. These military and political conflicts came to signify her intensely personal vision of loss and betrayal.[2]

With the introduction of historical context into the realm of private association, the atmosphere of a novel, always so important in Bowen's work, became charged with a new force. The insane, the homeless, and the surreal (in the shape of ghosts) intrude upon the drawing rooms and love affairs she depicted. The wars she endured became, then, not only abstractions but also emblems of what she detected to be wrong with the world and the century she inhabited. Her writing represents a lifelong attempt to trace what she perceived had gone wrong with her generation, which had "come to be made to feel it had muffed the catch."[3] She conveyed a similar sense of incompleteness in a letter to Virginia Woolf dated January 5 (1941). Bowen confessed that she felt "a sort of despair about my own generation—the people the same age as the century, I mean—we don't really suffer much but we get all sealed up."[4] Her inescapable proximity to these overlapping wars altered the way she described or imagined the smallest, most intimate details of character and setting, even in peacetime.

Born in Dublin in 1899 to parents Anglo-Irish on both sides, Florence Colley Bowen and Henry Cole Bowen, Elizabeth Dorothea Cole Bowen took her place in a family who had come to Ireland in 1653 under Oliver Cromwell. Her parents, expecting her to be a boy, had already chosen the name of Henry's father, Robert. The arrival of a daughter signaled the first time that, as she wrote in her autobiography, male heirs had "failed for the County Cork property."[5] By the fact of her birth, this only child of older parents became tethered to the mostly unspoken expectations of her property-minded family. She remembers her childhood home as being "at once unique and intensive, gently phenomenal" ("Herbert Place," 9). While she passed winters in Dublin, where her father practiced law, the Bowens ventured every summer to the family home, which dated from 1775, in County Cork. From the start her life was split between town and country, between present and past. And her fiction and her autobiographical writings draw vividly upon these first impressionable years, which she described as the most "acute" of her life.[6]

When Bowen was seven, the pattern of her life changed dramatically after her father suffered a form of nervous breakdown, which her biographer Victoria Glendinning has termed "anaemia of the brain."[7] Apparently, Henry Bowen had inherited the family propensity for attacks of nerves and depression and this siege necessitated solitary rest in a hospital outside Dublin. The combined strain from the simultaneous pressures of maintaining the estate while working on the Irish Land Commission and practicing law in Dublin had all contributed to his collapse. (The memory of his illness made a lasting impression on his daughter, who watched carefully for any manifestations of the family tendency toward mental instability.) In the winter of 1906 Bowen left her father and accompanied her mother to stay with relatives on the south coast of England. Sadly, she later noted her difference from preceding Bowens when she described herself as the first child in the family "to make the experiment" of living in England.[8]

An extended family of aunts and cousins on her mother's side surrounded the journeying Bowens on their arrival in England. As an adult, Bowen remembered that "all that could be done was done to make me think of England not as exile but as a new kind of treat" (*BC* 418). Despite her fond memories of those early years, at the time she reacted to the rawness of the double loss, however temporary, of her father and Ireland. The distinctive stammer, which never left her, first appeared at this time, and this hesitancy in speech became one of her hallmarks. Perhaps this difficulty was born of self-consciousness. From the outset Bowen sensed her difference from her English peers: her "sense of nationality showed itself" in her "wish to out-English the English by being impassibly fashionable and correct" (*BC* 420). While the Irish looked upon the Anglo-Irish as "an excrescence," the English believed them to be "an anachronism" for whom they had little patience.[9] After her death Howard Moss ascribed Bowen's particular predicament to the dilemma of being "Irish in England and English in Ireland." Her brand of what F. S. L. Lyons has called the "schizophrenia" of the Anglo-Irish became more pronounced as she tried to perpetuate what she judged valuable in her inheritance.[10]

Bowen represents perhaps the last writer who attempted to forge such a full compromise between two opposed traditions. Even the term *Anglo-Irish* has become part of the controversy surrounding Bowen's ancestors. Some critics, like Seamus Deane, have suggested that the appellation itself has become an anachronism.[11] The historian James C. Beckett defines the anomaly by arguing that the Anglo-Irish are "in fact Irish, without any hyphenated prefix; and the fact that they must be distinguished by some special term reflects the unhealed divisions of Ireland." It seems imperative to employ a study of the Anglo-Irish, or what R. F. Foster calls "the culture of the exaggerated attitude," to discuss Bowen's work because the phrase itself suggests the contradictions and paradoxes that continually divided her existence.[12]

Race, the term Bowen used to discuss the Anglo-Irish, derives from her conception of the cultural dimension of the word as that which defines a "geographical, national, or tribal ethnic grouping."[13] Deane postulates that to arrive at her stance, Bowen drew on the idea Edmond Burke had "promoted that the character of a race was formed by the conditions in which it had developed, the customs to which it had adhered, the mentality which it had inherited."[14] Her conviction that the strength of the shared experience of her ancestors justified the designation of a race distinct from both the Irish and the English affirms the same assumptions that so many other Anglo-Irish had held before her. She defined *class* in the same terms, grounding her fundamental comprehension of it in race, a position particularly evident in her study of the middle class in *The Heat of the Day*. The anachronistic socioeconomic distinctions that she drew contributed to her portrayal of the world as a polarized and precarious place.

The death of her mother in 1912 further jeopardized Bowen's already shaky bearings. Soon after suffering this traumatic loss, which she remembered as an eternity when she "should never trust life again," Bowen was sent to Harpenden Hall, a day school in Hertfordshire.[15] Later she enrolled in the Downe House School in southern England as a boarder. She obviously began to recover from her sadness because for the most part she recalled enjoying these schools, particularly the second, where she received a traditional classical education. On vacations she joined her mother's extended family in England, and, when her father healed, she once again began to pass her summers at Bowen's Court. The day she learned of the outbreak of the First World War she was, in fact, attending her first garden party at Mitchelstown Castle in Ireland.

During the troubled years from 1916 to 1922, which culminated in the Civil War, Bowen often spent time in County Cork, where she was briefly engaged to a British soldier stationed near her family's house. This first romance, combined with her own proximity to both the Anglo-Irish War and the Irish Civil War, strongly affected her outlook, as did the First World War. She became aware of this war when it engulfed her schooldays on the south coast of England. Simultaneously, the war brought a consciousness of guilt and heroism; she later said that she and her classmates "grew up under the intolerable obligation of being fought for." Using a familiar analytic categorization in her essay on "Downe House," she likened the world at war to her own age group: "The world seemed to be bound up in a tragic attack of adolescence."[16] When she left school in 1918 she answered the universal call to aid the war effort, heeded so strongly by her gender and class, by volunteering as a nurse for shell-shocked soldiers in a Dublin hospital.

Much later, Bowen reminisced about her formal education as a daughter of the Protestant Ascendancy, which consisted of reading widely but randomly, learning to write, studying history and drama, and appreciating how to get along with other people. She was to draw on the many facets of this far-ranging study. After the war had ended she interspersed her time in Ireland with trips to the Continent, noting her native country's affinity with the European tradition she admired. When she grew tired of travel, she acted upon her early interest in art and enrolled in the London County Council School of Art for a brief interval. After this unsuccessful and short-lived experiment she began to contemplate journalism. This course of inquiry led her to discover her gift for fiction when she wrote a few tentative and halting short stories while staying with a cousin in London. Characterizing these years in retrospect, she recognized that her eclectic search for an occupation seemed marked by her "flitting mind."[17]

The instability of Bowen's early years taught her to draw upon her imagination for a lasting reservoir of emotional enrichment. Fortunately, she had discovered in the turbulence of her childhood that she had a "wonderful visual memory."[18] Later, as an adult, she conceived of herself as a painter *manquée* who was "trying to make words do the work of line and colour" in her writing.[19] Other writers, such as V. S. Pritchett, referred to this trait: "You must be one of those writers who, like painters, actually see what they write as they write it. It stays for you to look at."[20] Recording her impressions in visual images became an imperative for Bowen. Just after the Second World War she claimed that "when I have nothing to write I feel only half alive."[21]

After a brief courtship Bowen married Alan Cameron in the summer of 1923, the same year that her first short stories appeared. Their union lasted until his death in 1952. He apparently answered some questions deep in her soul. She had written to him in the winter before their wedding, "There is something in you that can use up everything that is in me and still want more. —I suppose that is why I love you."[22] By virtue of her connection to Cameron, an employee of the British Broadcasting Corporation (BBC), she lived primarily in England, becoming a well-known inhabitant of a Regent's Terrace house in London who frequently entertained, among others, John and Rosamond Lehmann, Cyril Connolly, Stephen Spender, and Virginia Woolf. But she always maintained her identification with Ireland: Her father's death in 1930 marked the beginning of her ownership of Bowen's Court and the beginning of her long, arduous effort to keep the estate alive.

When Bowen appeared on the BBC radio show "Desert Island Disks" in 1957, she included among her list of essentials for life on an uninhabited island Beethoven's piano sonatas, Schubert, Mozart, Strauss, Bach, jazz, two decks of cards, a copy of *Emma,* and a kaleidoscope.[23] A love of music and the sonority of language, as well as her impish enjoyment of games, became her trademarks. Guests at parties at Bowen's Court often occupied their evenings with party games, cards, or Scrabble. When given the chance, Bowen would suggest her favorite game—one of her own invention called "Bad Parties"—which asked each player to compile hypothetical guest lists for the most disastrous dinner parties.[24]

Bowen's simultaneous vision of "the funniness, poetry, and near-brutality" of a social situation grew from a vivacious and energetic approach to life, which she subsequently filtered into her fiction.[25] Seán O'Faoláin understood her well when he called her "our great illusionist, sometimes her own self-hypnotist."[26] Yet, it was in her literary criticism that she left a most telling trail of hints, contradictions, and imperatives about the way she wished to be remembered. Although she believed strongly in the importance of "the critical faculty," which "no creative writer... can afford to lack," she distinguished this ability from skill in writing reviews or pronouncing judgments on value and character.[27] Typically, she deprecated her own powers of discernment, calling herself "at most, an impressionistic critic" who wrote criticism only as "a form of afterthought."[28] Not surprisingly, despite her proclivity for self-disparagement, her assessments of her own work were usually extremely shrewd.

Horrified at the possibility of being misunderstood, she once declared after reading several studies of herself which she lamented as wrong-headed, "if anybody *must* write a book about Elizabeth Bowen, why should not Elizabeth Bowen?"[29] She feared the intrusions of the words of others. In discussing Henry James, the writer who critics most often select as having influenced her, Bowen said in an interview in 1968: "I would never read him when I was writing. He's infectious, like a rash."[30] Much of her energy went toward inventing, and then protecting, the person and the writer that she wanted to be.

Above all, in commenting on her own work, Bowen maintained her belief in the primacy of her artistic purpose. No matter how great the emotional crisis facing her, she claimed that she always started by asking herself: "What effect is this having on me as a writer?"[31] Proud of her self-control, she hated the idea of being viewed simply as a quivering mass of female sensibility. When asked to pronounce on the distinctions between men and women, she enumerated women's gifts as "flexibility, ... quickness on the uptake... sensitiveness... and sympathetic attitudes towards the other person's point of view."[32] She remained vehement in her conviction that "great novelists write... from outside their own nationality, class, or sex."[33] Her literary criticism reflects her insistence both that the novelist must write outside her own "preassumptions [sic]" and that she must not sacrifice a moral viewpoint.[34] As a person determined to accomplish all that she set out to do, she had little time for the organized struggle for women's rights. In 1936 she decreed that while "a good deal remains to be righted... broadly, the woman's movement has accomplished itself."[35] Whatever her declamations, she remained sensitive to the particular difficulties women encountered in their lives. She often fashioned female characters who lead dull, quiet, and unsatisfactorily narrow existences. And, in her 1961 article

"Women's Place in the Affairs of Men," Bowen announced, "I am not, and shall never be, a feminist."[36] But, just as emphatically, the claustrophobic Lady Waters in *To the North* declares, "I do not believe in interests for women."[37]

Bowen included herself in the company of artists, rather than feminists. She eschewed membership in the tradition of women writers because the association, she feared, trivialized their work. Instead, she staked her claim to the realm of the geographic and creative, calling herself an "intuitive writer" who is "psychologically if not actually" a "regionalist," one concerned with a place but not provincial.[38] She explained, however, that she was "not a 'regional' writer in the accredited sense" ("Places," 35). Even though she feared that her Anglo-Irishness might underline the perception that her sphere was too narrow, she was proud of that identity, claiming that it gave her a special passport to cross many fictional borders. Her characters travel often and sentiently to real and imagined destinations. It was no accident, she said, that, "Bowen characters are in transit"; they move "*consciously*." They traverse "the Bowen terrain which cannot be demarcated on any existing map" because "it is unspecific." In the same breath she insisted that "topography" gives to fiction its "verisimilitude" ("Places," 41, 35, 34). Perhaps because she remained deeply attached to such real landscapes as southern Ireland and the south coast of England, she was unwilling to trust her recreations of them entirely because "the senses enter deeply into love of place, and the senses are unfaithful, easily won away" (*BC* 418). Hence, she took refuge in the creation of fictional locales that could not betray her.

When she began to write, she self-consciously acknowledged the public exposure entailed in practicing her private craft by disclaiming a relation between herself and her work. Throughout Bowen's novels, however, this issue weighs heavily. Lois Farquar, the heroine of *The Last September,* whose circumstances closely resemble Bowen's own, confesses that she does not want to write because "that's so embarrassing. Even things like—like elephants get so personal." Her confidante, a slightly older English woman, answers, perhaps sympathetically, "I know. I gave up reading—I'm sick of their personal elephants."[39]

Few book-length studies of Bowen exist, in part because the meaning of her work is difficult to grasp, to catalog, or even to comprehend; she saw to that. Restless and contradictory, her very reversals make for her continuing importance to any study of the literature of Anglo-Ireland, modernism, women, and, most important, war. Some of her best work, particularly the novels and short stories she produced concerning World War Two, demonstrate what Julian Moynahan has called "a scrupulous attachment to the highest Modernist standards . . . and an acute, sometimes devouring awareness of her own time and place."[40]

I am most concerned with the intersection in Bowen's work between this time and place as she reconstructed in fiction the rapidly modernizing age through which she lived. My study, which began all those years ago with a dust jacket picture of Bowen's Court, by necessity must involve not a few of Bowen's "personal elephants." As I have continued to read her work, I have come to realize that she must be seen in the context of the extraordinary events that she fictionalized. This book investigates the intersection of the poetics of loss with the politics of war through the writings of Elizabeth Bowen, a woman born on the eve of what has been called by many the century of "total war."

Acknowledgments

I would like to recognize the many kind and astute individuals who have made this book possible. My advisors and colleagues at the University of Michigan, James Gindin, George Bornstein, and Leo McNamara, have enriched the progress of my work since I first began talking about Elizabeth Bowen. I would also like to thank other Bowen scholars in England, Hermione Lee and Victoria Glendinning, for their generosity to a young American. For fellowships that supported travel to England and to the Humanities Research Center at Austin, Texas, and that made possible a year off from teaching, I thank the Horace H. Rackham School of Graduate Studies at the University of Michigan. My editor at the press, LeAnn Fields, has also been extremely resourceful.

At the many archives where I have worked I have been fortunate to have encountered intelligent and resourceful guidance. Cathy Henderson of the Humanities Research Center at the University of Texas at Austin was most cooperative. At the Berg Collection of the New York Public Library, the late curator, Dr. Lola L. Szladits, offered me imaginative assistance. Sally Brown and Ilse Sternberg at the British Library; Rodney Dennis, the former curator of manuscripts at Houghton Library, Harvard University; the staff at the Public Records Office at Kew (London); Michael Halls, the keeper of twentieth-century manuscripts at King's College Library, Cambridge; Mrs. Elizabeth Inglis of the library of the University of Sussex; David Burnett of the Durham University library; and Glenise Matheson of the John Rylands University Library of Manchester guided me sensibly and ably in my search through England for Bowen manuscripts. For continuous and indispensable assistance, I also want to thank the reference librarians at the University of Michigan and at Harvard University.

To those among my family, friends, and colleagues who have patiently and generously read and commented on the book in its varying stages, I give my deepest appreciation. My family and friends (all of them) have been wise and patient in their practical and philosophical guidance. I want to thank my grandmother, Irene Corbally Kuhn, whose family came from County Cork long ago and who first taught me to travel to Ireland in my imagination. For their critical faculties, their good humor, and their many gifts, I thank my mother and father. My husband, John, has lived with this project longer than anyone. To him I offer gratitude beyond measure for his insight and steadfast presence as reader, computer data retriever, joke maker, and stalwart companion in all adventures.

Grateful acknowledgment is made to the various individuals, libraries, literary agencies, and publishing houses for kind permission to quote previously published or copyrighted material.

Curtis Brown, Ltd., London: All previously unpublished Elizabeth Bowen material.

Faber and Faber, Ltd.: "Summer Night" by W. H. Auden, from *Collected Poems*. London: Faber and Faber, 1950. Reprinted by permission of Faber and Faber.

Rupert Hart-Davis: Excerpts from letters from William Plomer to Elizabeth Bowen.

A. M. Heath: Excerpt from a letter from Elizabeth Taylor to Elizabeth Bowen.

Mrs. Frances Hickson, for the Society of Authors: Excerpts from letters from Rosamond Lehmann to Elizabeth Bowen.

Houghton Library, Harvard University: Drawing of Bowen's Court. By permission of the Houghton Library, Harvard University.

Imperial War Museum, London: Fougasse [Cyril Kenneth Bird] drawing, "But for Heaven's Sake."

Macmillan Publishing Company: Excerpts from "Coole and Ballylee, 1931," by W. B. Yeats. Reprinted with permission of Macmillan Publishing Company from *The Poems: A New Edition,* ed. Richard J.

Finneran. Copyright 1933 by Macmillan Publishing Company, renewed 1961 by Bertha Georgie Yeats.

"A Nightingale Sang in Berkeley Square," written by Eric Maschwitz and Manning Sherwin, © 1940, The Peter Maurice Music Company, Ltd., London, England. Copyright renewed. Used by permission.

John Murray: Osbert Lancaster cartoon, "Of course, the work" from *More Pocket Cartoons,* published by John Murray. Copyright 1943.

Mrs. R. H. Oakeley: Excerpts from John Hayward's letters to Frank Morley.

Oxford University Press: Excerpt from letter from Gerard Hopkins to Elizabeth Bowen, by permission of Oxford University Press on behalf of the Society of Jesus.

V. S. Pritchett: Excerpt from a letter to Elizabeth Bowen.

Stephen Spender: Excerpt from a letter to Elizabeth Bowen.

The title is taken from "Mr. Edwards and the Spider" (1946) by Robert Lowell.

Every attempt has been made to trace the ownership of copyrighted material and to obtain permission for its use.

Contents

Chapter

1. The Lens of War 1
2. A Valiant Myth 13
3. "Innocently Abroad" 31
4. Tennis Parties and Ambushes 47
5. "The Map of Europe" 61
6. "A Madman on a Motorcycle" 83
7. Rifling the Past 107
8. "The Saving Hallucination" 129
9. Fictional Silences 153
10. A Fantastical World 169

Abbreviations 193
Notes 195
Bibliography 229
Index 249

Chapter 1

The Lens of War

War, loss, and destruction were familiar presences throughout Elizabeth Bowen's life from her birth in 1899 until her death in 1973. When she visited the Ballsbridge racetrack grandstands of the Royal Dublin Society as a young child, she made a Proustian association between that place and her first awareness of war.[1] As she recalled during the Second World War, the distant Russo-Japanese conflict penetrated the vagaries of her imagination because it made concrete her fear that "war had, that year, escaped from that locked strong-room of history into the present." Even though she was told that the battle was happening "at the unsafe other side of the world," that winter morning confirmed her inherent suspicion about the fragility of her universe: When the clock tolled at the grandstands, she knew that "time held war. The hour was more than my hour; within it people were fighting" ("Horse Show," 25, 26).[2] War continually altered Bowen's understanding of her world.

While Bowen endured the several preceding wars, the brutality and totality of the Second World War affected her with a new kind of intensity and urgency. She shared with her contemporaries the horror of a war that came so close to them. Virginia Woolf made the point in 1940 that she could "hear gunfire in the Channel. We turn on the wireless; we hear an airman telling us how this very afternoon he shot down a raider; his machine caught fire; . . . he was rescued by a trawler." Unlike earlier novelists such as Sir Walter Scott, who "never saw the sailors drowning at Trafalgar," or Jane Austen, who "never heard the cannon roar at Waterloo," the Woolfs could hear Hitler "as we sit home of an evening."[3]

Faced with a reality that could not be apprehended by means of conventional fictions, Bowen habitually addressed her own discordant attitudes by identifying continuities she saw stretching from earlier eras into her own time. Over the years she developed a firm habit of turning to the product of her imagination, writing, to allay the rawness of the everyday world. During the Second World War her self-appointed mission directed her to autobiography, where she traced the origins of the disasters: "From the declamation on the eve of the duel to the Nazi monologue has not really been such a far cry."[4] Such excavations of the palimpsest of history became the hallmark of her wartime writing. When Bowen discussed her enduring political allegiance to the Tory party, she returned to the realm of literature, citing her early reading of *The Scarlet Pimpernel* by Baroness Orczy as the agent that led her to "hate" the French Revolution and, consequently, wish to join this party of tradition.[5] The remove of fiction allowed her a means to distance herself from the conflicts, such as those surrounding the Anglo-Irish, that tested her natural political ambivalence. The landscape of war, which she perceived "more as a territory than as a page of history," appears throughout the work she created as the agent of resistance and salvation.[6]

In a discussion with V. S. Pritchett and Graham Greene just after the Second World War about the writer's relation to the outside world, Bowen declared, "You make a society each time you write a story"; "My books *are* my relation to society."[7] Impatient with the idea of a solitary artist mired in the lonely process of creation, she believed instead that "the artist's natural place is in the heart of human society."[8] To this end she worked to fashion intimate and sensible bonds that would link the external world with the one of her invention. This impulse continued, gathering strength after the wars she witnessed had ended. Indeed, she was still pressing for the connection between the inner and the outer when she wrote in 1957 that "the novel has never not been at grips with modern society."[9]

Always singularly sensitive to privation, Bowen's war writing examines the extended ramifications of many different kinds of destitution. The sense of bereavement works at many levels: loss of love between two characters, loss of voice, loss of understanding, loss of a mother, loss of a home, and loss of a country. The wars dominating her adult years all threatened the biggest of the Big Houses in Bowen's mind: civilization itself. The pressure of the Second World War "brought out her fullest powers" as a writer in a time "when what people *said* could not match the experience."[10] War's dislocations, both personal and social, forced the author to recognize her innate and continuing sense of the precariousness of existence, and she transferred this perception into her fiction.

Bowen's attitude toward war perhaps recalls the age-old Irish tradition of associating female spirits, like the valkyries, with "battle and death."[11] As the feminist historian Denise Riley has written, "war throws gender into sharp relief."[12] And in a similar spirit Virginia Woolf described in May of 1940 that "the army is the body: I am the brain. Thinking is my fighting."[13] Writing her treatise *Three Guineas* during the Spanish Civil War, Woolf postulated that "it seems plain that we [men and women] think differently according as we are born differently." She listed three reasons that compel men to fight: "War is a profession; a source of happiness and excitement; and it is also an outlet for manly qualities." Women, she argued, "can best help you to prevent war not by joining your society but by remaining outside your society but in cooperation with its aim."[14] Bowen's peacetime and wartime fictions reflect this interest, articulated by Woolf, in the implicit distinctions of gender invoked by war.

Both world wars posed and then underscored the questions regarding the relations between women and men that have continued to plague the Western world for much of the twentieth century. More specifically, total war was said to have "acted as a clarifying moment, one that . . . revealed systems of gender in flux."[15] Women like Bowen who lived through the nightmares of two world wars also benefitted from some of the social gains for women, such as the vote and new economic and social freedom. Although Bowen readily admitted that she was not a "feminist" (in this she parallels Woolf, who was a feminist, even if she herself "did not like the term"), she lived in a way that suggested her belief in the importance of the possibility of choice among opportunities for women.[16]

In her recent essay on women and war, Jane Marcus writes of the specific "ideological conjunction of women, war, and madness" which occurred in the lives of women who endured a world war, particularly those who emerged from the first.[17] Through a prescient fictional illustration of this observation, Bowen presents Cousin Nettie, the slightly dotty female character in *The Heat of the Day* (1949), as only partially aware of her world, glimpsed through a slit in the lace curtains. She has failed the expectations of her class, the Anglo-Irish gentry, by not being able to produce an heir for the estate. Cousin Nettie has been sentenced to spend her days knitting yards of woolens into unfathomable shapes at Wisteria Lodge, a rest home for the unstable. Hoping to keep her shielded from the war, her keepers warn her visitors not to speak of events occurring outside the lodge. Roderick, her nephew, who inherits the estate on the death of his uncle (in his role as the imaginary son), wishes to discuss this prospect with her. To the dismay of her vigilant guardians at the lodge, he arrives in uniform to have tea with his relative. Despite the fact that she appears protected from the hard truths of wartime life, comfortable in her loneliness and eccentricity, she seems to recognize more than we might like to admit.

A large number of some of the finest women writers of the period, such as Bowen, Rose Macaulay, E. M. Delafield, Winifred Holtby, Storm Jameson, Rosamond Lehmann, F. M. Mayor, Dorothy Richardson, Rebecca West, and Virginia Woolf, spent considerable energy describing or imagining women's and men's experiences of war.[18] This literature differs from that written during or about other wars because of the new importance that British women assumed with the onset of the Second World War. As Margaret Goldsmith wrote in a book published in 1943, *Women at War,* "For the first time in their lives thousands of English women have done essential work, have become a vital part of the society." She continued, "if the people of England refuse to allow their women-power to become stagnant and unused during peace, all these girls and older women ... will become an essential and constructive part of the peace as well." That was to take time. She pointed to the fact "that large numbers of [women] have gradually become more self-reliant, and have learned to use their own judgement and initiative." But she also recorded inequality; women who began in Civil Defense and Services were, at the start of the war, paid only two-thirds of what men received. Even in London at the beginning of the war there were "women wardens [who] were not allowed to patrol the streets." Needless to say, said Goldsmith, there was a "great outcry" at these injustices.[19] As the war worsened, these distinctions broke down as women had to assume new and more responsible positions in aid of the defense of the country and the manufacture of munitions.

But when those like Bowen gamely put on helmets and carried out their duties as air raid wardens a dramatic change occurred in the way men and women regarded one another, and these transformations could not help but make their ways into the fiction of these years. As Goldsmith wrote, "the whole attitude of the male population towards women in England has profoundly altered since the heavy raids, when the women demonstrated how fearless they could be. Englishmen are proud of their women... but I sometimes wonder whether, mixed with this pride, there is not in some of the men a feeling of sad regret."[20] She was right to wonder; daily life between men and women would not be the same again.

Images of death and violence ceaselessly menace the women and men portrayed in the novels and short stories Bowen produced so prolifically throughout her career. In *The House in Paris* (1935), a young girl, Henrietta, becomes an unwilling witness to the tears of her contemporary, Leopold. The young boy has been brutally disappointed by the news that he will not, after all, be meeting his mother for the first time in many years. His sobbing represents to Henrietta "all the tears that had ever been denied... for the man standing beside his own crashed 'plane, the woman tearing up somebody's fatal letter... people watching their family house burn, the general giving his sword up."[21] Bowen's choice of metaphors derives from war, from betrayal, from the burning of the family house—all experiences that darkened her personal vision.

In her fiction Bowen focused particularly intensely on what one of her characters describes as "the crack across the crust of life," flawed existence (*HP* 136). Some of the tension in her work, as she acknowledges, results from the fact that words can only represent an imperfect exchange, always subject to revision or misinterpretation. Emmeline, a young woman in *To the North* (1932), explains this dilemma: "one has to speak: words twist everything; what one agrees about can't be spoken. To talk is always to quarrel a little, or misunderstand" (*TTN* 194). The difficulty comes when the only shared currency in relationships is based on words, which form the elusive memories that Bowen's characters pursue. In a lyrical introduction to the retrospective middle section of *The House in Paris,* the narrator comments, "you suppose the spools of negatives that are memory... developed without being cut for a false reason: entire letters, dialogues which, once spoken, remain spoken for ever being unwound from the dark, word by word" (*HP* 67). Bowen's search for the buried link between memory and experience led her to write fictions that perpetually created and recreated the connections she saw among war, loss, and words.

Like the protagonist in *The Heat of the Day,* Stella Rodney, a middle-aged divorcée who is "younger by a year or two than the century," Bowen was almost the same age as the twentieth century.[22] Many of her characters, especially those Anglo-Irish who appeared in her fiction written in wartime, discover themselves entangled in an uneasy relationship with their present. The men are often middle-aged, too old for the Second World War but too young to have served in the First; they appear out of step with their times. And the female characters also recognize a discordance between their expectations for their lives, and the world as it is, as though they are dancing to a fading rhythm. Resembling her characters in this way, Bowen was always trying to discover just where she belonged.

When she began to frequent the London scene she became acquainted with Virginia Woolf, who described Bowen almost as an abstraction. In her diary entry for March 16, 1936, Woolf wrote, "I went to E. Bowen & I sat in her glass shining 'contemporary' room like a French picture—2 ladies looking out at the Lake."[23] After Bowen's visit to Monk's House in June, 1940, Woolf dissected her disconcerting habit of speaking, which "had a disintegrating effect: like a moth buzzing around a flower—her whirr of voice as she cant alight on a word." Woolf sketched her as having "a very honourable horse-faced, upper class hard constricted mind."[24] Perhaps Bowen sensed that she was being examined with a microscope. Cyril Connolly recalled in his memoir a conversation with Bowen where she talked of "the awfulness of women writers and the nastiness of her friend Mrs. Woolf."[25] To most observers, Bowen appeared a staunch member of the English upper class, and to a large degree she cultivated that image. She liked elegant mansions, expensive clothes, foreign travel, and fine food, perhaps as a result of her days in the Big House.

Yet the disjunction that Bowen perceived between the world into which she had been born and the one she afterward came to know was very real indeed. In fact, her first world, that of the Anglo-Irish gentry who wintered in Dublin and summered at the ancestral Big House, was already being eclipsed at the time of her birth. Its decline rapidly accelerated in the First World War and later in the Troubles, which soon devolved into the Irish Civil War.[26] For Bowen and her contemporaries, both English and Anglo-Irish, there seemed an identifiable moment when the world changed: August 4, 1914. Writing her biography of Roger Fry, published in 1940, Woolf claimed that "a break must be made in every life when August 1914 is reached."[27] For Bowen the date became a point of reference. She later described the days of September 1938 as being like "1914 but without even the illusion of 1914."[28] Those who belonged officially to "the generation of 1914" had been riding a series of crises that went back to 1895: the Boer War, Fashoda, the Russo-Japanese War, Agadir, and the Balkan wars.[29]

The belief that the world altered ineluctably in one instant obscured the fact that the world as Bowen had known it had been realigning itself all along. As one historian of 1914 put it, "the truth was that Ithaca had begun to change long before they had embarked for Troy."[30] For writers like L. P. Hartley, the mood that existed before 1914 could not be recaptured: "Wartime was a different kind of life from peacetime, nor have we in England ever recovered the pre-1914 feeling."[31] It seemed impossible, when a Second World War was raging, to forget the legacy of that first war when "the human imagination was one of the combatants."[32]

Writing in war carried with it many complications, hesitancies, and trials. In Paul Fussell's view, "if war is a political, social, and psychological disaster, it is also a perceptual and rhetorical scandal from which total recovery is unlikely."[33] For Bowen, war became more than a scandal. As her colleague Cyril Connolly complained, "we've got the race war, the class war, the age war, the sex war going simultaneously."[34] These various struggles intersected in Bowen, living and working as an Anglo-Irishwoman in London during World War II. She indicated some of the difficulties she encountered through her characters in *The Heat of the Day*, who utilize the methods of traitors to mask their own inadequacies and fears.

Because of its very nature, particularly in relation to the war of 1914–18, literary critics have often not known how to assess the literature that the Second World War inspired. Often the words produced during these years have simply been passed over, as less good than those about the First World War, as strange, prosaic, and banal.[35] Not only did the position of the observer or participant present obstacles to the writer in wartime, but so also did conceptions of language itself. Issues of censorship and control sometimes got in the way of the writer: a bombing was an "incident," and in Ireland the war was referred to only as "the Emergency." Such restrictions made clear expression more problematic than ever. In his analysis of what he calls the "silent" quality of World War II for its participants, Fussell points to the ideological focus of the war as being partly responsible: "if every element and utter impulse of society is busy eradicating wickedness, before long you will come to believe that therefore you yourself must incarnate pure goodness."[36]

The First World War served doubly as a reminder of what war could be and a cautionary note about the greatness of the literary work it had inspired. For those who had survived, that war was a sober reminder as they launched into the second. L. P. Hartley remembered that the course of the second war seemed lugubrious, indefinite: "sentiment and emotion lived on, as witness the hold that Armistice Day, November 11, 1918, still keeps on the public mind."[37] Yet Fussell has observed that it was only when the Second World War was over "that one could realize how near Victorian social and ethical norms the First World War really was."[38] Radically different from one another, the two wars affected entirely divergent sections of the population; while only 5 percent of the casualties in the first were made up of civilians, in the second the number rose to 44 percent.[39]

Bowen's wartime writing resonates with the generalized pain and horror engendered by her individual experience as a writer, a civilian, and a government employee. And in her estimation, she was rescuing the cultural and historical heritage that had shaped her as an individual through her writing and her wartime work. Ireland's choice of neutrality during the war tested her dual allegiance to both islands, as she alternately tromped through nights of air raids in London as a warden and then journeyed to Ireland as a reporter for the British Ministry of Information. While she identified strongly with England during the war, she could not forget the land that had supported her Big House, which represented for her, as for Yeats, civilization and harmony. Bowen's insistence on calling these imposed conquerors in Ireland a race echoes Matthew Arnold, who had once cataloged the distinctions between the English and Irish in racial terms: "the English race may be said, by one speaking favourably of it but not extravagantly, to be characterized by sentiment and perception."[40] By including her ancestors in a race, Bowen legitimated an intangibility.[41]

Bowen's Court, the house that she inherited in 1930 and memorialized in her fiction and her autobiography, had lost some of its luster by the time she became its owner. But this fading did nothing to diminish her fierce love for it; if anything, it strengthened her affections. Cyril Connolly remembered a house party with the Woolfs in the spring of 1934 where, to him, Ireland appeared "quite derelict, empty and down at heel. Elizabeth's house lovely but rather forlorn."[42] But for Bowen all definitions and standards originated from this house. She often referred to matters Irish by way of explanation, even in fictions set in other lands.

Her first novel, *The Hotel*, published in 1927, describes the excursion of English visitors in Italy as "going forward in the leisurely and spread-out manner called in Ireland 'strealing.'"[43] In the *House in Paris* the narrator tells us that there is "something in Ireland" that always "bends one back on oneself" (*HP* 90). Bowen remained the translator, trying to reconcile, or at least explain, the differences between the two cultures. In wartime her need to make the two cohere became even more urgent, leading her to create such novels as *The Last September* (1929), which focuses on the period of the Troubles in Ireland, and *The Heat of the Day* (1949), which describes World War II in England and Ireland. Her autobiographical study of her house, *Bowen's Court* (1942), and her memoir of her childhood in Dublin, *Seven Winters,* published in the same year, were all undertaken in wartime.

Life in Ireland was not easy for the Anglo-Irish man or woman after 1880. First there was World War I, the Great War, for the fighting of which many Anglo-Irish "suffered...half a century later." Closer to home, the Troubles, "a projection of the land wars of the nineteenth century," threatened to destroy both the Big Houses that were still standing and the adjacent communities.[44] When the Civil War followed, it meant only an intensification of the violence already dividing the land. Those writers who found their loyalties confused and their allegiances tangled, such as George Bernard Shaw, Oscar Wilde, and later Elizabeth Bowen, went into "exile."[45] Yet Bowen herself never left Ireland permanently; she returned again and again, seeking to preserve the many identities that war called into question for her. Although she sought to find the everlasting resolution of these personal struggles in Ireland, in fact there she learned of the existence of more uncertainties. When she returned to London, further quandaries awaited her.

By interrupting old rules, the Second World War turned life inside out in many dimensions. From the vantage point of the first months of war it seemed to many observers that all rationality had been suspended, only to let loose upon the world the kind of anarchy that Yeats had feared. In the first week of December, 1939, Virginia Woolf wrote in her diary: "There's no reason anywhere. Brutes merely rampant. This suspends one's judgement; makes it foolish even to discuss."[46] Through the many shifting moods of war nothing, either ordinary or extraordinary, appeared like itself. Those who wrote about the war sought to catch what it felt like to live on the home front in England, as if to make it real for a moment in memory. Richard Cobb describes the

> bored banality, the seediness of those dreadful years... waiting, forever waiting, mostly in queues, standing in overcrowded night trains that stop for hours in the middle of the black countryside, the frail consolations offered by the cinema,... the shabby, ugly, makeshift modes of war, headscarves, turbans, frayed overcoats, piled-up hair styles, cigarettes sold singly over the counters of pubs. The quirks and accidents and odd encounters of an emergency, the dull, dismal drudgery of the whole thing.[47]

In her short stories particularly Bowen speaks to these conditions of existence, makes them visual, and so conveys much the same sense as a painter at work.

When every day brought news of growing numbers of people killed or wounded and more buildings fallen it seemed difficult, if not impossibly selfish, to take time away from preserving life to chronicle it. Bowen mentioned the ceaseless fatigue that drained her, the constant strain imposed by nights on duty and endlessly interrupted sleep. The mere business of life took a superhuman effort, making the production of any writing, however brief, all the more miraculous. As Ronald Blythe has concluded, the war years were "unusually rich in first-rate short stories, and it is these, rather than the novels, which retain their spell."[48] Bowen's stories like "Pink May," "The Demon Lover," and "Mysterious Kôr" froze the intensity of the ghosts and the shadows on the home front for posterity. Blythe divides his collection *Components of the Scene: Stories, Poems, and Essays of the Second World War* into sections that evocatively convey some of the perimeters of wartime as Bowen also saw them: the City (which begins with Bowen's "Mysterious Kôr"), the Sea, Declarations, the Patient Khaki Beast, Confessions and Conclusions, and the Dark.[49]

Suddenly, it seemed that the war could not be apprehended as a whole; even the smallest details seemed impossible to interpret. The question that arose persistently was how to translate, or express, what those days felt like both for those living through them and for those who would come later. Daily, as people reflected on their own experiences by way of the usual mechanisms, they were disappointed. It was more than a little unsettling to see a wartime moment recaptured in images and words that did not ring true to the participants. Suddenly, the connection between artistic creation and the outer world seemed precarious at best. The critic Walter Allen observed early in the conflict "a halt amongst artists of all kinds in associating themselves with the thirties idea of art and action."[50]

Nevertheless, the individual voice still cried out sometimes in beauty and rage, and other times in more mundane tones, against the turmoil and the terror of the war. Although it was not easy to find the time, or the emotional energy, Elizabeth Bowen, Cyril Connolly, T. S. Eliot, Graham Greene, John Lehmann, Evelyn Waugh, and Virginia Woolf, to name only a few, continued to be both writers and participants in war. Some of them produced their best work during these years. In 1942, T. S. Eliot published "Little Gidding," a poem that, as much as any other work, celebrates the survival of the individual in the midst of death:

> That pointed scrutiny with which we challenge
> The first-met stranger in the waning dusk
> I caught the sudden look of some dead master
> Whom I had known, forgotten, half recalled
> Both one and many; in the brown baked features
> The eyes of a familiar compound ghost
> Both intimate and unidentifiable.[51]

Writers like Bowen responded to a twin impulse to preserve the world they perceived as under attack and to celebrate the individuals in danger of being lost in the crowd. Inevitably, war altered the contours of the terrain Bowen mapped over the course of her career.

Bowen's private understanding of the world as a dangerous and mysterious place contributed to the way she evoked war's effects in her fiction. As a particularly visual person, she took imaginary pictures of the images, which then remained forever in her mind. The fictitious houses she constructed replaced the unsteady ones that appeared to be crumbling around her. But in wartime, no one edifice or certainty can be trusted. In *The Heat of the Day* she described the "habitat" of love that the traitor Robert presents to his lover, Stella, in place of anything else (*HD* 90). Instead of strong, handsome, capable male characters, Bowen strung together a series of lame or enfeebled ones who serve as paltry substitutes for those who had lost their lives in the Great War. The female characters dwarfing these weaker men recall her observations in a 1936 letter to John Hayward: "Goronwy Rees tells me that though amiable I am heartless and see men as trees walking: perhaps in most cases I do."[52] In all her novels each sex realizes that, just as none of them can recreate the environment that bred them, neither are they sure they want to replicate their first abodes. In her writing, Bowen transferred the darkness she saw crouched in every corner of her emotional and physical landscape into the tension stretching between the ordinary and the extraordinary in peace and in war.

Chapter 2

A Valiant Myth

> The War dwarfed us and made us morally uncomfortable, and we could see no reason why it should ever stop.
> —Elizabeth Bowen, "The Mulberry Tree"

Elizabeth Bowen wrote a play for radio in the spring of 1949 entitled *A Year I Remember—1918,* in which the narrator exclaims, "I can't imagine myself without a war . . . the war's simply come to be a part of oneself."[1] World War I, as the first total conflict Bowen knew, weighed on her consciousness increasingly heavily throughout her life. During the Second World War submerged moments of the earlier conflict returned to her with renewed urgency. Her concern with the legacy of World War One pervades and shapes her short stories, her work for the BBC, her nonfiction, and her novels—*The Hotel* (1927), *The Last September* (1929), *Friends and Relations* (1931), *To the North* (1932), *The House in Paris* (1935), *The Death of the Heart* (1938), and, after the war, *The Heat of the Day* (1949).

A Year reflects Bowen's fascination with unearthing her remembrances of the Great War. The radio script passed quickly over her own admittedly dim memories of 1914, when the war "fed a restless wish for the grand" in schoolchildren, to recreate in detail 1918, the year when she stared "life in the eye" for the first time. Told by a "narrator" who resembles Bowen in outlook, expressions, experience, and sympathies, the voice records the conflicting messages the Great War conveyed to those girls who came to maturity during the war. While the narrator spoke of enjoying Union Jack handkerchiefs and "Tipperary," the long casualty lists daily increased her "debt" to "live well" and demanded that she be "worthy" of her symbolic "brothers" (*A Year,* 26, 4). The encroachment of mortality at Downe House School, where she herself was a pupil, was made all too real by the telegrams announcing the deaths of brothers, fathers, and cousins and by the sound of the guns firing across the Channel. As Bowen explained elsewhere, it was "not so much that we were determined to change the world. But it gave you the feeling that whatever you did, you should do it jolly well."[2]

The year 1914 acquired a mythical dimension in Bowen's imagination, a stature that increased when the Second World War loomed on the horizon. The first year of the Great War became synonymous in her memory with the disappearance of a long-established way of life: "confidence was broken by 1914: from then on, decline of love for the present went with loss of faith in it."[3] Her remarks echo those of her friend and fellow writer L. P. Hartley, who wrote that the First World War "shook one's belief in the essential goodness of humanity—the belief that all's for the best in the best of all possible worlds."[4] As her young narrator explained in 1949, "*I was a child before 1914.* History, to me, was a book closed—only to be taken out in the school-room." The sinking of the *Leinster,* the Irish mail boat, in October, 1918, destroyed the narrator's sense of security by making concrete the idea that war was "reaching out at random" (*A Year,* 1, 15). Bowen's later memoir, *The Shelbourne Hotel* (1951), pointed to the *Leinster* incident as one that left an indelible mark of the "boundless savagery of the war."[5] The narrator of *A Year* surmised that her first encounters with war led her to grow up "with *no* sense of safety," unable to be surprised by anything (15).

In her first novel, *The Hotel,* Bowen continued to dramatize the effect of the carnage on the living through the figure of Mr. Victor Ammering, who shares his ironic first name with another survivor of the war, Victor Rodney, a figure in her later book *The Heat of the Day.* The names of these two men suggest a familiar pattern in Bowen's writing which intensified in her later work, a Dickensian reliance on the representational possibilities of appellation. The first Victor, Mr. Ammering, is a young man displaced by the war who has gone to Italy "for a rest with his mother and father"; "unable to find a job since the War," he "was said to be suffering from nervous depression." A sympathetic character complains, "The War's come very hard on our generation, I don't think people understand a bit" (*H* 19, 48). The conversation taking place in the novel breaks down along lines of age.

A fellow guest in the hotel, Colonel Duperrier, views the postwar years bitterly, condemning people who "won't want [him] anymore" but who get upset when men like Ammering are "done out of" their "due" (*H* 48). Nor are Bowen's female characters (whatever age they may be) immune to the crippling effects of the war's casualties in their adjustment to life in peacetime. The mother of one of the main characters in *To the North* neglects her daughter in favor of the memory of her two slain sons to whom she had given "her whole heart" (*TTN* 11). Not surprisingly, the daughters also grow up emotionally injured. The men and women the novelist imagined all show themselves to be incapable of putting 1914 behind them.

As the distance between Bowen's generation and the Great War widened, she continued to try to assimilate what she called "the indictment of 1914" into her fiction.[6] In a story she wrote in 1934, "Firelight in the Flat," Bob Robertson, a beleaguered husband, appears "bitterly retrospective" for the tradition of warmth that usually emanates from an open fire.[7] Over time, Robertson fears his status as an ex-officer "counted for less and less." For Lois Farquar, the young heroine of *The Last September*, who had once cried for a "whole afternoon before the War had begun because she was not someone in a historical novel," the conflict allows her to believe that she is a part of history in the making.[8] Lois's lament prefigures Bowen's narrator's 1949 description of an earlier self: "For a whole afternoon in 1913, I wept out of temper and boredom. . . . Because nothing happened" (*A Year*, 2). In much of the fiction she wrote in the late 1920s and 1930s Bowen depicts the phantoms of those who have suffered either the fallout from their proximity to or distance from the war.

Bowen's portraits of the men who survive the war keenly reflect some of the ambivalence which dates from her own adolescence. The short story "Aunt Tatty" describes the visit of Paul, "a clever modern young man," to the country house of Eleanor, a girl he has met in London. Stifled by the chintz and mahogany that fill the air in the drawing room, he glimpses the images of the men who adorn the mantelpiece: "the brothers killed in the war, the dead father, the brothers in India, stood lined up in silver frames, staring at nothing frankly and fearlessly."[9] The judgments emanating from these sepia-tinted photographs cause Paul to feel guilty to be alive and woefully inadequate in comparison to the heroism displayed by Eleanor's male relations. He fears he will not be a suitable substitute for the men the family has sacrificed.

Written from the vantage point of 1926, the story scrutinizes the heritage of death which stalks the survivors. After Paul clumsily proposes to Eleanor he puts words to the silent disapproval he senses from her family: "'Think what your brothers would have thought'—that would be your mother's last shot. I shouldn't have got on well with your brothers, Eleanor" ("Aunt Tatty," 271). Damned by his insecurity about whether he can satisfy the high expectations that result from surviving the slaughter, he becomes mired in self-flagellation and apprehension while Eleanor, having lost brothers in the war, feels guilty in another way about the fact that she was spared by an accident of birth.

The First World War also echoes through Bowen's 1931 novel, *Friends and Relations*. The book begins with a wedding during a summer "when men were so few."[10] But it is in one of her most successful novels, *The Death of the Heart,* that Bowen takes up the legacy of the war more directly through the portly figure of Major Brutt, one of the few adults who shows kindness to Portia, the young orphan. By the time Bowen wrote this novel, she had attained a perspective on the war which allowed her to study the lasting details of its social ramifications. Drawn to the vulnerable young girl, the major senses that Portia is also excluded from the posh circle surrounding her. By bestowing jigsaw puzzles (with military themes) and other such treats upon her, he demonstrates his solidarity with her against the cruel adults who ostracize them. Eddy, Portia's half-brother, takes a dim but sadly realistic view of Brutt as a "1914-1918 model," or a "make" for whom there is now "no market." In assessing Brutt's failure, another character notes snidely that he was "not . . . unlucky in having had the war to do so well in" because, despite his amiability, he will "never amount to much."[11] Thus, through even the smallest exchanges, the characters express their conviction that the war has altered everything and their supposition that postwar society has closed ranks against those who returned maimed from battle.

When Bowen wrote that Sarajevo marked the end of an age, she spoke preeminently of that year when the existence of the Anglo-Irish "became a little thing; from 1914 they began to be merged, already, into a chapter of a different history." As a young girl, she had attended what she remembered as one of the last glorious celebrations of the Anglo-Irish, the Mitchelstown Castle garden party held on the afternoon of August 5, 1914. On the expansive grounds of this stately mansion, the hardier members of the Anglo-Irish had "rallied" and "renewed" themselves in a brave show of festive silks and parasols. Through the transforming lens of the Second World War Bowen emphasized in writing her family memoir that, "if the Anglo-Irish live on and for a myth, for that myth they constantly shed their blood" (*BC* 437, 436).[12] Such a fête as that Mitchelstown party became one of the many sustaining fantasies of her Anglo-Irish heritage. In her autobiography she vividly recorded the cherished magical remembrance:

> it was an afternoon when the simplest person begins to anticipate memory . . . it was agreed [that this afternoon] would remain in every one's memory as historic. It was, also, a more final scene than we knew. Ten years hence, it was all to seem like a dream—and the Castle itself would be a few bleached stumps on the plateau. . . . Many of those guests, those vehement talkers, would be scattered, houseless, sonless, or themselves dead. (*BC* 436)

During World War II, when "War as we now know it encloses [us] in its immense to-day," Bowen's memories of the earlier conflicts made the afternoon at Mitchelstown seem all the more elegiac (*BC* 437).

Like many of the characters she created, Bowen expressed a strange guilt about her distance from the Great War. She blamed this sense of isolation on her sequestration in Ireland where news "travelled slowly," where she claimed she did not ever remember hearing "the word war" before August 5, 1914. In recalling the days immediately preceding the outbreak of that war, she described playing with her "dollshouse" and earnestly hoping that the weather would clear in time for her party at the castle. Her childish response to her father's announcement that England had declared war on Germany—"Then can't we go to the garden party?"—illustrates what she later described as her remove from the "real world" (*BC* 434, 435).

Even at that early moment in her life, however, she had begun to scrutinize war's effect on her landscape. When she and her father drove along the "bye-roads" on that Cork August afternoon, she remembered, "the War already gave them an unreal look" and they glared whiter than usual. As war increasingly colored her outlook, she became more determined to recall the reaction to the First World War in Ireland: It was greeted as an "earthquake-shock to a theatre inside which the drama grows unbearably tense" (*BC* 435, 426). Although she recognized that "it may be too much to say that the German march into Belgium averted an interior war in Ireland—but everything looked that way," she viewed the onset of the First World War as "something of a 'relief' to Ireland in crisis" (*BC* 426; *SH* 181).

Just after Bowen learned in November, 1918, that peace had been declared she gazed out of the windows of Bowen's Court, scanning the "empty landscape" for signs of change. To her chagrin, her research yielded no results. She dated her stricken realization that she might have "grown up without having the capacity to feel" to the narrator in *A Year* who experienced this "vacuum of peace." A kind of terror at what she considered her emotional retardation haunted her, and, after the "shock" of peace had set in, the play's narrator arrived at an understanding of the concept of grief as "the missing of unknown people" (*A Year*, 18, 19). The gulf she sensed separating her from the contemporary currents further complicated the basis of her allegiance to the Anglo-Irish.[13]

Surviving the Great War imposed on Bowen, as on her generation, a sense of having been spared for something special, of having an unnamed responsibility to the future. According to her narrator in *A Year*, who defended the "mess" that she and her contemporaries had made of the "blank page" they had been handed at the end of the war, "it was not because we did not care enough. We cared too much. In our nervousness we left behind us nothing but nonsense and gaps and blots" (19). Bowen was constantly demonstrating that those who had been born at the turn of the century had begun life with the deck stacked against them. While in *The Heat of the Day* she would harshly implicate several of her contemporaries as spies and traitors, she also created many corrupt and cruel characters in her interwar fiction.

In spite of its sustained influence upon her life, Bowen never devoted an entire work of fiction to the First World War, perhaps on account of her self-proclaimed remove from it. Because of the enormity of the First World War, and the smallness of her part in it, she never was able to grasp it entirely in a sustained fiction. Hence, it enters into her work by way of shadows and hints and reproving glances from handsome young men in frames on mantelpieces. While never in the foreground, the war remains a steady but saddening fact that lonely women and injured men must acknowledge, whether they wish to or not.

On looking back to the First World War on the eve of the second, Christopher Isherwood wrote, "We young writers of the middle twenties were all suffering, more or less subconsciously, from a feeling of shame that we hadn't been old enough to take part in the European

War. . . . I was obsessed by a complex of terrors and longings connected with the idea 'war.'"[14] For his female contemporaries this intermingled sense of loss and frustrated desire loomed larger. Many legends grew up surrounding the memories of the Great War; first and foremost came the conception of mythmaking itself. The war dominates the imaginations of later generations through such powerful images as "the lost generation"; the myth of July, 1916; the battles of the Somme (1916 and 1918); the myth of the "loss of innocence"; and the myths of the "lost imperial splendour."[15] When faced with such epic tales of conflict, stories of explanation and justification rushed in to fill the inevitable vacuum of tragedy. The slaughter of a generation of a certain class of young men became associated in memory with the Edenic fable of the shedding of naïveté, and, thus, pain became equated with beauty. Pictures of dapper blue-eyed young men who marched bravely off to fight for their country, who were felled in the trenches, became etched indelibly in the imaginations of a generation of young women and men.[16]

As they gazed ahead, the fabled world of their own making shimmered on the far side of war with the perennial promise of better days to come. But when the battles dragged on, men and women, particularly the latter, who had gone to work outside the home for the first time during the war, hoped "that society would be transformed once peace came."[17] Just as the war's beginning had seemed an "apparent thunderbolt," shot from the cloudless skies of the glorious summer of 1914, distracting England from a multitude of domestic problems, the end of the war portended answers.[18] Disillusionment with the conflict, which started in 1915 and reached a peak in the summer of 1916, grew to new proportions as the fighting continued without an end in sight.[19] Mythmaking and story telling became the only means available to comprehend the inconceivable sorrow. The tales that people invented to outlast the unendurable illustrate the differences between the way men and women approached the First World War.

Women's reaction to the Great War has often been overlooked; since they did not take an active part in the actual battles, it has been a temptation to conclude that they remained aloof from the whole situation. Yet, they too wrote about the guilt, losses, and disruptions, indeed devastation, of an entire way of life.[20] That women felt and understood the war differently is undeniable, but so also is the fact that they grieved. Many of them described their responses to the First World War in poems, stories, and, particularly, novels. In traditional studies of the literature of this war, however, such as Bernard Bergonzi's *Heroes' Twilight* and Andrew Rutherford's *The Literature of War,* women figure scarcely at all.[21]

Virginia Woolf, writing in January, 1916, wondered how long the war, which she characterized as "this preposterous masculine fiction," would keep on "without some vigorous young woman pulling us together and marching through it."[22] By so labeling the war, Woolf acknowledged the barriers dividing male and female experience that are so often built in wartime. Indeed, she contributed to a myth persisting from the First World War, that is, "that the experience of battle was incommunicable; you had to have been there."[23] Vera Brittain's romantic and self-indulgent memoir of the era, *Testament of Youth* (1933), sold 120,000 copies in six years and was reissued as recently as 1978.[24] In writing this reminiscence of the First World War Brittain referred to the absence of women's voices from the narratives of the generation of 1914. After she read the books by the beautiful young men, Siegfried Sassoon and Robert Graves and Edmund Blunden, she asked melodramatically: "Why should these young men have the war to themselves?... Who will write the epic of the women who went to war?"[25]

In facing the first global war, women discovered themselves caught in a treacherous confluence of competing cultural expectations. The socioeconomic patterns of women's lives mirrored the enormous upheavals caused by the war. Typically, in response to wartime conditions the "marriage rate took an upward leap" in 1915, and many women began to work outside the home.[26] Despite the apparent benefits contained in these advances, to the dismay of the suffragettes the majority of them were only temporary. As the historian Arthur Marwick explains, "many of the economic effects of the First World War were concealed by the onset of the depression."[27] Moreover, when the war ended, whatever lives women had staked out for themselves became subject immediately to the reconfigurations necessitated by the returning soldiers.[28]

The conception of woman as comforter, provider, and healer sought its natural outlet in the picture of a young girl, dressed in a starched white uniform tending the wounds of the often delirious soldiers. Women like Bowen flocked to the call of nursing, to the reassurance that they could be of service during wartime. Upon leaving school in 1918 she returned to her native Ireland, and like the narrator of *A Year I Remember—1918,* Bowen worked as "a pink, rattled, inexpert V.A.D." tending to shell shock victims who impressed her as having their "inner queerness a little heightened." The narrator remembers being "a young person who didn't know what to make of the world yet... like a rabbit in the middle of the road" (*A Year*, 5, 14). She describes from memory what some recent feminist scholars, such as Sandra Gilbert, have seen in the "rhetoric and iconography of nursing in the First World War." The female nurse, Gilbert argues, presents an image of women as the "triumphant survivors and destined inheritors," a picture in stark juxtaposition to the maimed men to whom they minister.[29] The nurse in Bowen's novel *The Heat of the Day* appears as "a kindly middle-aged woman" who cared for the veteran, Victor Rodney, until his early death closely following his divorce from Stella (*HD* 83).

It took time, however, for the experience of war to be assimilated into fiction, whether written by men or women. Not until the end of the 1920s did books on the war, many of them autobiographical in nature, begin to be published in large numbers.[30] Bowen's novel *The Last September*, which appeared in 1929, reflected the trend toward reconsideration; in this same year at least twenty-nine books on the First World War came on the scene.[31] Like so many others, she was shaping the experience of war into some recognizable fictional form. Bowen concentrated on how the women and men of 1914 reconciled themselves to whatever awaited them on their return from battles, hospitals, factories, ships, and in some cases, at least figuratively, from the dead.

In her interwar fiction, Bowen frequently evoked the chasm separating the years following the First World War from that fateful August. Often her characters continue as though nothing has happened and their lack of awareness brings on their ruin. Karen Michaelis grew "up in a world of grace and intelligence," in *The House in Paris*, a world "in which the Boer War, the War and other fatigues and disasters had been so many opportunities to behave well." This refusal to feel is closely associated in Bowen's fiction with a certain kind of "pre-war" existence, best lived "in one of the tall, cream houses in Chester Terrace, Regent's Park." Furnished with the props necessary for this sterility, the houses boast old volumes of *Who's Who*, a bust of the Duke of Wellington, "engravings of the Virtues in action," a service lift, old directories, and a gas fire (*HP* 69, 68, 99). Often, the author intimates that, despite their apparently oblivious natures, the residents live blindly because they cannot feel deeply; they have trained themselves to avoid the sensation of pain. Yet, in her novels of the later 1930s Bowen suggests with growing vehemence that the suppression of perception itself is responsible for the darkening horizon.

When Karen Michaelis attempts to discuss her mother's sorrow at the death of her sister, Aunt Violet, Mrs. Michaelis "sat nobly in the armchair, eyes fixed on the second page of the *Spectator,* behaving as she had behaved in August 1914." Raised in this environment, Karen can only begin to accept that her mother's "resistance is terrifying; she would rather feel me almost hate her than speak. The good morale of our troops won the war" (*HP* 192). The seeming non sequiturs that Karen joins together betray some of the tensions stemming from the war which separate generations. Mrs. Michaelis's willful ignorance of her daughter's emotions causes Karen to return to the platitudes she had relied upon in time of war. But at the same instant that Karen, as a dutiful daughter, is appalled by her mother's "resistance," she grudgingly admires the exactitude of Mrs. Michaelis's "well-lit explanations of people." Sadly, the clinical sharpness of her mother's photographs lack humanity: "Like the classic camera, she was blind to those accidents that make a face, a scene that scene." In her careful "anti-romanticism" Mrs. Michaelis reduces the murkiness, the mystery of life and love, to their most minimal contours (*HP* 125, 126). Of course, her daughter embraces what she sees as the core of life at the same time that she begins to reject her mother's chilling observations.

Just as Karen remembers the way her mother behaved during the Great War, the war also becomes a way to situate Markie Linkwater's family in Bowen's earlier novel *To the North*. The wartime economy offers the vulgar Dolmans, Markie's sister's family, a rare opportunity which they seize. By arrangement, Markie lives in a flat at the top of his sister's house, in a state where "delicacy did not exist." The house appears miles away, at least socially and spiritually, from the elegant terrace houses that Bowen usually portrays. Bound by convenience rather than affection, Markie and his sister devote their energies to "exacting hard terms from each other without compunction." But the arrangement satisfies them in an odd way: "The Dolmans, whose minor economies were remarkable, could keep on their large rather disagreeably imposing house whose lease had been purchased for almost nothing during the War" (*TTN* 66). In Bowen's hierarchies those who are stingy with their money or their hospitality compromise not only their physical comfort but also their moral rectitude. When Emmeline Summers, the young heroine of the novel, visits Markie's flat for the first time, she duly notes that the servant turns off the hallway light "before she was up the first flight." This obvious sign of parsimony bothers Emmeline when she realizes that the servant's action reflects the attitude of her employer, who says proudly, "I never waste anything" (*TTN* 66, 67). The war has set the scene for an awkward upset in social relationships. Bowen makes it clear that Markie and his family do not inherently belong in the house they happen to inhabit. Their ignorance of this fact only underlines their gracelessness and inappropriateness.

Beyond turning social distinctions upside down, the war lingers, altering every aspect of life. The presence, or possibility, of war is so embedded in the characters' minds that it offers a continual point of comparison, a ready supply of metaphors. At a cocktail party an obstetrician returns to Shakespeare's description of England as a place "built for nature by herself, Against infection and the hand of war" (*TTN* 130). Even spheres traditionally associated with the giving of life (such as gardens or obstetrics) seem connected to death. In *To the North*, at the grimly regimented girls' school that the plump and ungainly Pauline attends, the girls' "gardens were planted like rows of neat little graves." And, during an awkward conversation with Pauline's uncle Julian, the widow Cecilia Summers has another nightmarish vision that "an enemy army seemed to be marching from the garden" (*TTN* 77, 166). The carnage of the Great War lurks unexpectedly in the minds of the survivors. In a letter to Julian, Cecilia writes snidely that her family's country house, Farraways, "isn't a morgue, only like a nice Italian cemetery with photographs on the graves." She cannot escape the impress of war; returning from her trip to Italy by train, Cecilia sees her new friend Markie superimposed against "a flying background of battlefields under new culture" (*TTN* 176, 11). Even though new crops are being planted, images of graveyards linger in Cecilia's imagination.

Cemeteries cover the Italian landscape that the English visitors have come to tour in Bowen's first novel, *The Hotel*. Cordelia, another member of Bowen's cast of untamed and ungainly prepubescent girls, discovers a burial ground on her walk with Sydney Warren, a place where "the rank and file of small crosses staggered arms wide in the arraignment of sunshine." On their excursion Cordelia shares her preference for "Italian graves; they look so much more lived in." Sydney, preoccupied by her recent misunderstanding with the young clergyman James Milton, replies pointedly, "They would certainly be more difficult than others to get clear of." While contemplating the graves and the deaths they memorialize, Sydney is overcome by "the treachery of a future that must give one to this ultimately." As a young single woman facing a varied array of possibilities, including marriage, she can see only instability and the threat of loss: "The present, always slipping away, was ghostly, every moment spent itself in apprehension of the next, and these apprehensions ... promised to make the past barren enough should she have to turn back to it" (*H* 86–87).

Sydney's haunting preoccupation with death and the futility of life contrasts sharply with Cordelia's fascination with the logistics of the cemetery. She has no trouble speculating about the practical problems associated with the Italian custom of disinterring those who cannot afford to pay for their permanent burial. Instead, she leads Sydney to the area she prefers, the "very nice corner" the English occupy in the cemetery "where more discreet memorials had been hewn into shapes better suited to granite than to Carrara marble." When Miss Pinkerton, another guest in the hotel, arrives carrying narcissi to a headstone, Sydney and Cordelia greet her with appropriate warmth. Apparently, this dutiful woman is heading for the grave of the cousin of a friend who "was an Admiral." Before she can finish her homage, with childlike openness and curiosity, Cordelia asks, "Isn't he an admiral still?" Frustrated and annoyed when Sydney admonishes her and drags her away, Cordelia wonders aloud, "Why shouldn't I have asked that?" Sydney answers hesitantly, "Because Miss Pinkerton doesn't know" (*H* 89–90). The problem is, neither does Sydney.

The visit to the graveyard in the Italian countryside provides Bowen with an opportunity to examine women's different responses to life as it has been altered by war. Cordelia, too young to have thought much about the war, approaches the cemetery with the irreverence and inquisitiveness of a child. Unfettered by the knowledge of the rituals of mourning and prescribed attitudes toward the dead, she enjoys the visit as providing a valuable source of information. For Sydney, poised at an uncomfortable juncture in her romantic life, the graves symbolize too much feeling; they provoke troublesome questions she would rather avoid. Finally, the respect and reverence shown by Miss Pinkerton illustrates the conventional manner in which one honors the dead. To appease her friend's grief, she pays tribute to a fallen English admiral unlucky enough to be buried far from his homeland.

The Hotel depicts the survivors of the Great War making peace with themselves and with the situations they encounter. The young people, in particular, declare themselves to be disoriented and wandering. Victor Ammering stands at the center of the group of young adults escaping

England, each for his or her private reasons, to the temporary haven of a winter at an Italian hotel. In response to Colonel Duperrier's insistent question "*Can't* young Ammering get a job?" Joan Lawrence explains, "No he can't . . . It worries him awfully." Despite the standard wisdom that youth should be "idealistic," she argues, "I suppose *we* can't help feeling that, considering how hard things are on us, we aren't really so bad." Fairly mystified by this lecture, the colonel casts his lot with Victor: "I personally can understand very well how hard this is on Ammering—having nothing to do but rot about here for a winter. At his age it would have driven me clean off my head" (*H* 48).

Poor Victor has fallen prey to the ministrations of the three Lawrence girls, daughters of a doctor staying at the hotel. They manipulate Victor as though "he were a marionette," giving him an assortment of parts in their imagined scenarios (*H* 32). To the reader, he appears somewhat nondescript, like his contemporaries, who seem to be about the age of thirty with a "(Public School and University Education, active, keen sportsman, good general capacities), who advertise their willingness to try anything in the Personal column of *The Times*." Although he cannot secure gainful employment in England, abroad he can play tennis or dance and talk "most beautifully about the War" (*H* 19). Older guests, like the pompous Mr. Lee-Mittison, find him at best superfluous, an assessment made clear by his exclusion of Victor from his picnic with the Lawrence girls. Ignoring efforts made to detour him from the outing, Victor wanders near the picnic site, like a stray dog or an unwanted child, as Veronica, one of the ruder Lawrence girls, announces: "Oh, we don't want Victor up here, . . . he's such a bore" (*H* 39). Victor's ostracism from such small social occasions suggests his more important exclusion at home and in Europe from the postwar society at large.

Victor, like many other male survivors of the war, in the eyes of Bowen's female characters appears incomplete. Sydney Warren gives her dim opinion of Victor as "rather a dreary young man" (*H* 98). When Veronica deliberates whether or not she should marry him, she belittles the significance of her choice because, although several possible husbands are waiting in England, "there's not really much to choose between any of them." Rhetorically, she asks Sydney, "Do you think perhaps men aren't what they used to be?" To the women's dismay there do not seem to be enough men at the hotel to go around. Eileen Lawrence remarks, "What a pity we have used up all the men!" (*H* 102, 127). Unfortunately for the women, they do not know what else to do with themselves besides scout for men, and circumstances at the hotel do not cooperate in this venture.

After the war, for those who relied on the event to give meaning and definition to their lives, the sense of loss and disorientation became even greater. Another of Bowen's interwar stories, the 1934 tale "The Disinherited," relates the saga of a man who has murdered his mistress.[32] After her death he confesses to his shortcomings: "I saw you had me bought up. A motor salesman who didn't do big business and didn't have money and started to have tastes he didn't have money for." In his *ex post facto* analysis he refers to himself as "a war gentleman after the war," saying pathetically as he addresses the dead woman, "you'd have liked me then in the war." Here the war has become the material that fuels his fictional rendition of life. As he explains, the war gave him definition and oriented him, for in those days he "could see how things were" ("The Disinherited," 396, 395). Now, he loathes himself and all those who have called his bluff in the postwar world. He joins the ranks of the walking wounded, male characters who stumble around the obstacles that the war has left behind.

Bowen's 1938 novel, *The Death of the Heart,* vividly portrays another veteran of the First World War, Major Brutt, a man who is nothing like the brute his name suggests. In fact, he appears worrisomely vacant, "like an empty room with no blinds, his imagination gapes on the scene, and reflects what was never there" (*DH* 45). There is something childlike and pathetic in the way he clings to his memories of the war. Trying to force his way into the drawing rooms of Regent's Park, he depends upon his war experience to guide him. When asked, for example, if he knew a certain Robert Pidgeon, he assures his hosts at Windsor Terrace that, although "he is not a chap, of course, that I should ever have met if it hadn't been for the War," the two shared the mutual fate of having been wounded "on the Somme" and subsequently went on leave together (*DH* 47). Ironically, his obsession with his war experience separates him from the company that he so eagerly wishes to keep.

Lost to his contemporary world, or at least on a prolonged leave, Brutt cannot satisfy the exacting demands of the inhabitants of Windsor Terrace, the Quaynes. Thinking that he might be useful to their friends, the Peppinghams (who are looking to employ an agent in Shropshire), the Quaynes invite Brutt to join their lunch party. In a painful series of forced attempts at conversation Anna Quayne gives him "hoop[s]" to jump through when she raises his management of a rubber estate in

Malay. Mrs. Peppingham, also making gestures to keep the patter going, underlines her sure sense of class: "With all these social changes, I sometimes fear that's a lost art—managing men, I mean." During lunch Brutt is showing himself not able to be manipulated by his hosts. In their eyes, he is even less impressive when the talk turns to political affairs. Mrs. Peppingham gets a little flustered when she attempts a hasty distinction between "hero worship," which she concedes only "leads to dictators," and the appropriate respectfulness of employees. Throughout the conversation, Brutt's ominous silence begins to make the Quaynes nervous that he might appear to be "a Red." When his quiet demands an explanation, he genially acknowledges his state of indecision, his preference for listening, and his lack of qualifications for contributing to this debate (*DH* 276, 277, 278).

In contrast to the timidly inadequate Major Brutt, other characters in Bowen's novels, such as Karen Michaelis's brother in *The House in Paris,* appear relatively unscathed. He seems to have "come safely through the war to marry a nice woman with property in the north" so that he can manage the holdings, hunt, occasionally publish "clever satirical verse," and try "artificial manures" (in that order) (*HP* 70). For those like Brutt who do not have such ready-made lives waiting for them on their return, the years leading up to the Second World War become much more treacherous and dislocating. Some of those who came back apparently victorious, namely *The Hotel*'s Victor Ammering and Victor Rodney, Stella's first husband in *The Heat of the Day,* could not surmount the multitude of setbacks endemic to their postwar situations.

In her fiction Bowen demonstrated her belief that women had to think about their existences using different standards from the ones men employed. Loss dominates the lives of many of her female characters, and photographs of the war dead, victims of victory, adorn many of the rooms Bowen portrayed. The women who honor these men lose part of themselves in their preoccupation with the past. Too often, the mothers of slain sons neglect their surviving daughters while they worship their memories of the dead. Frequently, the surviving sons perceive themselves as less wanted, less significant than their departed brothers.

The short story "The Last Night in the Old Home" explores the nostalgically fragmented feelings of one family on the eve of a move from their long-occupied house. Surveying the leftover bits and pieces of their lives, they come across tag ends of their days there—extra buttons, gloves, reminders of an era that has ended in a silence that "echoes" through the halls.[33] The sentimental mother has saved all the family letters to be read aloud and, after that has been completed, "only the best, the jauntiest and most eloquent [were] put away in dispatch cases." This family encounters much difficulty in putting to rest their grief for their own war dead. Once they have dismantled the usual paeans, such as their framed photographs, they are left only with letters, reminders of their deceased brother Adrian's presence: his "had been kept, because he was dead." Jealously, his remaining brother, Henry, compares this reverence with their lackadaisical attitude toward him: "Had Henry been dead, his [letters] might have acquired some kind of morbid value" ("The Last Night," 371). He is not alone in his awkwardness in the face of the loss of a loved one.

Bowen's fiction of the interwar years is replete with women who, in rushing toward life, have had to overcome great tragedy. The young widowed mother in the short story dating from 1936, "Tears, Idle Tears," has "a horror . . . of the abnormal," resulting from her sorrow when her husband, a Royal Air Force (RAF) pilot, "died two days after a ghastly crash, after two or three harrowing spaces of consciousness."[34] Carefully, she has pieced her life together over the five years since that tragedy. Her friends remark upon what they see as her "gallantness" in not remarrying and in keeping up her life as she does. She helps a friend with a shop in Surrey, breeds and sells puppies, and devotes "the rest of her time to making a man of Frederick," her son ("Tears," 487, 483). Her child's masculinity becomes paramount to her, and his dissolution into loud and unattractive tears in the middle of Regent's Park greatly embarrasses her. He cries often, apparently, which worries her and makes her feel "ashamed." Once she wrote, but never sent, a draft of a letter to an advice column, describing herself as "a widow; young, good tempered"—"my friends all tell me that I have great control" ("Tears," 481). The humiliation of such a public revelation thwarts her request for help. Yet her son's childishness makes overt what she fears, namely, that all may not be right with the environment she has fostered for him.

Children in Bowen's stories often fall prey to adult desertion or disinterest and repeatedly appear as orphans or half-orphans. "The Tommy Crans," an Irish short story dating from 1930, depicts a young boy named Herbert, who spends "his first Christmas Day without any father."[35] His relatives in Dublin try to sweep him up into their festivities and whisper about his toughness: "He had seen his mother off, very brave with the holly wreath, in the cemetery tram." Herbert gamely tries to join the new celebratory scene, which is filled with the stench of gunpowder from a toy gun and the fragrance of winter hyacinths. The mood of the story evokes the faraway and untenable loneliness of children in an adult world. Herbert, "fat, with spectacles, . . . felt deformed a little from everyone knowing about his father" ("The Tommy," 350). As is true for so many other children in Bowen's fiction, the death of a parent has indelibly scarred Herbert.

Daughters in these stories and novels also miss their absent fathers terribly. Henrietta, the orphaned, ungainly, and talkative child in *The House in Paris,* boasts proudly about her father, Colonel Mountjoy, who, as she likes to imagine, has served valiantly in the army. It is a source of pride for Bowen's female characters as well—this knowledge that their relatives have participated in the defense of their country. But a particular kind of regret often tinges this reverence, stemming from the characters' inability to take part in combat. Naomi Fisher, the quiescent daughter in *The House in Paris,* explains to the inquiring Henrietta that her "father was a captain in the English artillery," adding with satisfaction, "The Fishers were always soldierly" (*HP* 43). Typically, Henrietta sees Captain Fisher's image in the oval photograph that Madame Fisher treasures.

English girls entertain other fantasies about war. In "Charity," a short story first published in Bowen's second collection, *Ann Lee's and Other Stories* (1926), two young girls play together.[36] Rachel introduces her friend Charity to a secret spot on the roof of the bicycle shed. There Rachel has a "ring of terribly secret thoughts" where she imagines that "the school was on fire, or there was nearly a bathing fatality. Sometimes there was a war on, and, as none of the men were brave enough, they were both going to fight" ("Charity," 193).[37]

Throughout her fiction Bowen explicitly takes up the supposed state of "civilization" which produced such a conflict as the Great War, and its carnage and devastation. Paradoxically, given her own ancestry, she blames much of the problem on the whole process of colonization, undertaken imperiously and without respect for the "native" culture. Mr. Lee-Mittison in *The Hotel* is treated harshly. This character brags about his days as a conqueror in Malaya to impress naive young girls bred on dreams of empire and domination (*H* 40). Such arguments recur with increasing moment in Bowen's fiction of the Second World War. Stories like "Ivy Gripped the Steps" take a focused backward glance at the years surrounding the First World War. Because Bowen and her generation were forced to live with its effects, they came to accept, reluctantly, its physical scars, and they endured the psychological ones.

Bowen's stories recount the sad tale of the men who, after having survived the war, display an array of invisible as well as visible scars. They are often lonely, misplaced, displaced, and, if not physically injured, at least mentally troubled. Discussing their field of marriage prospects, the women in *The Hotel* express their concern about this state of affairs: Where are the men? and who are they when we find them? For Veronica Lawrence, trying to decide whether or not to marry Victor, the inauspicious start to a romance that she knows she can dominate troubles her: "What is the use of a man one can kick?" (*H* 102). These wounded veterans, as Elaine Showalter has noted, formed a "shocking contrast to the heroic visions and masculine fantasies" inspired by "the British Victorian imagination."[38] Particularly during the Second World War, but also for many years before and after it, Bowen created men and women who had been irrevocably altered by the events of these years. The ghost of a war victim appears as late as 1955, in her novel *A World of Love*. For her and for many of her characters, August, 1914, would continue to divide two eras of history. When she recognized the permanence of this boundary, she entered into her adult life.

Chapter 3

"Innocently Abroad"

In the years immediately following the First World War Bowen settled in London where she began to write short stories in earnest. An old connection with the headmistress of Downe House School led to her acquaintance with Rose Macaulay, the well-known literary figure, who took an interest in the young writer and offered her an entrée into a network of publishers and writers. Frank Sidgwick also took Bowen's work seriously, and in May, 1923, he published *Encounters,* her first small collection of stories. Although the edition did not sell well, being in print delighted her as it acknowledged that she might make a name for herself in the city that she had imagined as a young child in County Cork. She conveyed some of her amazement at learning of the contract in a letter to her fiancé, Alan Cameron: "Still, Mr. Sidgwick is not a fool and I suppose he wouldn't take them if they were rotten."[1]

After their August marriage in a small church in Blisworth, Northamptonshire, Bowen and Cameron began their life together in this county where Cameron worked as a member of the BBC Educational Commission. Six years older than she, he had served as an officer in the First World War and had suffered gas poisoning. Despite the discrepancy between their experiences, he was someone with whom she could be herself; she explained to him, "I think I loved your *you* long before I saw it in relation to my *me.*"[2] Her friends, particularly her literary ones, did not pretend to understand the attraction between the two newlyweds. Peter Quennell described their union as "mysterious and unexpected."[3] But acquiring the stability of a home through marriage proved fortuitous for Bowen's development as a writer. The life that they established provided her with those essentials that Woolf enumerated in *A Room of One's Own:* space, time, and money. Later in life

Bowen recounted with relish one ritual begun in these years: She would settle down in the morning at her writing desk with a glass of lime juice by her side, a cigarette in her mouth (she chain-smoked), and bare forearms so that she could feel her skin crossing the paper as she wrote.[4]

Their sojourn in Northamptonshire did not last very long. When Cameron was appointed secretary for education in the city of Oxford in 1925, they moved to that university town. For a person like Bowen who had little postsecondary schooling, the chance to befriend academics such as David Cecil and C. M. Bowra satisfied some of her quest for a life of the mind. Thoroughly at home in this new environment, she impressed Bowra as someone whose "presence" and "authority" could enable her to become "head of a women's college at Oxford or Cambridge."[5] Reminiscing about this era in 1953, Bowen wrote to her friend Alice Runnells James that these years were "the best ten" of her life and "the friends made at that time had a special dearness."[6] The move to Oxford coincided with a deepening seriousness about her own writing, and, thus, she devised a stricter schedule for herself to protect against the mounting demands associated with membership in a community. She established a pattern that she followed for most of her life, devoting mornings to writing and afternoons to volunteer groups such as the Women's Institute. Yet, even though she readily adapted to this routine in England, she kept her ties to Ireland. She and her husband traveled often to Bowen's Court where they always celebrated Christmas with her father and his second wife, Mary Gwynn, whom he had married in 1918.

When Bowen described her first attempts at writing short stories, she identified "the sensation of desperate and overweening enterprise, of one's entire being forced to a conclusive ideal." She claimed these many years later that those feelings had stayed "constant" for her in her work. As she fashioned lived or imagined experience into the stuff of fiction, she came up against a realization that, for her, "reality was the books I had read."[7] Repeatedly, she was fabricating a world for herself and her readers composed of characters and landscapes that closely resembled, but that she insisted were not, the places and figures she had known.

"Some time ago" Bowen "had understood . . . that nothing became real for her until she had some time to live it over again."[8] In a 1923 short story, "Coming Home," which Bowen referred to as "transposed autobiography," she describes the tribulations of a young girl named Rosalind.[9] When the child returns home to find that her mother is unexpectedly out, she becomes stricken with a panic that suffuses many of Bowen's characters and clouds their excursions into the surrounding society. On their quests they become preoccupied with solving the difficult puzzles of their identity. The characters in *The Hotel* attempt their self-analysis in a faraway land, a circumstance which itself causes them to feel foreign. Eileen Lawrence, who is visiting the hotel with her family, asks rhetorically, "Isn't it funny that for everybody there seems to be just one age at which they are *really* themselves?" (*H* 126). Bowen's fiction of the 1920s describes some of her most memorable characters, those who embark on a journey toward self-discovery in their passage to adulthood.

Bowen continued to produce short stories steadily; when her second collection, *Ann Lee's and Other Stories*, appeared in 1926, it received more favorable reviews than her first volume. Encouraged, she began *The Hotel*, her first long work of fiction, which was published in 1927. Taking confidence from a successful foray into this genre, Bowen next tackled a subject nearer the bone in her second novel, *The Last September*. This book explores country house life in southern Ireland during the uneasy fall and winter of 1920–21, a choice of subject she later explained resulted from her realization that Ireland seemed far away from her life in Oxford. She recounted that, increasingly, the country of her birth began to appear

> immensely distant ... more like another world than another land. Here I was, indeed, arrived at the kind of life I had vaguely dreamed of long ago. ... Yet, when I came to the work of my second novel, it was the vanished era which took command—nor is it hard, at second thought, to see why. The writer is like the swimmer caught by an undertow.[10]

The challenge of re-creating the history she had witnessed in Ireland beckoned to Bowen. As she discussed the relations among the English, the Irish, and especially the Anglo-Irish in the ugly years between the Troubles and the Civil War, she drew upon a newfound skill in language and portraiture. Lyrical and poignant, the novel elegizes without sentimentalizing an ordered society jeopardized by unleashed anger, widespread inequity, and raging guerrilla violence. When the book appeared in 1929 it received high praise as her most accomplished and substantial work to date. The attention she devoted to her novels, however, had not caused her to abandon the short story, which she often thought of as a warm-up, or sketch, for longer fiction. The individual tales in *Joining Charles and Other Stories* (1929) gathered collective strength from the more mature and distinctive tone of Bowen's writing at the close of this first postwar decade.

Particularly sensitive to, even obsessed with, what they call the "atmosphere of the age," Bowen's characters remark upon infinitesimal variations of tone and mood. Her short stories often chronicle the observations of not-so-innocent bystanders who sternly judge other's choices. "Daffodils" (1923), for example, depicts the relations among three cruel pupils and their spinsterly teacher, Miss Murcheson. The intimate details of this older woman's life provide a source of mirthful speculation for her students. While she is laboriously grading a set of their essays on the inspiring topic of the story's title, she grows impatient with their canned answers: "They get their very feelings out of books. Nothing ever surprises or impresses them." And yet, when she hears the girls' familiar laughter on the street outside her window she startles herself by inviting them inside. After a strained conversation, during which the students surreptitiously survey Miss Murcheson's domestic surroundings, they decline her offer of tea. When they leave, one of them pronounces with smug superiority, "Miss Murcheson has never really *lived*."[11] Neither the mean pupils nor the barren spinster seem to have arrived at a comfortable accommodation with their lives.

For the characters in the stories collected in *Encounters* (1923) any institution such as marriage that might be perceived as constraining becomes subject to debate and analysis. In "Mrs. Windemere" (1923) Esmée, a fashionable young woman, runs into an elegant older woman she has met earlier in Italy. Sharing an unexpected lunch together in London, Mrs. Windemere urges Esmée to take a lover. She bases her argument on the idea that Esmée's husband, Wilfred (whom the older woman has never met), does not seem to be "generous" about letting his wife travel alone or have her freedom. Esmée protests, but not before her companion can suggest an invitation to the country to inspect Wilfred. When the young woman hesitates, trying to forestall the plan by mentioning the impending arrival of "Wilfred's relations," Mrs. Windemere "tenderly" calls her a "little *caged* thing." However confining, marriage has its rewards; after Esmée asks for the bill Mrs. Windemere capitulates by saying pitifully, "I haven't got a Wilfred."[12]

Mrs. Windemere belongs to a familiar group in Bowen's fiction that includes the lonely, meddling older woman.[13] The middle-aged Mrs. Kerr in *The Hotel,* mother of Ronald, exerts a similar kind of influence over Sydney Warren. During an afternoon outing Sydney reflects that the excursion feels like "being given tea by an aunt at the zoo," to which Mrs. Kerr replies, "I only wish you had been taken more to the zoo" (*H* 114). Sydney's choice of metaphor, that of a place where animals live in captivity, signifies the sense of closed opportunities and constraints that many of Bowen's younger characters, especially the women, note in this decade.[14] That their elders scrutinize them and tell them how to live, or how not to live, often makes them feel trapped. For the restless women who are unhappily contemplating being engaged or divorced the metaphor of the zoo, or the cage, seems inescapable.

Beneath the surface of lives that seem restrained and controlled some of Bowen's 1920s characters convey more emotion than is immediately apparent. Sometimes the characters' responses even verge on the macabre. The beginning of "Recent Photograph" (1926), for example, vividly describes the murder of Mrs. Brindley by her husband, who "cut his wife's throat with a razor . . . afterwards turning in for the night with his head inside a gas oven, having mitigated the inside's iron clemency with two frilly cushions."[15] After the nearsighted Mr. Brindley survives this ordeal his story becomes the province of a young reporter who dreams of using the tale to make a name for himself on the local paper. The gruesome tone of "Recent Photograph" implies that cruelty and death do not take place very far from so-called everyday life.

Bowen does not draw a very wide line separating the dead and the living in her short stories from this period. "Telling," a story dating from 1927, was first published in *The Black Cap,* a collection of stories compiled by ghost fancier Cynthia Asquith.[16] The story recounts another murder, that of Josephine, a beautiful young woman, by Terry, her former boyfriend. On the night of a dance at his family home Terry realizes his total frustration with the staleness of his life. Terry drinks too much and has never been able to perform in the arena that his more capable brothers and sisters effortlessly command: "Again and again he'd been sent back to them all . . . from school, from Cambridge, now—a month ago—from Ceylon. 'The bad penny!' he would remark, very jocular."[17] When he spies someone else kissing his onetime girlfriend at the dance his sense of impotence overpowers him, producing a homicidal rage. Maniacal with hatred and jealousy, he takes Josephine to the chapel to demand if she believes in him. She only laughs, and he sees the one being who has "made him a man" deserting him and belittling him ("Telling," 327, 326). Driven by his lack of belief in either himself or his future, he stabs Josephine with an African hunting knife. He has found the weapon, a symbol of colonial conquest and totemic masculine potency, hanging conveniently in the dining room.

His insignificance to his family becomes sadly obvious as his narrative of murder falls on deaf ears. When he announces, "I've killed Josephine in the chapel," his brother does not even listen ("Telling," 329). His relatives appear more preoccupied with supervising the cleanup of the party than with noticing what is occurring around them, a typical response for the Bowen characters of this decade. Their myopia causes them to be unable to see anything untoward, like Josephine's dead body. They look askance at any interruption, large or small, of their own routine-bound existences.

Most startling to the reader, however, seems the complete lack of perspective, or sense of proportion, apparent in the attitudes of so many of Bowen's characters in these interwar years. When in "The Working Party" (1929) a gathering is to be held at Combe Farm, the young hostess Mrs. Fisk becomes nervous and agitated. Newly married, she is eager to earn the approval of the local clique of women, and before the party she even gets down "on one knee for a moment by the large mahogany bedstead and prayed that all might go off well—nay, showily."[18] The climatic moment of the affair occurs at teatime: At the instant that the tea is to be served the cowherd Cottesby, who had "a heart," collapses on the stairs outside the kitchen. Mrs. Fisk regards his presence in the central hallway as a logistical nightmare threatening the ceremonial presentation of the tea. Whatever happens, she cannot let the service be interrupted: "'There's a man dead on the stairs,' she keeps thinking and 'they'll each want a third cup'" ("Working Party," 292, 295).

The thin barriers between the real and surreal lend an air of the bizarre to this social ritual. Frozen in a paralysis of feeling, the terrors that threaten to explode from within are kept at bay by the strictest exercise of will. Ghosts become subject to the same rules of convention and control. In the 1929 story "Foothold" a character asks, "have you noticed that one may discuss ghosts quite intelligently, but never any particular ghost without being facetious?"[19] Social protocol no longer offered the protection it once did, leaving the characters adrift in a world readjusting itself after war.

Other echoes of dislocation reverberate from the First World War.

Frequently, the women stand teetering on the brink of marriage, hesitating at the critical juncture between domesticity and the nebulous possibility of a "career." In "Requiescat" (1923) Mrs. Majendie, a stately widow, says mournfully to her husband's friend Stuart (who may have been the major's lover), "men make better things for themselves out of life than we do."[20] Repeatedly in Bowen's fiction, women like Mrs. Majendie have to reconstruct their lives without the aid of a spouse. Her women also find themselves adrift in the realm of marriage, the conventional bower for nurturing and sustaining women's lives. "Joining Charles," first printed in the *Royal Magazine* in 1926 as "The White House" and later revised, takes up the case of a recently married woman, "young Mrs. Charles," who is visiting her husband's parents.[21] She is staying with his family while her husband looks for a house for them in Lyons. The fixtures of marriage, such as the obligatory photograph of Charles on her chest of drawers, "from which the young wife, falling asleep or waking, had turned away her face instinctively," only cause her to feel empty ("Joining Charles," 223). Her avoidance of this image prefigures a scene in a later novel, *The Heat of the Day,* when Stella Rodney tries to escape the reproachful glances she imagines emanating from the static face of her husband.

Embedded in her husband's family, Louise, or the young Mrs. Charles, becomes ensnared by the myth of the son that the household has cultivated. Louise longs to express the pain deriving from her marriage to the supposed paragon, a union which has not turned out as she expected. She wishes to say aloud, "I'm unhappy. Oh, help me! I can't go on. I don't love my husband. He's grand, but he's rotten all the way through—." Of course, in a house devoted to celebrating Charles she cannot make such an admission. Charles's mother breaks the cold silence when she hesitantly cautions her daughter-in-law at the end of the story, "If things should be difficult—marriage isn't easy. If you should be disappointed—I know, I feel—you do understand?" ("Joining Charles," 227, 230). Ironically, when she is presented with the opportunity to speak, the possibility of self-revelation becomes all the more implausible for the young bride. To admit her unhappiness would be to surrender to a force Louise does not yet want to recognize.

Although Bowen's fictional young women commonly debate marriage as offering the alternative to whatever disagreeable situation they find themselves in, Mrs. Charles offers compelling proof of the flaws inherent in this institution. Particularly when the marriage has been welcomed as the only available solution to the question of what to do next, it draws criticism. The 1925 short story "The Parrot" describes an impatient young woman named Eleanor, who has become a companion to the older and more feeble Mrs. Willesden only because of the girl's "immense ineffectuality."[22] She resembles the caged bird featured in the story who cannot outwit her jailors except through luck or accident. After carelessly leaving the bird's cage open one day, Eleanor stares at herself in the mirror and speculates about her future: "although she was quite ready to marry anybody who seemed at all suitable, and thus escape from life with Mrs. Willesden and the equally odious alternative of using her brains, nobody, even of the most unsuitable, had so far presented himself" ("The Parrot," 113). While Eleanor muses on this dearth of opportunity, the parrot flies the coop.

Her search for the bird lures Eleanor outside the walls of Mrs. Willesden's gloomy residence to the house of neighbors, the Lennicotts. Mrs. Willesden had often shared her disapproving view of these people, telling the girl that he is a novelist but that his books are so "improper" and dull that she would not shelve them in her library with Eleanor in the house. Although, according to Mrs. Willesden, Mr. Lennicott lives with a woman, "it is not even known that they are the Lennicotts, but *he* is a Lennicott, and she is *called* Mrs." Eleanor feels trepidation about approaching this den of sin where the parrot, being no fool, was ineluctably drawn. To situate these characters, Bowen turns to the literary tradition for definition: "Mrs. Lennicott" greets Eleanor "uncomprehendingly, but with an air of earnest effort, as though she were a verse of Georgian poetry that one could not possibly understand" ("The Parrot," 115, 116). This confrontation between the conventional and the modern explains Eleanor's encounter with the surprisingly kind, though distracted, novelist who manages to retrieve the ornery parrot from the roof.

The domestic crisis ensuing from the bird's escape provides an opportunity for Eleanor to journey forth from the closed rooms that bind her. A metaphor for Eleanor, the parrot flew free of her captors to a place of apparent beauty and freedom, but she chose a land where she cannot remain. When Eleanor brings the parrot in to Mrs. Willesden the next morning the girl must get up her nerve to confess that it had got away. Mrs. Willesden, mistakenly assuming that Eleanor had captured the bird on her own, exclaims: "if strange people had caught him, even people quite respectable and honest, it would have put me in an embarrassing position—under compliment, I mean" ("The Parrot," 123). There are no such easy answers for the companion. Unfortunately, Eleanor remains the captive of a cranky old woman, a victim of her own lethargy.

In *The Hotel* Bowen expanded upon many of the ideas about the relations between the sexes she had been alluding to in her short stories. Focused primarily on women, it tells the tales of Sydney, Mrs. Kerr, Miss Pym, Miss Fitzgerald, and the young Lawrence daughters, who embody many differing female voices. Sydney and Veronica often debate about their own sex, with the former explaining that "women . . . are all tentacles, they absorb and stretch feeling." Veronica adds plainly, "I do think men are pathetic." Locating herself in the discussion between the modern and the old-fashioned that runs through Bowen's fiction—the dichotomy that Eleanor and the Lennicotts represented in "The Parrot"—Veronica declares, "I'm not modern. . . . Tell me what you think will become of me" (*H* 99). Reducing tangled issues to pithy remarks, the characters express the contradictions common in an era when women and men were uneasy about how to adapt to a complicated and quickly shifting postwar world. The women find their new situations of strength perplexing but seem surprisingly ready to abdicate the responsibility of making choices for themselves.

Many of the women in *The Hotel* appear able, even eager, to put the harshest criticism of their own sex into words. Sometimes they parody damaging stereotypes, and in so doing they echo the author's perennial concern with the dangers inherent in labeling and categorizing. When Mrs. Kerr and her son Ronald are discussing the relations between the sexes, their conversation centers on a much-disputed fear prevalent after the First World War that women had become too aggressive and warlike. Mrs. Kerr admits to Ronald, "I cannot disentangle myself from the idea that it isn't right for a woman not to be a little barbarous." Her tentative manner indicates her discomfort with the conception that women might be taking too much charge of their own destiny. Ronald comments in a measured way, "You see, [women] can . . . they can *canal* the natural forces." With alarm, his mother replies that *she* does not recognize these "forces" in herself. Playing with stereotypes, she says, "you would hate me to be rational. It's forbidding and horrible in a woman, I think" (*H* 95).

Part of the social atmosphere Bowen explored in *The Hotel* evolved in reaction to the mercurial changes in women's occupations prompted by the war. The women in this novel often appear disoriented and useless, as they bat back and forth various pastimes that might occupy them. As the historian Carol Dyhouse has argued, "The First World War only temporarily increased women's participation in industry"; an era of strong disapproval toward married women working either in professions or industry followed.[23] Bowen's female characters often question the advisability of their working outside the home, and the query becomes more pressing in the later novels. Eileen Lawrence, the daughter of a doctor, speculates that "it might be an advantage to a girl to have some kind of career, though she might not want to stick with it" (*H* 126). When another vacationing Englishwoman, Mrs. Aherne, tells her husband "what men really want," he interrupts her to say, "I do wish you wouldn't generalize about men."[24] Such mindless declarations are seen as promoting many of the misunderstandings that keep the sexes from forming heartening unions in Bowen's fictions.

From the start the conversations that take place in *The Hotel* set up the expectation that, as women decide how their lives can mesh with men's, they will surmise what it means to be a woman. Early in the novel, when the smothering Mrs. Kerr and the unconventional Sydney Warren are discussing the "sensational" quality of women's lives, Mrs. Kerr blurts out, "I'm not a Feminist, but I do like being a woman" (*H* 11). Like many other Bowen characters, Mrs. Kerr enjoys her stature as a woman while refusing to align herself with any kind of political or social movement. Recoiling from the idea of organized action on a large scale, Bowen's fictional females prefer to work from within the specificity of their own lives to alter the status quo. They utter small protests against the rigid hierarchical arrangements that too often prevent them from fulfilling their talents or realizing their dreams.

The Hotel, which concentrates on men and women and the gaps between them, suggests the impossibility of a contented marriage. When Sydney observes the dull silence emanating from the couples in the dining room, she wonders at the oddity of the expectation that demands "that men and women should be expected to pair off for life" (*H* 18). Sydney, who dreams of becoming a doctor and has come abroad to recover from the strain of studying for examinations, still finds herself embroiled in the question of romance. Veronica Lawrence, another quester, asks Sydney, "Does it seem to you . . . that this world is entirely divided into rather stupid men and very silly women?" (*H* 98). But, later in the novel Sydney reluctantly becomes engaged to a newcomer at the hotel, the Reverend James Milton.

After an outing in the Italian countryside when her fiancé becomes distraught at the scene of Italians cruelly beating a horse, Sydney backs out of the engagement: "The crisis brought out in him at the expense of his rationality all that was latently English" (*H* 159). Later Sydney confesses to her old friend Mrs. Kerr that she had been untouched by the act of cruelty. Occasionally throughout the novel, some such incident allows the shutter of consciousness to snap open, if only for an instant. As a rule, Bowen keeps this intimate emotion in her characters hidden. When she allows it to surface it precipitates a deluge of confusion, as in this instance when Sydney abruptly cancels her plans. Although she is, like the Lawrence daughters, ostensibly "modern," she does not find the girls entirely congenial, and eventually Mrs. Kerr, who never finishes the books Sydney carefully selects for her, gets on her nerves. When Mrs. Kerr's wandering son Ronald stops at the hotel to break up his journey between the Continent and Oxford, he puts words to what others have been wondering: "There is nothing now to prevent women being different . . . and yet they seem to go on being just the same. What is the good of a new world if nobody can be got to come and live in it?" (*H* 110).

Not accidentally, the soul-searching that Bowen's characters indulge in takes place in Italy, a place where they feel severed from their personal pasts. They exist in a suspended state at the hotel. Expressing his frustration with things as they are, a voice in the hotel's drawing room complains: "Nothing definite seems to happen at all—I mean, of course, there is always politics, but that goes on and on, so one begins to lose interest." One character even claims that hotel time is different; the "idyllic evenings" seem "agonizingly meaningless" as the traveling Britishers realize that they have no purpose other than escaping England and seeking the warmth of the sun (*H* 119, 129).

Obviously, the characters rarely know what they are missing, but the more self-conscious ones such as Mrs. Kerr acknowledge: "I do nothing at all all day long," a forthright declaration that she claims protects her from the "feeling of rootlessness" (*H* 95). Travel and foreign adventure, activities that are usually associated with the widening of horizons, seem only to narrow the lives of the English wayfarers at this hotel on the Italian Riviera. On "the edge of Europe," or not so "innocently abroad" (like Lady Elfrida in Ireland in *To the North*), the residents approach the unfamiliar hesitantly, and only when fortified with the mainstays of the English experience (*H* 118).[25] On her walk, the quintessential Englishwoman, Miss Fitzgerald, had taken "everything that, abroad, an English lady takes out with her"—that is, "coloured straw satchel, the native umbrella, the golf jersey, the net bag supplementing the satchel." And although Sydney's cousin Tessa has seen much of the world, her exposure to so many vistas has not altered her fundamental perception that "there was only one view" (*H* 7, 155). By depicting her characters as clinging tenaciously to their Englishness, Bowen comically circumscribes them until they cannot see past their own faces.

Concerned not only with defining the English abroad, Bowen was also beginning to come to personal terms with them at home. In April, 1923, she had complained to Cameron, "England does look nasty from the outside, doesn't it?" Nevertheless, she began to write more frequently of the English from the inside, but often retaining a certain distance.[26] One story in particular, "Human Habitation," dating from around 1926, makes this perspective apparent. A university student named Jameson tours the countryside with his college friend, advising his companion that "one should get to know the English Country as more than a poetic abstraction and its people as more than a political entity."[27] When developing her characters, Bowen defined them clearly as people and as representatives of certain national traits and outlooks.

While England and the English, wherever they may be, stand as the focal point in much of her fiction of the 1920s, Bowen increasingly began to explore the cultural misconceptions separating the Irish from the English. Italy and elsewhere in Europe stood at one pole from England, while Ireland remained at the other. In one of Bowen's first stories about Ireland, "The Back Drawing-Room," initially published in 1926, a man tells a story about visiting his cousin in Ireland. Just as he gets started on his account, his wife exclaims, "Ireland unforgettably and almost terribly afflicted me. The contact was so intimate as to be almost intolerable. One lives in a dream there, a dream oppressed and shifting." In this story within a story Mr. Henneker takes his listeners on a tour of Ireland both in the midst and in the aftermath of civil disturbance. They venture to a place in their minds' eyes where the "country" looked "dilapidated and rather depressing."[28] The narrator tells of stumbling across the gates of an estate and finding himself in a back drawing room that smells of geraniums and musty wallpaper. There he realizes that he is seeing ghosts, that the woman he sees does not see him. Terrified, he retreats speedily to his cousin's house.

When Mr. Henneker recounts his story to his relatives no one believes him; they make clear to him that the Big House that once stood where he describes it was burned in the Troubles and that the Anglo-Irish inhabitants have scattered to Dublin or England. In "The Back Drawing-Room" Bowen begins to acclimate her readers to the avenues, houses, and walls of the Anglo-Irish that she evokes in *The Last September*. Seán O'Faoláin describes the long, winding walls of the estates as the "barrier" that the Anglo-Irish "erected" to imitate the one that "originally existed between Normans and Gaels."[29] As Bowen began to traverse this countryside in her short stories, she turned her gaze on the people of her race, the Anglo-Irish. Because she herself had necessarily come to regard travel and transience as commonplace early in her life, others who had to leave their homes started to move toward the center of her fiction. As the listeners in this short story hear the tale of ghosts and desolation, they learn Mr. Henneker's view of the Anglo-Irish: They are like "plants one's pulled up"; "They've nothing to grow in, or hold on to" ("Back Drawing-Room," 210).

Some Bowen characters have no idea what home means and, thus, are unable to miss this mythical place. One such character is Louise, the young wife in "Joining Charles" who has "been able to boast until quite lately that she had never been homesick." As she encounters the "fullness, this intimacy and queer seclusion of family life" for the first time, she suffers sudden pangs of alienation ("Joining Charles," 224, 223). The internal workings and rhythms of the daily life of a house appear bewildering and sometimes magical from the outside. When Mr. Lennicott's companion first meets Eleanor in "The Parrot" she exclaims, "Of course, one sees the houses, but it is difficult to realise, isn't it, that they have insides and that they really mean anything!" ("The Parrot," 118). It is apparently Bowen's view that preconceptions (or misconceptions) about what goes on inside houses can erect walls between people that are frequently impermeable.

Often in Bowen's fiction houses can exert a force larger than characters who inhabit them. A story that first appeared in *Encounters,* "The New House" (1923), focuses on a middle-aged brother and sister who have just moved into a house they purchased with their earnings and proceeds from their mother's estate. Their relocation means not only a change of address for them but also suggests a gesture toward upward mobility.[30] Herbert, the fastidious brother, feels intimidated by the gracious gentility the new house represents, so much in contrast to the "small brick villa" where they had until then spent their lives. At times he fears that the new house is "sneering at him," making him feel defensive about being a "parvenu." His sister, Cicely, regards the change of scene as liberating. In the disorder of the unsettled house she realizes that her old life pinned her down, "even the way the furniture was arranged at No. 17 held me so that I couldn't get away." Freed by this temporary suspension of routine, she recognizes that it is time to accept the suitor who has been proposing to her repeatedly. She had been hoping that he would pop the question so that she could "get away before this new house fastens on to me." Herbert views her abandonment of him as a betrayal. Her departure sets his rusty imagination "into movement," and he comforts himself by envisioning the new drawing room cast in the warm and sustaining light of family life. Defiantly, he asserts that he and his fantasy family "could do very well without Cicely's escritoire" ("New House," 56–58).

Few rooms in Bowen's fiction glow with this cozy light. Since so many of her characters live in perpetual motion, they have difficulty stopping long enough to transform a house into a home. Often, they are responding to some real or perceived lack in their own childhoods. The adults question whether they have provided good homes for their offspring; in *The Hotel* Mrs. Kerr wonders aloud whether she has "deprived" her son Ronald "of something." She asks him mournfully, "how long is it, I wonder, since you and I have kept house?" (*H* 95). Because the hotel can mimic a home but can never be one, it appears to Sydney to resemble a doll's house. She wishes that its front "could be swung open on a hinge" so that the inhabitants could be observed, in the kitchen, the library, and the spare room (*H* 69). Just as Cicely flees from her brother in "The New House," Sydney bolts from her engagement, fearing the routine demanded by the mundanities of domestic routine, either in the doll's house or the hotel.

Life abroad dissolves into a series of disconnected moments; the sheer transparency of relations in the hotel evokes an uncertain and claustrophobic atmosphere. Sydney, who can detect the veneer, still admires its sheen but worries that if the facade is removed nothing important will remain underneath. When she breaks her engagement with the clergyman she exposes the charade at the hotel for what it is. The characters who stay there must come to recognize its temporality and impermanence, its inability to engender life. They cannot accept that in their flight they resort to lives of vagueness, loneliness, and a barely submerged despair. The consequences of their rootlessness can be more damaging than they are willing to admit.

Like figures in a doll's house, they look to a child at the hotel as "hardly alive!" But as Sydney reasons in her rejoinder to this exclamation, "Well, you don't know what may not be happening to them" (*H* 81). Such rootless travelers and restless wanderers as these guests in *The Hotel* appear throughout Bowen's novels of this decade. In her next novel, *The Last September,* she fixed her attention on an extended examination of southern Ireland, where she began to locate her own origins.

Chapter 4

Tennis Parties and Ambushes

When Bowen wrote the preface of *The Last September* for its reissue in 1952 she confessed that "[this work] is nearest to my heart. This novel had a deep, clouded, spontaneous source. It brims up with and is rendered to a degree poetic by experience I had had in my early youth."[1] Set in September, 1920, in a Big House called Danielstown, which bears a strong resemblance to Bowen's Court, the book relates the story of a love affair played against the Anglo-Irish War. Clearly, the author's interest rests on this internal conflict. The First World War appears only indirectly: A child finds a "prewar" tennis ball under the bushes at a party, an officer's wife suggests a chorus of songs from the "Great War," and we hear that a young woman's first fiancé has been killed at the battle of the Somme.

The atmosphere of the novel is suffused with the bitterness of the struggles lasting from 1919 to 1921 known euphemistically in southern Ireland as the Troubles. In a direct borrowing from actuality Danielstown becomes caught in the guerrilla war when, from December 6, 1922, until March 22, 1923, fire destroyed 192 Big Houses.[2] The novel depicts Bowen's intense reaction to her proximity to the battles tearing apart southern Ireland. While she had never seen any of the sites of the First World War, she knew well both the scenes of the Irish ambushes and arson fires and some of the combatants. When writing in 1951 of the transformations of war she had known, Bowen noted certain changes she had observed: In 1916 "battles were associated with battlefields, not yet cities. To that extent, in spite of the Great War, the Edwardian concept of civilization still stood unshaken" (*SH* 186). On the other hand, the irregular and clandestine nature of the Anglo-Irish war preoccupied her. By setting her second novel in an Anglo-Irish Big House much like Bowen's Court, Bowen announced her readiness to engage, at least metaphorically, in the bitter struggle that marked her own years of adolescence in a nation itself fighting for independence.

In her preface to *The Last September* Bowen explained that color and light both "play their part in my plots." Nowhere is this more evident than in this novel, where a distinct and sharp pattern of images of battle and fire bring the disparate and scattered events of war to its core (*LS* viii). An awareness of shades and degrees of light becomes (as it does in much of Bowen's work) an index of the characters' moral stature. Her technique represents tremendous advances over her initial experiments with longer fiction. She self-consciously relied on the same structural device she used in her first novel, *The Hotel,* grouping the characters and the action under one roof (*LS* xviii). Paralleling personal dramas with the Anglo-Irish War, however, as she does in the later novel, makes for a more compelling story. Through her characters Bowen explores the continuously painful relationship between Ireland and England, the function of the Anglo-Irish and the meaning of their Big Houses, and the disturbing prospect of war, while she examines the confusing process of becoming "grown-up." Written when Bowen herself was twenty-eight, *The Last September* allows an intimate perspective on Lois's entrance into adulthood, which, like Bowen's, has been made all the more difficult by the wars enveloping it.

From her Oxford study, where she wrote *The Last September,* Ireland seemed far away. Yet, she recalled that in the process of writing she felt as Woolf had when she was at work on *The Waves,* submerged "like the swimmer caught by an undertow" (*LS* x). Bowen later explained in her preface that, with "perhaps the exception of *The Heat of the Day* which could but attach itself to what had become 'historic' fact," *The Last September* was the only novel she wrote which is "deliberately set back in a former time." She became transfixed by a past where the "Troubles troubled everything" and re-created in "fiction torn from the texture of history" an altered rendition of her own coming of age (*LS* ix, xi, x). By paying careful attention to making these former days accessible to an audience inhabiting a very different time, she included such details as "in those days, girls wore crisp white skirts" to emphasize the historical nature of the novel. She attributed the scrupulousness of her technique to her "fear" that the reader might "miss" the view of being "aware of looking—backward, down a perspective cut through the years" (*LS* 3, ix).

The Last September concentrates upon the story of the romance of

Lois Farquar and Gerald Lesworth (whose name puns on *worthless*), a British soldier stationed nearby at Clonmore. Defiantly blurring the fine distinction between fiction and autobiography, Bowen later pointed out that Lois "derives from, but is not, myself at nineteen." Lois, the niece of the Naylors, Danielstown's owners, embodies the enduring problem for Bowen of the relationship between the course of her own life and those of her literary creations. Her retrospective preface insists on the distance from and the connection between the novel and her own circumstances: "The book . . . is neither autobiographical nor in any way a transcript of *conscious* happenings." While *The Last September* attains much of its power from its proximity to Bowen's experience, she takes characteristic pains to stress that, although the story "could have been true, [it] is not" (*LS* ix, viii, xii).

Most closely, the novel scrutinizes the Anglo-Irish, those members of a disintegrating gentry who seem unable either to see or to assimilate what is happening around them. While Lois suffers from moments of blindness, her aunt has more consistent difficulty. As the days shorten, the mistress of Danielstown, Lady Naylor, "wished for clear, steady light" in the evenings. The lack of electricity in the house becomes yet another deprivation she bemoans as the lot of an Anglo-Irish woman, leading her to compare her situation to that of an acquaintance in England "whose brain was all shreddy with rabbit-combing and raffia" but who "had had electric light for years, just from living in England" (*LS* 207). Lady Naylor's conviction that electric light would illuminate her world becomes only one of the many fictions sustaining her tenuous existence. Clarity of vision and insight can come to her, in the novelist's view, only when she and her husband realize and accept what is happening around them—that the world they know is vanishing. Only when they stop denying that they are living in a war zone can the Naylors begin to perceive their existence through clear lenses. Like several other novels written in the 1920s and 1930s, *The Last September* investigates the demise of the Protestant Ascendancy through the image of the Big House and its residents.[3]

The flirtation between the young Anglo-Irish girl, Lois Farquar, and the Britisher, Gerald Lesworth, functions as a microcosm of the larger political and social conflicts developed in the book. At nineteen Lois is casting around for something to do with her life; Gerald regards her as having "no idea what she was." Surrounded by adults who discuss her future prospects insensitively, she avoids their predictions: "She didn't want to know what she was, she couldn't bear it: knowledge of this would stop, seal, finish one" (*LS* 57, 70). This adolescent Lois, who endures a time of "impatience, frivolity, lassitude or boredom," resembles the young Bowen, who endlessly asked herself "*what* I should be, and when" (*LS* viii). Lois, apparently drawn to a career as an artist (as Bowen once was), contemplates going to art school. When a family friend tells her that they hide ammunition in the plaster casts of sculptures in Dublin, the prospect becomes more exotic and romantic. Unlike her cousin Laurence, a son of the Protestant Ascendancy who is being educated at Oxford, Lois has no obvious opportunities open to her save marriage, and Laurence's apparent better fortune often makes her jealous.

While Laurence frequently has his eyes trained on a treatise by Locke or a book on Nigeria, he is also eager to engage in heated debate over the current political situation. Lois, in contrast, spends her days wandering around the house, arranging flowers, and daydreaming. Despite her cousin's admiration of his own ideas, he nonchalantly views his exclusive formal education as his right. Bowen portrays Lois, on the other hand, as crippled by the dearth of avenues to the future for someone of her gender and class. In her vagueness she resembles many of Bowen's earlier female characters. Particularly, she brings to mind the feckless Eleanor in "The Parrot," who wants someone else to decide her fate for her. The formlessness of Lois's future underscores the uncertain years ahead for the Anglo-Irish, whose power and numbers were rapidly fading. The Protestant population in southern Ireland declined by one-third between 1911 and 1916.[4]

Laurence does not encourage Lois about her ability to thrive in the world that stretches beyond the gates of Danielstown, and she herself fears her isolation. On the same evening that a Royal Irish Constabulary (R.I.C.) barracks at Ballyrum "had been attacked and burnt out after a long defense," resulting in several deaths, Lois had been daydreaming, "cutting a dress out, a voile that I didn't even need, and playing the gramophone." When she realizes what she was doing at the time of the skirmish, she asks Gerald pointedly: "How is it that in this country that ought to be full of such violent realness, there seems nothing for me but clothes and what people say? I might as well be in some kind of cocoon" (*LS* 54, 56). With Gerald, or more precisely, because of him, Lois begins to realize that she is isolated not only from the future but also from the present. Yet she fears what may happen if she becomes too dependent on him.

Lois and Gerald's love affair epitomizes the misunderstandings and bitterness that separated the Anglo-Irish and the British. As Bowen explained to her friend, the novelist William Plomer, *The Last September* describes the "equivocal position" of a Big House family in whom "interest and tradition should make them support the British. Affection ties them to the now resistant people of their surrounding community."[5] Gerald is caught in this struggle for Lois; after he has been on duty all night in the countryside, he comes to Danielstown to declare to Lois, "You know I'd die for you" (*LS* 110). From that moment on, if not before, the reader realizes that Gerald will indeed meet his death while defending people who do not think they need to be protected, leaving behind the girl who thinks she might love him.

When the young pair attends a dance at the British barracks at Clonmore the wind blows with "a sinister energy in this fixed and angular world." After he kisses her she does not have the two reactions she had expected, "outrage" and "capitulation," which epitomize the Anglo-Irish attitude toward the English. Instead, she shrinks from the emotional intensity of the situation by concentrating on remembering the social protocol of who should speak first after "a kiss had been, not exchanged but—administered" (*LS* 188, 189). That Lois and Gerald cannot forge a true union, either sexually or emotionally, is an inevitable component of their sad story and is equally so in the larger one being played out around them.

The dance spins out of control as the young lovers run up against obstacles partly of their own making, namely the question of Gerald's proposal to Lois. Each becomes fearful of loving too much, or of appearing vulnerable. In a scene that foreshadows "The Demon Lover," a short story Bowen wrote during the Second World War, Gerald presses the buttons of his uniform against Lois as he embraces her. Instead of reacting to the physical discomfort, Lois thinks about the pain that results "from not being understood." When she returns from the dance Lois has to face the further consequences of the conflicts between her love for Gerald and her family's wishes. Lady Naylor disapproves of her niece's socializing with the soldiers, commenting tartly that, if they spent more time dancing "and interfered less, I daresay there would be less trouble in the country" (*LS* 191, 203).

Lady Naylor reveals herself to be a meddler and conniver when she pays a clandestine visit to Gerald to deter him from pursuing Lois.[6] Superficially, she regards him as an inappropriate choice for her niece since his military status forbids him to marry. But more disturbing to her are the vagaries of his social and economic class; she complains to a friend, "His mother, he says, lives in Surrey, and of course you do know, don't you, what Surrey *is*. It says nothing, absolutely." Gerald's mysterious pedigree perplexes Lady Naylor: "Of course, I don't say Gerald Lesworth's people are in *trade*—I should never say a thing like that without foundation.... No, I should say they were just villa-ry" (*LS* 68). The conclusions Lady Naylor draws about Gerald's family presage the ones Stella reaches about Robert Kelway, the traitor who dominates Bowen's later novel *The Heat of the Day*. In both cases, the men's roots are held to blame for their later transgressions.

Lois becomes furious when she learns that Gerald did not muster a more assertive defense when her aunt intruded into their affairs. He can only explain his response by muttering, "I ... I don't know." Lois at that instant "saw him standing confused, like a foreigner with whom by some failure in her vocabulary all communication was interrupted" (*LS* 236). No matter how well he plays the part of the savior-soldier come to rescue a backward country, it becomes clear to Lois that the enormous distance between them can never be lessened, largely because of the self-absorption that prevents her from understanding the larger context surrounding them.[7]

Laurence, like Lois, cannot situate himself anywhere in this controversy. But this remove bothers him. Although he fears the violence of war, he also dreams secretly of being somehow involved in the drama: "the neglect of the raiders' pricked his egotism." He alleviates his sense of detachment from the events around him by questioning Gerald intently: "How is this war of yours really going? Do you realise I know nothing—this might all just as well be going on in the Balkans. I sometimes rather wish that I were a gunman" (*LS* 132, 113). Despite the time he has spent being educated at Oxford, Laurence still shows himself an Irishman when he bristles at Gerald's defense of the imperial rationale for "civilisation" and nationality. Their conceptions of civilization fundamentally clash. Laurence sees it as "an unemotioned kindness withering to assertion selfish or racial; silence cold with a comprehension in which the explaining clamour died away" (*LS* 114, 115). But his neat rationalizations do not deepen his comprehension of what constitutes his "side," and he expresses consternation at this absence. He is called upon to define his position when Marda Norton, a visitor from England, asks him, "How far do you think this war is going to go?" Revealingly, he chooses to denote his stance by referring to a negation: "our side—which is no side—rather scared, rather isolated, not expressing anything except tenacity to something that isn't there—that never was there" (*LS* 100).

Those Anglo-Irish Laurence typifies, who came of age at the same time as the Easter Rising of 1916—when Yeats wrote that "A Terrible Beauty is born"—were especially confused.[8] Laurence derives his identity from both England and Ireland. This Anglo-Irish ambivalence reveals itself repeatedly in *The Last September* in personal dimensions, as when Peter Connor, a young Irishman the Naylors have known forever as their neighbor, is reported as missing. Peter (who was thought to be stealing arms) is captured by Gerald, who boasts of his prowess while Laurence listens silently to the details of the incident. His uncle, Sir Richard Naylor, by contrast, becomes flustered when he hears about it and betrays conflicting reactions: "His mother is dying. However, I suppose you must do your duty" (*LS* 113). He can only conceive of the situation in individual terms and responds by sending luxurious grapes to Mrs. Connor, a token of sorrow. When the abstractions of war are brought home in human terms they horrify both sides and emphasize the intractable passivity of the Anglo-Irish. They appear helpless to ward off violence or to bring the bloodshed to an end.

Eventually, Mr. Daventry, a subaltern at Clonmore who is already "beginning to hate Ireland," appears at Danielstown to report that, while on patrol, Gerald has been killed instantly in an ambush. The household responds to this news in its usual muffled way, by embracing conventional gestures that obscure any private emotions. Lady Naylor puts aside her earlier dislike of Gerald and writes to his mother in Surrey to console her with a description of "how happy his life had been [in Ireland]. He quite beamed, really; he was the life and soul of everything." Lois, in contrast, briefly attempts to discover what Gerald's death means to her and why it has occurred. She tries to talk to Laurence, saying, "there are things that one can't—," but her cousin's obvious indifference silences her. Finally, she reduces the complex conflict to the selfishly simplistic outlines that make sense to her: "He loved me, he believed in the British Empire" (*LS* 254, 252).

As symbols, Lois, Gerald, and Laurence embody the novel's study of the crosscurrents that flowed between the Irish and the English in the difficult autumn of 1920. Bowen portrayed the damaging misperceptions that handicapped both the British and the Irish as they engaged in a war that made no fundamental sense either to the Anglo-Irish or to the

British, who were their supposed defenders. For the first time in her own fiction Bowen was exploring the divisions of nationality as they had impinged upon her own experience. The characters in her novel are caught in various traps contrived from their lack of comprehension of their citizenship in either personal or political terms.

The Anglo-Irish in *The Last September* find themselves particularly vulnerable to what Bowen often termed a state of "suspension." Lois's mother, Laura, who dies young, is successful in England because "she was too Irish altogether for her own country." Her daughter falls heir to the same mixed nationality to the point that "she could not conceive of her country emotionally: it was a way of living, abstract of several countrysides, or an oblique, frayed island moored at the north but with an air of being detached and drawn out west from the British coast." While the main subject of the novel is ostensibly the war of independence, or revolution, Bowen also considers the related topic of what it means to be Anglo-Irish. Thus, Lois's indecision about her future devolves not only from the situation of the country where she lives but also from the perception that, in her words, "I don't live anywhere, really" (*LS* 18, 37, 194). Her indeterminateness about what home is highlights the spiritual and emotional flux that suffuses her.

Lois is not the only one at sea about where she belongs. Usually, Sir Richard Naylor manages to ignore the reality of the surrounding situation, successfully not noticing what goes on around him. That he might have to alter his pattern of life at the request of anyone else annoys him profoundly. Although at night he dreams of being a member of the Black and Tans (the British police force known for their brutality), he observes the ordinary daily routine of the household, a captive in his own country (*LS* 133). He and the older residents of Danielstown who will not revise their views are the objects of some of Bowen's harshest criticism. Clearly outdated and old-fashioned, their desire to live securely within sheltered pasts becomes as harmful as their inflexibility. While they think of themselves as brave, they appear merely ludicrous, mindlessly carrying out rigidly unchanging customs in the middle of a war, refusing to acknowledge that the lines of battle have long been established.[9]

Vehemently, Bowen censures the British as well as the Anglo-Irish for their narrow-mindedness in *The Last September*. Her later autobiography, *Bowen's Court*, conveys conflicting emotions about the principle of home rule, which grew out of the battles of these years, and its effect on the Anglo-Irish; she calls it "that fatal principle of separation—still damaging to us—... in Ulster the Protestant Ascendancy was a living fact; in Munster, Leinster and Connaught, it had become, within the last fifty years a ghost only" (*BC* 430). But the Britishers in her earlier novel do not distinguish themselves as attractive residents in Ireland. Betty Vermont, the wife of the commanding officer at Clonmore in *The Last September,* symbolizes what for the Anglo-Irish are the despicable qualities of the English outlook. As if suddenly compelled by an attack of conscience, Mrs. Vermont warns other gossiping wives that, although the Anglo-Irish are "different" from the Irish, they still have "got feelings" (*LS* 192).

Bowen's dramatization of the behavior of the British entourage stationed at Clonmore indicates one view of the British attitude toward the "natives" among whom they were compelled to live. Mired in self-fashioned stereotypes, Bowen's Britishers contort their observations to match their narrow preconceptions. The officers' wives are among the worst offenders. At a tennis party at Danielstown the obnoxious Mrs. Vermont exclaims in loud surprise, "Aren't they hospitable!" Mrs. Vermont "was not disappointed in Ireland. She had never before been to so many large houses with so small a sense of her smallness. Of course they were all very shabby and not artistic at all" (*LS* 40). For her, Ireland is in desperate need of improvement. If she were living permanently in the country, she proclaims, she would spruce up the grimy facades with sparkling white paint.

Throughout these social occasions, an underlying uneasiness pervades the superficially pleasant exchanges between the officers' wives and their Anglo-Irish hostesses. Mrs. Carey, a loyal inhabitant of a Big House, thinks to herself that Mrs. Vermont is "a little person" while she urges on her another piece of chocolate cake, which is a specialty of the house at teatime. Mrs. Vermont censures her own thoughts, stopping herself from telling a story about a Ford car "because in Ireland they seemed to like Fords so seriously." Instead, she says in false admiration, "I do think you're so sporting the way you just stay where you are and keep going on. Who would ever have thought of the Irish turning out so disloyal[?]" When even she realizes she has gone too far, she hastily amends her sermon with predictable and unnecessary clarification: "I mean, of course, the lower classes!" (*LS* 53).

Nervously, she goes from bad to worse as she recalls the childhood repertoire of Irish songs sung to her by her mother, who "always said [the Irish] were the most humorous people in the world, and with hearts of gold." She gives away her limitations even more, adding, "though of course we had none of us ever been in Ireland." Mrs. Vermont feels compelled to justify the official nature of her presence in Ireland in order to validate her important role in the British occupation: "you see we didn't come over to enjoy ourselves, did we? We came to take care of all of you—and of course, we are ever so glad to be able to do it" (*LS* 53). These awkward social lies mirror the more damaging political ones each nation is spinning. Neither side can see through its mask to the other.

Laying bare the heart of the hostility between the two countries, Bowen interjects a piquant satirical humor into the bitterness of the dialogues between the English and the Irish. Mrs. Vermont typifies the rudeness of a British busybody matron on the loose in Ireland, eager to peer into the private lives of any natives she may surprise. One day, she ventures into the countryside with her friend Mrs. Rolfe on an excursion to see Danielstown, or what symbolizes for her "a lovely old Irish home." Laurence, who is at home when they arrive, does not mistake their motives for an instant and deliberately fulfills their ridiculous expectations of the locals, saying with a straight face, "Yes, we are quaint, really" (*LS* 242). The scene conveys the sensations of being the watcher and the watched as the Englishwomen tour the perimeter of the house.

When the women look through a window and see Sir Richard Naylor in the library, Mrs. Vermont declares that he is "such a type," while her companion wonders aloud if he is a knight or a baronet. They do not trouble to hide their dissatisfaction with the lukewarm hospitality offered by the Naylors, exclaiming huffily, "When one thinks these are the people we are defending!" Snidely, they tell Sir Richard that they are admiring his "darling cows," yet they leave Danielstown clucking that the Naylors are "going down in the world," noting the damp and unused drawing room (*LS* 242, 243, 244, 246). As much as women like Mrs. Vermont begin to seem despicable for laughing at the shabbiness of Danielstown, Sir Richard appears equally far from a realistic appraisal of the scene.

Just when Bowen seems about to damn the Anglo-Irish for their aloofness and indifference, something stops her, causing her to suggest instead a respect for their unyielding perseverance. The residents of the Big Houses in *The Last September,* as in actuality, live under the constant threat of nighttime arson by Irish rebels (Sinn Féiners). When the Naylors go to bed they bolt the doors against raiders who might appear at their gates. Sir Richard dreads an attack, but Laurence cannot stifle his excitement. Hearing that the nearby Castle Trent has been raided, he hopes that Danielstown will be next. Lois is more ambivalent; she views Danielstown as the only approximation of home she knows.

While the inhabitants of Danielstown try to ignore the war, armed conflict pervades the country. It makes its presence known, cutting wires, arousing suspicions, and causing such alarm that those who had never locked their doors bolt them securely every night. Nothing seems safe, but more than ever the Anglo-Irish labor to keep up the pretense that all is normal. The Naylors decry deaths and ambushes as "the horrible thing" while taking their tea in the cold drawing room. Lois's friend, the more classical Livvy, expresses her disappointment with her future fiancé, the subaltern David Armstrong (whose name suggests an obvious contrast with Gerald Lesworth), when he cannot attend the gymkhana at Mount Isabel (another nearby Big House) because he has to be on duty; he, in turn, explains pointedly that such service is "what we are here for," in case she has forgotten (*LS* 54, 43). It seems all too easy to lose sight of what purpose the British are serving.

Insulated inside the Big House, Lois frets that Marda Norton, the English visitor, will judge her life to be boring or pathetic. She hesitates to show Marda her drawings for fear that the sophisticated woman from across the sea will think them childish or dull. Her sense of self derives from her belief in the house, and, thus, she hopes that Danielstown may also impress an outsider. Yet she knows its powers are limited: "already the room seemed full of the dusk of oblivion. And she hoped that instead of bleaching to dust in summers of empty sunshine, the carpet would burn with the house in a scarlet night to make one flaming call upon Marda's memory" (*LS* 121). Lois's desire for fame through apocalypse can be read as her yearning to secure a place in a world other than the dying one she has inherited at Danielstown.

Bowen insists upon the house's sudden temporality and weightlessness through the language of the novel as the ideals it once embodied break down all around it: "The vacancy of the sky" penetrates the "defenseless windows" of Danielstown. At Mount Isabel, the mountains beyond the house are "sheathed in pink air," while "the cream facade of the house [is] like cardboard, high and confident in the sun—a house without weight" (*LS* 172, 143). It becomes, in some respects, like the vision of the hotel that Sydney longs for, one where the front has been unhinged to reveal the contents.

As the Naylors hold up their heads proudly, finally able in the midst of this tragedy to look straight ahead, they see the world redden around them. Bowen's repeated reference to the shades of crimson they perceive telegraphs the impending season of loss. The novel's setting in early autumn underscores the cycle of death and demolition that the internal events of the story symbolize. The house, like others nearby, loses its mass in direct accordance with its residents' decline in moral stature. Danielstown appears to shrink in vitality, a diminution that impresses Lois on her return from the dance when she sees "twenty dark windows" that "stared over the fields aloofly out of the pale grey face of the house." However much Lois loves it, the house is filled with emptiness as a "reservoir of obscurity" (*LS* 197, 79).

The novel follows the season of mourning as its action moves from the autumn into the winter of Anglo-Irish discontent. On the apocalyptic February night in 1921 when Danielstown does indeed burn, Sir Richard and his wife watch the inferno, which "in the light from the sky" enables them to see "too distinctly." The moment when "the door stood open hospitably upon a furnace" raises the blindfolds from the Naylors' eyes. What they see leaves them shaken and weakened for they recognize it as the death knell of their position in Ireland. In a bitter, ironic twist, the tradition of Anglo-Irish hospitality which Bowen celebrated has led the arsonists right to the doors of Danielstown, Castle Trent, and Mount Isabel: "it seemed, looking from east to west at the sky tall with scarlet, that the country itself was burning" (*LS* 256, 255). The red here, instead of representing the promise of the flowers, suggests the flames of Dante's inferno.

Such wanton destruction was not unfamiliar to Bowen, who would later recall in *Bowen's Court* the spring night in 1921 when "three Anglo-Irish houses in our immediate neighbourhood—Rockmills, Ballywalter, Convamore—were burnt by the Irish. The British riposted by burning, still nearer Bowen's Court, the farms of putative Sinn Feiners—some of whom had been our family's friends. What now?" (*BC* 439–40). Although Bowen could destroy the residence in *The Last September* in the name of greater freedom—because, she explained, it "violently, serve[d] to free [Lois]"—she could not murder its inhabitants, for that came too close to home. By relying on her distinction from Lois as the "daughter of the house from which Danielstown was drawn," Bowen emphasized the distance she placed between her own existence and the lives she invented in the novel. This fictional exercise enabled her to reexamine without fear of exposure her emotions as an Anglo-Irish descendant in a storm of troubles. She, like Lois, who "had to surmount adolescence during the First World War, reacted against any excessive tax, any strain or demand made upon feeling. To the core, we were neither zealots nor rebels" (*LS* xii).

Bowen later explained in her afterword to *Bowen's Court,* written in 1942 while another war raged, that by teaching herself to imagine the family house in flames, she survived the instability of its tenure during the Irish revolution. Paradoxically, by burning the house in her fiction, she ensured its immortality by etching its image in her heart. Like other uprooted Anglo-Irish, she discovered painfully and deliberately how to separate her traditions from their grounding. The still sweet peas in silver bowls atop mahogany tables and the steady dinner gong that assured the continuance of the life within Danielstown remained parts of their creator. Tenuous symbols of an even more shaky universe, these metaphors for order, beauty, and tradition grounded Bowen's hunt for her own roots in the midst of the chaos of war. Her early training served her well. Subsequently, she spent her life seeking images of security and tranquillity, while simultaneously imagining them being destroyed by fire.

Chapter 5

"The Map of Europe"

> The new masters of the world created Le Touquet and Juan les Pins, fought each other for oil and reparations, blamed each other for the slump, and wandered blandly and ignorantly over Europe with a dark blue suit, letter of credit, set of clean teeth, and stiff white collar.
> —Cyril Connolly, "Writers and Society, 1940–43"

After burning the Big House in *The Last September* Bowen charted her own fictional course through the 1930s, one that included sterile houses, cold hearths, and hearts in disrepair. The characters she created wander the countryside aimlessly, either in search of their origins or in restless exile from them. When they do alight—to establish their own domestic routines, often in cramped modern villas on ugly housing estates—the structures they acquire do not become homes in the Burkean sense of the word. That is, they do not imbue integrity, tradition, harmony, or proportion; their residents mature without the ability to love. Like a hearth, Bowen saw, the human heart could go dramatically wrong, on both a small and on a large scale. These inadequate houses provide only temporary shelter for the typical Bowen collection of orphans and stray children who grow up without an understanding of themselves or of anyone else.

For the adults, locked in marriages or relationships that do not sustain them emotionally, the bond of wedlock offers only a poor substitute for love. The women appear either lost, vulnerable, or devouring of the enfeebled men who ask to accompany them on their journeys. The marriages they attempt rarely produce children (a fact which sometimes creates anxiety); and the only births result from adulterous affairs. Without this hope for the next generation the future looks bleak. This hopelessness emerged as Bowen began to point her fiction toward the events in Europe that clouded the horizon. Increasingly, she was preoccupied with the effects of race, class, and gender on the inheritance she felt was in danger. In her fiction of this decade, she dissects the characteristics of the English, the French, Jews, and the Anglo-Irish. Once again she analyzes the fundamental juxtaposition between the English and the Irish; she described it in *The House in Paris,* written in 1935, as a relation that "remains a mixture of showing off and suspicion, nearly as bad as sex" (*HP* 94).

A house in Ireland dominated Bowen's own life in the 1930s. When her father died in the spring of 1930 she became the first woman to inherit Bowen's Court since its completion in 1776. The legacy of the ancestral home dramatically colored, and in a sense controlled, her life. Bowen described herself as a philosophical descendant of Edmund Burke, the guardian of a tradition, an ideal, and all of the best that remained from the past. She looked to the eighteenth century as the heyday of the Ascendancy when such admired figures as Burke had defined her so-called race.[1] In reality she had come into possession of a large, cold, and outmoded house that still had hip-baths instead of indoor plumbing and only candles for illumination.[2] Her share in the estate included the house but little capital to run it. Consequently, finances became a greater worry than they had been for previous Bowens who had let what money and land there was trickle away in gambling, legal struggles, and spasmodic gestures toward the upkeep of the estate.

Bowen's ownership of the house suffused her life with the atmosphere, or "time-colour," of what she viewed as the glorious days of the eighteenth century when the Anglo-Irish tradition had become firmly established.[3] Many historians affirm her view, arguing that the Anglo-Irish Big House had lost most significant political meaning and economic power by the end of the nineteenth century, when it "entered upon its long Indian summer as a cultural memory and myth."[4] According to Bowen, the year the house was built, 1775, marked the apogee of her family's membership in the race.[5] The family located its faith that its members could make a continuing life in Ireland in the actual stones of the house. R. F. Foster maintains in his *Modern Ireland, 1600–1972* that "the Ascendancy built Big Houses in order to convince themselves not only that they had arrived, but that they would remain." A Big House built about the time of Bowen's Court cost approximately thirty thousand pounds to construct; such an investment carried weight in its demonstrated intention to endure and prosper.[6]

The Irish connections embodied in Bowen's family estate made for incessant contradictions, and even endowed her life in England with something of the fantastical nature Virginia Woolf mocked when she asked, "Oh, you, when are you going back to your ancient Irish castle?"[7] By referring to Bowen as an "Irishwoman, at least one sea apart from English traditions," the Irish writer Seán O'Faoláin, who was a longtime friend, wisely detected the opposing forces inherent in her Anglo-Irish origins. These came to the fore during the 1930s, an era when she epitomized the contradictions O'Faolain used to describe her: "Heart-cloven and split-minded . . . consistently declaring herself born and reared Irish, residing mostly in England, writing in the full English tradition."[8]

Obviously, Bowen found the anomalies in her inheritance stimulating. As the century turned thirty, she embarked upon her most prodigious period of literary production. In these years she widened the scope of her career by becoming known as a frequent (if overly generous) book reviewer and a clever essayist. She wrote for such journals as the *New Statesman and Nation*, the *Tatler*, the *Spectator*, and *Cornhill* magazine and was the drama critic for Graham Greene's short-lived publication *Night and Day*. While she appreciated the recognition and income generated by her reviews for the *New Statesman* and the *Tatler*, she complained to Virginia Woolf that the job was "a perfectly awful business."[9] Although she often fretted that this work cut into her fiction writing, this decade still represented her most prolific years as a novelist. She not only wrote a great deal, but much of it was accomplished and adventurous as she continually widened her compass.

Bowen situates her characters in England, Europe, and Ireland. *Friends and Relations* (1931), her intricate study of a love triangle, represents her first try at basing a novel entirely in England. She explained that this new locale demanded a different kind of style. The book's narrowness and hesitancy show that the experiment was still in its early stages. After Woolf read the book she warned Bowen that the emotional and linguistic inversions of the plot resembled the work of someone who was "trying to throw a lasso with a knotted rope."[10] Bowen attempted to combat allegations of parochialism levied against this book in her next novel, *To the North,* published in 1932. In an atmosphere that combines emotional subtlety and melodrama, she parallels the states of consciousness of several upper-middle-class young adults living in London with the political tensions of the continent. Encouraged by the critical acclaim given to the book, she was also pleased when her collection of short fiction *The Cat Jumps and Other Stories* met a similar reception in 1934.

The House in Paris, which many called Bowen's most important novel to date, appeared the following year. Through studying several generations the novel examines the varying conceptions of nationality and race expressed in the French, Jewish, Irish, English, and Anglo-Irish temperaments. *The Death of the Heart,* which rivals *The Last September* as Bowen's most complex and skillful prewar novel, came out in 1938, the same year she was elected a member of the Academy of Irish Letters. Her subtle exploration of Portia, the young orphan who lives with her selfish guardians in a London terrace house, merited much attention. The complexity of the work inspired William Plomer to share his idiosyncratic admiration of her accomplishment: "I sometimes feel inclined to compare you to a circular saw."[11] It was to be her last novel for eleven years—until after the Second World War had passed and she had gained the necessary distance from the events she wished to fictionalize.

Bowen and her husband moved to London as a result of his appointment to the Central Council of School Broadcasting at the BBC in 1935. Installed in No. 2 Clarence Terrace, a townhouse in Regent's Park, Bowen began to move in a sphere of London cultural life which included such figures as Virginia Woolf, T. S. Eliot, Rosamond and John Lehmann, Cyril Connolly, L. P. Hartley, V. S. Pritchett, and Graham Greene. Despite the apparent ease with which she entered into this circle, Bowen often encountered bouts of insecurity which lingered from the instability of her early years. Woolf recorded an early visit from Bowen: "Miss Bowen, stammering, shy, conventional, to tea."[12] When Woolf got to know Bowen better, she, like others, admired her and appreciated her kindness. After Bowen agreed to loan her house to Woolf's niece for a party to benefit the Artists' Committee for Spanish Relief, Woolf thanked Bowen for her "amazingly generous" offer.[13] Although she came into her own during this decade, she would continue to comment on "how this can take it out of you" in articles like "Manners" and "How to Be Yourself, But Not Eccentric."[14]

It was not long, however, before Bowen became known as an engaging hostess who matched sharp wit with ingenuity and a gift for improvisation. Anthony Powell remembers in his memoirs that he first met her when he had accepted her invitation to return to her house for further sustenance after a characteristically inedible dinner at the Connollys'. He told the story of their rummaging through the basement kitchen for some ham. Without her glasses she was very nearsighted:

> "Some people complain of cockroaches in the basements of these Regent's Park houses," she said. "Your parents do, but they say their cook doesn't mind a bit. She just stamps on them. I never seem to see any here." In one of the sinister Dr. Fu Manchu stories . . . [the doctor,] by the use of hypnotism, causes the wallpaper of a room to appear to be writhing with huge beetles. That was just how Elizabeth Bowen's kitchen floor looked at that moment.[15]

Guests upstairs at Clarence Terrace never complained of boredom or of not having enough to eat. Once she had established herself congenially in London and had made many English friends, she readily adapted to the British outlook.

Bowen's review of the 1936 show at the Royal Academy demonstrated what she called her ability to embody a "race within a race," as she wrote simultaneously from without and within her nationality.[16] As a Britisher she could write "no one is fonder of art than we English," which she then schizophrenically followed with the comment of a foreigner: "The English must be the most alarming race on earth; they ride down a minority so unconsciously."[17] Only in the hindsight induced by the Second World War could she appreciate that, as a Protestant child in Dublin, she had belonged to the Anglo-Irish: "the unquestioned rules of our being came, in fact, from the closeness of a minority world."[18] In the same memoir she explained that she "took the existence of Roman Catholics for granted. . . . They were, simply, 'the others,' whose world lay alongside ours but never touched." She learned quickly as a child to be "too discreet to ask" about the differences between the Catholics and the Protestants; the question "appeared to share a delicate, awkward aura with those two other differences, of sex, of class" ("Sundays," 49–50). But she continued her ambiguous relationship with Ireland during the post-treaty years (as Ireland tried to learn "how to be herself"), at the same time that she came to appear increasingly at home in England.[19]

Bowen's energy for both social life and literary production seemed boundless, and her work began to draw significant public recognition. Repeating the rhythm of her childhood patterns, she spent the majority of the year at Clarence Terrace with summers and Christmas holidays at Bowen's Court. She counterpointed her rich intellectual life in England with more bucolic stays in Ireland. There, she ran the estate and entertained lavishly, thus realizing her romanticized vision of herself as an Anglo-Irish landowner. In a letter to William Plomer she described the "perfect" evening of the Hunt Ball, held at Bowen's Court: "it was what I used to imagine when I was ten that a party here ought to be like." Electric light had been rigged up for the night, and so she saw the "blaze inside" for the first time. The borrowed velvet curtains transformed the usually shabby drawing room into an elegant salon for a few hours. In the next paragraph of her letter, Bowen related (in a typical stream of consciousness) some of her recent and eclectic reading, which included e. e. cummings's latest work, *The Enormous Room*.[20] And, although she was kept very busy with chores and her work at Bowen's Court, she sometimes journeyed to Dublin. Here she met William Butler Yeats, "who was an angel," both "less showy and more mellow" than she had expected.[21] This constant interplay between her various responsibilities gives just one measure of the several different lives she pressed into one.

When the number of years that she spent in England began significantly to outnumber those she had passed in Ireland, Bowen insisted with growing frequency that her heredity remained "more powerful" than her environment.[22] The waifs and strays who wander through her fiction, particularly in the novels and stories of the 1930s, reenact Bowen's own battles with herself over her hybrid origins. As the orphan Portia Quayne fights to make a place for herself among the indifferent adults in *The Death of the Heart,* the narrator remarks matter-of-factly, "The need to attach themselves makes wandering people strike roots in a day; wherever we unconsciously feel, we live" (*DH* 147). The change in pronouns in the middle of this observation shows the shifting attitude of the fictional narrator toward displacement.

Bowen was fond of saying that the only place she really felt at home was in the middle of the Irish Sea, between Dun Laoghaire (formerly called Kingstown) and Holyhead. Lois Farquar, in *The Last September,* experiences the indeterminacy of being Anglo-Irish and seasick and "locked in misery between Holyhead and Kingstown." Not only does the rocking of the boat make her ill, but her journeying and homelessness cause her to feel that she is "enclosed in nonentity, in some ideal noplace perfect and clear as a bubble" (*LS* 109). About her own crossings between England and southern Ireland, Bowen once claimed she could sense a "differentiation of atmosphere" when she arrived in her native country.[23] For her characters who embark upon the same trip in novels such as *To the North*, *The House in Paris*, and *The Heat of the Day*, the sea passage also symbolizes a search for definition.

Bowen's fiction usually took place where she was living emotionally, which did not always correspond with where she happened to be. The settings of *Friends and Relations*, *To the North*, *The House in Paris*, and *The Death of the Heart*, as well as her short stories from this decade, reveal some indication of where she placed herself in relation to the larger world. London, the British countryside, Ireland, Rome, Paris, Milan, Hythe, and Waikiki (a villa on the south coast of England) form the backdrops for the novels she wrote during these years. Like Emmeline Summers, the shortsighted travel agent in *To the North* who never felt "the map of Europe... far from her mind," Bowen acknowledged Europe's proximity (*TTN* 27). While she viewed the distances separating these worlds as simultaneously expanding and shrinking, she traversed the Continent, Ireland, and England in her fiction. The geography of her imagined worlds suggests the pressure she saw the events in Europe applying to the islands of England and Ireland.

As Bowen looked to the foreboding future, she was hoping, like many others, that there would not be another war. She transformed these threats from the outer world into an inner and violent struggle among her characters. Her transferral bears out what Virginia Woolf argued in her 1936 essay "The Artist and Politics," that affairs of state must perforce encroach upon the creative life: "Obviously the writer is in such close touch with human life that any agitation in his subject matter must change his angle of vision."[24] This shift in perception meant that Bowen increased the turmoil troubling her characters as they lived in a world that seemed the same but, in fact, differed radically from any they had encountered before. They respond to this alteration with restlessness and dissatisfaction, which keeps them moving from place to place in a ceaseless quest for some elusive fulfillment.

The characters in Bowen's 1930s novels remember the legacy of dislocation left by the First World War, but they are shortsighted (perhaps unavoidably) about the possibilities the future might offer. They vacillate between speculating on what may come and deliberately choosing to live exclusively in the present. In *To the North* Emmeline is, unfortunately for her business as a travel agent, "short-sighted in every sense" (*TTN* 25). Like other Bowen characters, she is usually the last to recognize the intractable connections between her choices and the ruin she brings upon herself. As the 1930s progressed, Bowen became braver in talking more directly than before about questions of morality and responsibility. *To the North* (which appeared the year after the more insular *Friends and Relations*) shows Bowen concentrating on the general degeneration of integrity and loss of idealism, a state of affairs she had been deploring for a number of years. The novel describes two sisters-in-law who share a house in St. John's Wood, Emmeline and Cecilia, who are related through Cecilia's early marriage to Henry Summers, Emmeline's brother. Henry has died of pneumonia after only one year of marriage, and Cecilia assumes the position of the glamorous young widow.

Unable to remain any one place for long, Cecilia often travels to the Continent where she and her fellow tourists look back on England with "uncertain thoughts of home" (*TTN* 5). This attitude suggests the antipathy to England that many other characters in Bowen's interwar novels confess to harboring.[25] While abroad, Cecilia is briefly attracted to Mark Linkwater, a young Englishman who resembles Cecilia in that neither of them has "nice character." Cecilia soon abandons Markie for her previous romantic interest, Julian Tower, but not before she has introduced Emmeline to Markie. Quickly bored after her European jaunt Cecilia yearns to join her mother in America; she imagines herself as a Columbus, seeking new sights. When her travel plans to the new world go awry, she wishes that she were still in Italy at sunset; she always wishes she were somewhere else.

Wherever she goes, Cecilia leaves devastation in her wake; her chance encounter on the train leads to Emmeline's ill-fated romance with Markie. Toward the end of the novel Cecilia's aunt, Lady Waters—who resembles her predecessors Mrs. Kerr in *The Hotel* and Lady Naylor in *The Last September*—remarks sternly to Cecilia, "In future I hope you may travel with Julian, or have more ties: no good has come of your running about alone." Earlier she has complained that Cecilia has a habit of picking "up the oddest acquaintances" (*TTN* 221, 15). Lady Waters is, of course, referring to Emmeline's affair with Markie, a liaison she finds distasteful. For the first time in a longer work of fiction Bowen takes up a tabooed sexual relationship explicitly. Markie and Emmeline go on a jaunt together to Paris and later in the novel spend a weekend at a borrowed cottage in Devizes.

In the country, Markie and Emmeline disagree over every detail, unable to achieve harmony anywhere. She wishes to spend intimate evenings by the fireside, while he insists that they dine in public at the local inn. His selfishness brings on their undoing because, unluckily, a friend of Lady Waters spies them dining together. Shortsighted both literally and figuratively, Emmeline cannot see that Markie is simply using her while he continues to be involved with other women such as Clara, a lower-middle-class shopkeeper. He is consistently selfish in his attitude to both women. Yet Emmeline allows herself to be manipulated by Cecilia as well as Markie. While she is away with Markie, Cecilia and Julian overcome their inertia and decide to marry. Immediately, she summons Emmeline to London to hear the news in person. Annoyed by the intrusion, Markie opposes Cecilia's request, but Emmeline feels obligated to honor it. With so little sense of herself, she cannot help but feel incomplete and unsure of what she would like to choose; she lets herself be dominated.

The final dissolution of the affair comes on their return to London when Emmeline realizes that Markie is still seeing Clara. Wrapping herself in her pride, Emmeline pours all her energy into her travel agency. Its slogan, "Move dangerously," predicts what lies ahead for her. Her meddling sister-in-law cannot leave her alone and invites both Markie and Emmeline to a dinner party. Afterward, Emmeline, who likes to drive, volunteers to give Markie a ride. This fatal last journey has been heavily intimated throughout the novel—in Paris by a wild taxi ride and on this last trip when she takes dangerous curves too fast and too carelessly. Markie keeps coaxing and then begging her to slow down, to stop, but she, hell-bent on her mission, refuses; she keeps going until her myopia gets the best of them and they die instantly in the crash. The submerged quarrels in *Friends and Relations* surface in this collision in *To the North* by destroying those who move too fast without being able to see the road ahead.

Bowen's female characters often drive recklessly at night, but this is the only such trip that ends in fatality. In "The Disinherited" (1934), one of her best short stories of the decade, the ruthless Davina motors frantically to a party down avenues concealed by darkness, possessed by the thought "that events led nowhere, crisis was an illusion, and that passions of momentary violent reality were struck off like sparks from the spirit, only to die" ("The Disinherited," 407).[26] And Emma, the adulterous wife in the wartime short story "Summer Night," who is most unlike her Austen namesake, also careens through the Irish countryside to meet a stolid lover on a darkening twilight night.

Impatient and dislocated, the characters in *The House in Paris* also cross the Channel, the Irish Sea, and traverse England in various irresponsible and feckless pursuits. This novel represents Bowen's first attempt at the three-part structure, resembling a lyric poem, that she was to favor in her wartime short stories. The novel begins in the present, slides into the past, and returns to bring a widened perspective to where it began. The plot leads us on a journey through a morally dubious world where a single act of unconsidered passion ruins many lives. An international group of characters—Karen Michaelis, a young Englishwoman; Max Ebhert, part French, English, and Jewish; the Frenchwoman, Madame Fisher; and her daughter, Naomi Fisher, who is half-English and half-French—enmesh one another in a series of crippling ties. Madame Fisher, mysterious and intense, runs a pension for young English girls like Karen who travel alone to the Continent. Daughter of a Regent's Terrace house, Karen has been born to breed another generation of tall, well-heeled young women. Not given to anything out of the ordinary, most of the time, she becomes ensnared by an exciting but ultimately damaging love affair with Max.

Although Max and Karen are each engaged to someone else (he to Naomi Fisher, she to an Englishman, Ray Forrestier), they pursue their ardor for one another with a reckless passion that recalls Emmeline's affair with Markie in *To the North*. After all is said and done, Max kills himself in guilty recognition of the hurtful choices he has made, and Karen bears his son. She becomes one of the only Bowen women to become pregnant in the course of a novel. Even then, she abandons the child. Despite her gestures toward a new life, the consequences of this romance continue to cloud Karen's life; even many years later she can think of little else besides Leopold, the child she has not seen since his infancy. This son, who has nothing to inherit, remains caught in a transient domain where a collective of adults in Italy foster his care. Karen perpetually worries about how Leopold is being raised: "But I must see some way for him to live. . . . But if he is like Max and me he would hate that—hate exile, hate being nowhere, hate being unexplained, hate having no place of his own. Hate me too, because of all that" (*HP* 207). When Karen eventually weds Ray, the marriage has too many impediments from the start to satisfy her by offering a replacement for Max.

Both "refugees," Karen and Max gravitate to one another because they are "glad to find themselves anywhere. He had been right in saying they were not rooted. . . . They both had the hybrid's undefendable shyness that no one else can gauge." But like other lovers created by Bowen, they have been raised with divergent values: "Their worlds were so much unlike that no experience had the same value for both of them." Consequently, their views of the past clashed; his was "political," hers, "dramatic." They bring to mind some of Bowen's descriptions of the Anglo-Irish who cannot settle in any one place; together, they understand their alienation. Long after Max's death Karen is haunted by the house in Paris which "so possessed her that nothing was real that happened outside that" (*HP* 119, 155, 206). The novel begins with Karen's decision to meet Leopold, then age eleven, at that house. Losing her nerve at the last minute, she realizes that this vestige of the past will be too painful for her. Instead, she sends her husband to meet her son.

The fictional children Bowen creates frequently suffer the effects of their parents' reckless and selfish decisions, growing up without adults who love them. Another Bowen short story, "Maria," published in 1928, portrays a young "motherless girl, sensitive, sometimes difficult, deeply reserved."[27] Her aunt, Lady Rimlade, in trying to assuage her own guilt about not offering a home for the child, searches for a permanent place where she can stay. But Maria is painfully aware of the situation and announces with precocious formality: "I suppose no one, who has not been in my position can be expected to realize what it feels like to have no home." Unwilling to let her elders get away with their callousness, she observes shrewdly, and calculatedly, "So often carelessness about a girl at my age just ruins her life" ("Maria," 409). In *The Death of the Heart* Bowen pursues at length the implications of such neglect through the story of an orphan left homeless among self-involved adults who do not particularly care what happens to her.

Although neither England nor the Continent can provide anything like what Bowen would have described as a real home for her characters, young or old, travel between the two becomes a compulsion for many of them: "the tip of a long magnetic wave from the Continent touches the Victoria platform whenever a boat-train starts" (*HP* 129). Emmeline takes pride in her agency's knowledge of "what to avoid, what to do in the afternoons anywhere—Turkestan, Cracow—what to do about mules, where it's not safe to walk after dark, how to tip" (*TTN* 23). To show she keeps her word, she routinely plans such elaborate excursions as dispatching a congregational choir to Paris, trying to make contact with Intourist, the state travel bureau of the U. S. S. R., and arranging for travel to Palestine.[28]

Emmeline even manages such logistical wonders as sending notes to welcome clients when they arrive at their destinations. In the office, she sticks flags into the maps to designate her travelers' positions. When the tourists return, she arranges to hear reports of their journeys. Since neither Emmeline nor her business partner, Peter Lewis, themselves travel, these became more than just interesting accounts. Markie, who has never had Emmeline's best interest in mind, does encourage her to withdraw as matters worsen in Europe. But his attitude toward her occupation makes her self-conscious: "Emmeline had to admit that this whole affair of careers for women did sound rather funny, the way Markie saw it, not unlike a ladies' race at regimental sports." She clings to the idea that she can assert control through her neat tabulations and clever schemes. In an environment on which "strain at home and in Europe . . . were gravely written," travel functions as a means for maintaining the illusion of normalcy for Emmeline and her clients (*TTN* 221, 177). It also provides an excuse for Emmeline to evade control over her own life. Although she knows train schedules everywhere in Europe by memory, she cannot see what is happening in her own heart.

In this "restless age" the characters' incessant travel appears in large measure attributable to their dissatisfaction with the places they call home (*TTN* 170). These domiciles stand far away from the Big House that anchored Bowen's imagination. The majority of buildings dotting the landscape of the 1930s, either Victorian redundancies or modern monstrosities (products of the author's distaste for ugly villas), do not symbolize the values of tradition, integrity, and harmony which she celebrated. The houses she builds in her fiction of this decade cannot contain the dissatisfaction that the characters continually express; they remind their visitors of the coldness of their hearths, their spareness resulting from their proprietors' lack of character.

Farraways, the late nineteenth-century country house that offers a retreat from London for the characters in *To the North,* fails to provide the sustenance offered by Bowen's Court or Mt. Morris in *The Heat of the Day*.[29] Instead of offering an atmosphere that will heal all these walking wounded, the interior of Farraways seems to regard its guests with "a sardonic indifference." Since the house has not known any acts of kindness, it cannot return any favors. Resembling a number of other such houses Bowen described in these years, Farraways seems to have faded; its drawing room has seen "weeks of oblivion and shut-up silence" (*TTN* 155, 167). It recalls the "masterless" house in "The Disinherited," which is described as dilapidated, a place where "things are not what they used to be" ("The Disinherited," 386). Bowen's structures mirror the moral bankruptcy and emptiness of their English owners.

In the 1930s, Bowen began to portray the Big House as an alternative to the failed English country house in a pattern the author would amplify in her fiction of the Second World War. Karen Michaelis (Forrestier) tries to escape the fatal hold of *The House in Paris* by gravitating to her relations who reside in southern Ireland. Of all the novels Bowen wrote during this period this one most significantly concerns Ireland. Karen remembers her trip "up the tidal river to Cork"; when as the plot spirals into the past she kept asking herself "what next?" instead of being satisfied with the present. Despite the announcement of her engagement to Ray Forrestier, who has departed for "the East as secretary to a very important person on a mission so delicate that it must not appear to be a mission at all," Karen is dissatisfied with London "where everybody [knows] everything." Responding to a sense of uneasiness, she writes to "the most unconscious of her relations," Aunt Violet Bent, who lives in County Cork. Through reviving this connection, Karen hopes "to rescue something at any price," and the minute she leaves London reassurance comes to her (*HP* 67, 68).

Karen's choice of destination surprises the Michaelises, who never have understood why her relations, Aunt Violet and her second husband, Colonel Bent, have not settled somewhere like Devonshire. Later Karen will learn firsthand that her aunt has been too "wild" to stay in a London terrace house. Yet, Ireland seemed very far away to the Michaelises, although they "all knew Florence well": "'Abroad' was inside their compass. But the idea of Aunt Violet in Ireland made them uncomfortable; it seemed insecure and pointless, as though she had chosen to settle on a raft." Before she lands, when Karen is looking at the landscape of Cork from the steamer, she notices Ireland's affinity with the Continent (a point of view Bowen always stressed). To Karen's eye the land in Cork "looked like a hill in Italy faded; it stood in that flat clear light in which you think of the past and did not look like a country subject to racking change" (*HP* 75, 70).

Once in Ireland Karen learns that the country does not seem as isolated from either the past or the present as she has fantasized upon her arrival on that beautiful April morning. Colonel Bent tells her confidentially that her aunt is facing a cancer operation; the odds are not good. Nor has the past been easy. Colonel Bent's Big House, Montebello, like Danielstown, has suffered one of the most terrible fates a Bowen house could encounter: It has been burned in the Troubles. With the "compensation money" for the destroyed home the Bents have bought Mt. Iris, a smaller house. This new domicile contains many images of the idealized past: a "photograph of [Montebello] as it used to be, in winter, a grey facade of light-reflecting windows, flanked each side by groves of skeleton trees." But, then, outside the bathroom door a visitor encounters "ghastly black staring photographs of the ruins" (*HP* 74). Colonel Bent talks about the glory days of Montebello and takes pride in the fact that the stables were built of "cut stone." In its total effect Bowen's description fashions the place into the familiar classic Georgian Big House.

It is not long, however, before what Karen fears most overtakes her, and, although she is caught in a vortex of emotional turmoil, she seems immune to feeling. When she receives the news of Naomi Fisher's engagement to Max in Ireland, she realizes with a start that "all pleasure in looking seemed to have left..."; "she wanted the unkind ease of feeling again." As she thinks about departing, she accepts the futility of wishing she had not come to Mt. Iris in the first place; "the cold zone crept forward everywhere." Even in Ireland, which has seemed a shelter from reality, life's predictable pain is present. Karen discovers that Ireland can intensify one's emotional responses; "It upsets one," she writes to her fiancé (*HP* 88, 89, 90). But when she wishes to leave Ireland, indeed believing she could stay no longer, her departure is difficult. After boarding the ship she descends to the dinner deck to avoid one last look at Rushbrook. Back in London she can safely rationalize that this is where she "really belong[s]." What she is searching for—herself—continues to elude her, no matter where she turns.

The characters live in an atmosphere of uncertainty, particularly anxious over the many misunderstandings occasioned by the social, economic, and national terms of *race* and *class*. In the case of Karen and Max, "Talk between people of different races is serious; that tender silliness lovers employ falls flat. Words are used for their meaning, not for their ring" (*HP* 171). As Bowen becomes interested in tracing the sources of human motivation in her fiction of these postwar years, she examines both national and racial characteristics, often blurring the distinctions between the two. Frequently, she uses the word *race* where *culture* or *nationality* would be a more obvious choice. An understanding of these influences began to prey upon her in the course of the decade, and this obsession culminated in her voyage to discover her origins through autobiography. The title of the resulting book, *Bowen's Court*, places it securely in the cultural and, as she would have it, racial tradition of the Big House in Anglo-Ireland.

Bowen's fiction of these years, like her autobiography, shows her engaged in some of her strongest analysis about the meaning of birth and place in the world. During her most concentrated period of living in England, she delves deeply and sometimes wickedly into the character of "the English" with the ear and eye of someone who had been born elsewhere. In her fiction the English excel at not noticing things, at being oblivious, sometimes with disastrous consequences. When the imperturbable Cecilia realizes that her luncheon guests have heard her complaining about them on the telephone to Julian, the subjects of her meanness react accordingly: They "had exchanged less than a glance and, all raising their voices, maintained a strenuous conversation till she came back. They were not English for nothing" (*TTN* 115). Bitter quips about the cultural parochialism of the English are scattered throughout *To the North* and *The House in Paris,* echoing some of the sharper asides in *The Last September.*

Leopold in *The House in Paris,* for example, sees his stepfather, Ray Forrestier, only as a type, as one of a breed of identical Englishmen "who stand back in train corridors unobtrusively... in a dark-grey suit with a just visible stripe, light-blue shirt, deep-blue tie with a just visible stripe, a signet ring of some dull stone." This generic man, a member of a group the author often satirized, could be assured to have "a composed unclear romantic evenly-coloured face with structure behind it, a slight moustache two tones darker—and, if you look down, deeply polished brown shoes." We know exactly how he looks and how old he is; in fact, he is always the same age, "the Englishmen's age" of thirty-six (*HP* 239). Bowen had begun to concentrate her attention on characters of her own generation, like Emmeline, a "step-child of her uneasy century" (*TTN* 63).[30]

More pointedly, in these novels Bowen portrays the English as plagued by provincialism. Henrietta, an ungainly child in *The House in Paris,* displays the perennial English fear of French water, convincing herself that it smells and feels different from other water. Leopold is amazed by the very Englishness of Henrietta. Her copy of the *Strand* magazine "perplexed" him "with its rigid symbolism, Martian ideology." Because he does not possess the cultural background, it is neither funny nor comprehensible: "His passionate lack of humour was native and untutored; no one had taught him that curates, chars, duchesses, spinsters are enough, in England, to make anyone smile" (*HP* 28). Bowen's own status as an outsider leads her to isolate what makes this turn of mind so alien to this child.

Leopold takes after his father in his unfamiliarity with the British. In a scene that foreshadows some of the exchanges about patrimony in *The Heat of the Day*, Madame Fisher tells Leopold that "in one thing, you have the advantage of him, Leopold: you know it is necessary to have a father, he did not know it was necessary to have a son." Once on a picnic with Naomi Fisher and Karen, Max declares: "English good-natured jokes seem to me terrible; they are full of jokes about mortification—the dentist, social ambition, love" (*HP* 225, 120). Naomi Fisher, herself half-English by virtue of her "soldierly" British father, chooses to sidestep this comment by busying herself with the picnic preparations. She says in deference to her own heredity and to her English friend Karen, "I think that humour is English courage." When Max arrogantly counters that he finds it "ostrich courage," Naomi asks him not to "be anti-English." Later in the picnic (when Max and Karen are alone together) she discovers that Max has been in England more than she has supposed—"long enough to learn what you say when no one speaks." He had lived there for three years but never learned to speak "naturally." Frustrated by the gap that separates his thoughts from his articulation of them, he explains that, when he uses the unfamiliar language, "it never fits what I mean" (*HP* 43, 121, 127).

Max represents yet another aspect of Bowen's sensitivity to the fact that the events in Europe during the 1930s are bringing the war closer. He is the only Jewish character to appear in Bowen's longer fiction, although in "The Disinherited" Bowen touches on Semitism. Marianne's mother tells her daughter that "the little Jewish girl was not a lady, and ever since then Marianne had thought of the extraordinary with contempt" ("The Disinherited," 383). In *The House in Paris* Bowen investigates Max's religious and cultural heritage much more completely, defining his Jewishness as observed through English eyes blinded by stereotypes. Mrs. Michaelis claims that Max is impossible to understand; she wonders whether the match between Naomi and Max could be successful: "there is always that touch—Jewish perhaps—of womanishness about him that a woman would have to ignore and yet deal with the whole time" (*HP* 124). Mrs. Michaelis shows her own narrowness and her obsession with racial markers in her discussion of Max's Jewishness. When she catches Karen in lies about her affair with Max, she warns her daughter against him, further implying what Madame Fisher had hinted earlier, that Max might only be using her: "But you have behaved like an infatuated woman, an 'easy' woman, and he is a very astute man. No Jew is unastute . . . he can see for himself that you are very much wealthier [than Naomi]" (*HP* 195).

Bowen analyzes other stereotypical thinking when, for example, she describes an encounter Karen has on her return trip from Ireland. On the boat she meets a woman known simply as "Yellow Hat" and inadvertently finds herself drawn into a discussion about her own identity. "Archly," the woman in the Yellow Hat ventures, "I'd like to bet *you're* not Irish" (she has spotted Colonel Bent seeing Karen off at the pier). The woman seems intent on drawing Karen into a discussion of the English and the Irish, saying, "I guess you think we're all mad?" Karen answers the woman's question nonchalantly: "No, not specially. Why?" To which Yellow Hat says, "Well, we are, . . . Mad as hares. Reckless and mad and bad—that's what they say, you know: there's no harm in us." After splitting a bottle of wine, Yellow Hat fulfills Karen's own preconception as "one of those decent pink pious racy girls who screech a good deal, speak of their fathers as Pappy" (*HP* 93, 94). After Yellow Hat learns that Karen lives in London she says, "You're quieter-looking, if you'll excuse my saying, than most London girls. I never care for their style." Karen recognizes that "she must look to Yellow Hat like something on a Zoo terrace, cantering round its run not knowing it is not free, and spotted not in a way you would care to be yourself" (*HP* 97). Both Karen and Yellow Hat are perplexed by their encounters with an individual rather than a collection of generalities.

For Bowen, Karen cut a familiar figure, belonging to "the class that in England changes least of all. The Michaelises live like a family in a prewar novel in one of the tall, cream houses in Chester Terrace, Regent's Park." The author satirizes the family's "goodness of heart; they were not only good to the poor but kind to the common, tolerant of the intolerant." Yet, the values Karen had been raised with are implicated as responsible for the insularity of her outlook. Although the Michaelises are not at all "snobbish" or "over-rich, over-devout, militant in feeling or given to blood sports," they are unable to feel genuinely for anyone else (*HP* 68, 69). Emotionally stunted, they recall Lady Waters of *Friends and Relations,* who stubbornly clings to the idea that God meant for England to be an island.

Despite their parochialism, but perhaps all the more tragically because of it, the Michaelis family fits well into a certain elevated level of society: "They are not rococo, as the aristocracy are supposed to be, or like the middle classes, tangles of mean motives: up against no one, they are hard to be up against." According to Angela, Ray Forrestier's sister in *The House in Paris,* he had "that touch of inbreeding" that would make his marriage to Karen so "promising." To Karen's dismay Angela confirms this belief that "it's better to inbreed than marry outside one's class." Karen's ambivalence about such a claustrophobic existence culminates in her affair with Max. She is simply not contented with the situation of her class; the noiseless servants who bustle around irritate her. After she learns of her Aunt Violet's death, she wishes to be alone, away from Braithwaite, the parlor maid who "was clearing tea away with a concerned face—if she did not know, she knew there was *something* to know" (*HP* 69, 134, 137). Yet Karen is not willing to forsake all the comforts she has come to regard as her right.

Many other characters share with Karen the contradictions and hypocrisies Bowen believed indigenous to the middle class wedged between two warring strata. The narrator in the short story "A Walk in the Woods" (1937) remarks "there is no poetry for the middle class woman in her middle years."[31] The class conflicts that emerge in this decade often begin with what Bowen regarded as the antipathy between the upper middle-class and everyone else, or they derive from such characters as Oliver who announce themselves completely outside the system. The spoiled son in "The Disinherited," Oliver "despised the rich and disliked the poor and drank to the bloody extinction of the middle classes" ("The Disinherited," 389).

The illusory nature of Bowen's characters' journey for meaning recalls the extended analogy she develops to describe what happens after fire destroys a Big House. The new residents of these new houses, such as Mrs. Watson, the young woman in the 1936 short story "Attractive Modern Homes," notice an emptiness: "She had never needed imagination herself, but now felt, for the first time, its absence in other people." These "estates" seem all the more inadequate because of their ironic imitation of a landed estate. In these stories, Bowen continually imagined houses changing hands, being sold, being bought by people who could not appreciate them. This recurring nightmare would come true many years later in the case of her own house, Bowen's Court. During the 1930s, while she was accustoming herself to the reality of owning a Big House, she was always preparing for its loss. Her 1934 short story "The Last Night in the Old Home" describes the sad state of dissolution that descends on a house that is being vacated.[32]

Men's and women's inability to form lasting and satisfying relationships in Bowen's fiction results in large measure from her conception of the character of the age, a conception that was increasingly disillusioned and stubborn. The heart, like the house, became a barometer by which Bowen measured the atmosphere around her. Literally organic and life-giving, the heart could convey much of what she could symbolize through the structure of a house. The word *heart* appears constantly in her works of these years, often in a sarcastic and deprecating way, and, as the 1930s lengthened, her use of the word grew more despairing. "The Cat Jumps," a ghost story dating from 1929, describes the Harold Wrights, a modern family who had "light, bright, shadowless, thoroughly disinfected minds." Because they "were pious agnostics" who "read their murders only in scientific books," they dared to buy a large house, Rose Hill, also the site of the gruesome Bentley murder ("The Cat," 362).

The story catalogs the Wrights' crusade to transform the house into a home. At a house party one of their guests, Muriel, entertains the company with her rendition of the Bentley murder: The husband had killed his wife and put her pieces everywhere; a hand appeared in the library, and he "put her heart in her hat-box" ("The Cat," 367). The novel Bowen wrote toward the end of the decade, *The Death of the Heart,* is much less flippant about the misuse of the heart and the ideas responsible for disfiguring the past. Trapped in a barren house, Portia becomes "like a bird astray in a room, a bird already stunned by dashing itself against mirrors and panes" (*DH* 308). In a short story, "The Same Way Home," first published in December, 1938, Bowen chronicled the despair of a weak woman who was always "setting her heart on things" she could not have. When Bowen revised the story for its reprinting in *Living Age* in February, 1939, she changed the title to read "A Queer Heart."[33] As she developed her uses of the metaphor of the human heart, she refined a technique she would rely on even more heavily in her novel of wartime, *The Heat of the Day*. In the 1930s she was still experimenting with mirroring the emotional passages of the characters with events in the external world as she expanded what she had first attempted in *The Last September,* using relationships as the weather vanes of political barbarism.

Bowen, like Virginia Woolf, delineated the worsening of the international crisis through disruptions in the private lives of her characters. In Woolf's last novel, *Between the Acts,* which she wrote between early 1938 and February, 1941, the world keeps interrupting the pageant of English history whose performance the novel records. Bowen, in reviewing the novel, declared that the drama "is a sort of war itself . . . the confrontation of two armies, the actors and the acted upon." She particularly admired the way Woolf had "integrated plot and vision."[34] One of the central characters, Isa Oliver, who is "the age of the century, thirty-nine," wonders "what remedy was there for her at her age," for she is, like her contemporaries, "book-shy" and "gun-shy."[35] The frenetically creative pageant maker, Miss La Trobe, tries to make the observers realize that in their role as audience they are "caught and caged": "They were neither one thing nor the other; neither Victorians nor themselves. They were suspended, without being, in limbo."[36] Like Portia Quayne in *The Death of the Heart,* Woolf's spectators in this novel feel in-between, hesitant, and confused while suffering their own deaths of the heart as the external world appears to crumble around them.

The well-known events of these years unfolded: In January, 1933, Hitler came into power; in 1934 Austrian social democracy was crushed; in 1934 right- and left-wing extremists fought it out in Paris; and in July, 1936, the Spanish civil war erupted. Bowen's contemporaneous fiction churns with predictions of an unattractive or disagreeable future. In *The House in Paris* Angela Forrestier wonders about the days to come: "No doubt I shall live to see the poor children nationalised, or married in a laboratory. But while we *have* names, not numbers, I think it's nice to be like what one's like, don't you?" (*HP* 134).[37] Portia Quayne, who keeps trying to assemble the jigsaw puzzle that Major Brutt has given her, is one of the many characters who tries to decipher what the future might bring.

In *The Death of the Heart,* the last novel she completed before the war, Bowen examined the crevasses she saw appearing in her generation, fastening on the mistrust and betrayals that she saw splitting such spiritual fortresses as home and family. She was mourning not only the passage of an age but also the loss of a stable social structure in which sensibility, sentiment, and faith in a common moral code consistently mattered. Although she would describe the Second World War as "the most interesting period of [her] life," she would later claim that the war came about because these qualities no longer seemed essential.[38] In reaction to the disintegration threatening all she valued and cherished, when war became more probable she turned to autobiography to make her peace with where the years had taken her so far.

Chapter 6

"A Madman on a Motorcycle"

War is a tin-can tied to the tail of civilisation.
—Cyril Connolly, "The Ivory Shelter"

The writer and editor John Lehmann retrospectively pointed to the 1930s as a time when "promised beginnings had failed again." Cyril Connolly, in his backward glance, had "reached the specific conclusion that the 1930s had been a failure."[1] The long, halting beginnings of the Second World War made its onset seem all the more sadly inevitable. Virginia Woolf wrote in her diary on September 30, 1938, in reference to the Munich crisis, that "the obvious feeling everywhere was We don't want this war." A kind of terrible resignation followed the events of mid-March, 1939, when Hitler had annihilated the Czechoslovakian state. After the series of "dress rehearsals" that Virginia Woolf described movingly in her diary entries as winter changed to spring, the quandary became, as she phrased it, "How to go on, through War?"[2] By the first week of September, 1939, these abstractions had dissipated as the turn of events forced practicality to the foreground. For many, writers and nonwriters alike, the urge to express what they were feeling proved almost universal.

Bowen told Woolf early in the war that she lived in a "stupefied excited and I think rather vulgar state."[3] Because Bowen was not a diarist and at best only a sporadic letter writer, she saved her commentary on the day-to-day events and emotions of the war for her fiction and essays. All through these works lies Bowen's sorrowful sense that somehow she had failed her inheritance. Others echoed her sentiments, including Vere Hodgson, a London resident who kept a daily chronicle of her life throughout the war which was published under the title *Few*

Eggs and No Oranges; in May of 1941 after Westminster Abbey and the Houses of Parliament had been hit by German bombers she wrote, "I can see all our ancestors looking down reproachfully; saying: 'we gave it to you. You have not guarded it as you received it. You have failed your trust—even those who loved it best.'"[4] In her autobiography, Bowen worked out her own responses to the war, the failure she saw marking the present.

When war came it became all the easier to lament the injurious decade that had led up to it. On the first of September, 1939, Lehmann wrote: "I had the feeling that I was slipping down into a pit, clutching at grass on the ledges but failing to stay the accelerating descent into darkness." Yet, in the midst of this danger he saw much beauty. When he looked out of his flat in Mecklenburgh Square, just down the street from the new quarters of the Hogarth Press, on "hauntingly lovely" mornings he recollected "the silvery barrage balloons floating high in the sky above the tall plane trees, still and dream-like."[5] Some observations were made even more poignant by the recognition that the whole populace feared for the end of civilized life. On the sixth of September Virginia Woolf wrote, ". . . the mind seems to curl up & I become undecided. . . . This war has begun in cold blood. One merely feels that the killing machine has to be set in action . . . of course all creative power is cut off."[6] Everyone anticipated what was to come in the shape of personal demons.

Later that same fall Evelyn Waugh pondered the situation: "They are saying, 'The generals learned their lesson in the last war. There are going to be no wholesale slaughters.' I ask, 'how is victory possible, except by wholesale slaughters?'"[7] During the early days after the declaration of war on September 3, 1939, the threat of total destruction loomed as rumor chased rumor in anxious speculation. By the following summer of 1940 after the fall of France, when German bombers first appeared over England, Woolf admitted that for the first time she understood "completely" what being "in the war" meant: "The feeling of pressure, danger horror. . . . The worst of it ones mind wont work with a spring next morning [*sic*]."[8] As the terrible fact of war became reality, it made overall comprehension impossible and women such as Vere Hodgson, as well as those who wrote for a living, began to look at what was being lost, perhaps in hopes of preserving it in memory if nowhere else.

Almost from the moment the war commenced, writers in particular found themselves asking, throughout their journals and their letters, differing versions of the same question: How can this be happening? One year into war Lehmann inquired, "Did one ever imagine one would come to accept so much so quickly?" He had the feeling in the fall of 1940, which he described in a letter to Isherwood, that "life has changed so much and so fast already, like one picture fading into another in a film."[9] This figure of overlapping images seemed continually to collapse upon itself, giving a curious and unsettling fluidity to existence. The London woman, Vere Hodgson, memorialized the dreams of a fire watcher who sees a red glow of incandescent terror, illustrating "how this fire-business does work havoc on the subconscious." These nighttime delusions seemed all the more unreal and remote for her when, in a London park on a warm June day that same spring, it was difficult to think "about the war, as everyone looked so happy enjoying the flowers and the sun."[10] During the long, tedious middle years of the war it felt to many city dwellers as though "everything in the war seemed to be happening on a distant rim." But when the bombing was resumed with a vengeance, once again war occupied everyone's consciousness. Whether the fighting was near or far, Lehmann wrote of "the trance-like feeling" that characterized for him and so many others the endless duration of the war.[11]

The volatile and always changing relationship of literature to politics became even more highly charged in wartime. Chief among the concerns that artists articulated was that the fact of armed conflict might obliterate creative life. As Virginia Woolf saw it, "Art is the first luxury to be discarded in times of stress."[12] Many chroniclers of the scene described the terrible toll that the endless sensation of living with danger extracted. Apprehension over the continuation of the life of the mind became intertwined with a generalized perception of a dimming of all hopes for humankind. Of necessity, life grew even more complex for those artists and writers who were pulled into the demanding routine of wartime service. Evelyn Waugh, for example, put in several years of eccentric but dedicated military duty, taking part in the botched invasion of Crete, serving in Yugoslavia, and occupying various bureaucratic posts in England. But he ended up recording in August, 1943, "I wrote to Frank [Pakenham] very early in the war to say that its chief use would be to cure artists of the illusion that they were men of action. It has worked its cure with me.... I don't want to be of service to anyone or anything. I simply want to do my work as an artist."[13] For women and men alike the nature of wartime commitments left them torn between their desire to fulfill their private creative impulses (in conjunction with their fear that they could not) and what they saw as a more public responsibility to their nation.

Some of the concern that surrounded the production of literature during the war in London can be attributed to what W. J. Bate has identified (speaking of another century) as "the burden of the past."[14] In this case it was the legacy of the First World War. At the start of the Second World War literary pundits were swift to point out the shabby nature of contemporary war literature. Connolly, in his essay "Writers and Society, 1940–1943," observed that "war poets [or substitute writers in general] are not a new kind of being, they are only peace poets who have assimilated the material of war."[15] More recent critics have echoed these harsh assessments of the writing the British produced during the war. Some have refused to believe that anything emanating from the Second World War could improve upon or match the eloquence associated with the aftermath of the first. Paul Fussell, for one, characterizes and contrasts the "loquacity" of the "Great War" with "something close to [the] silence" he views as "the byproduct of experience in the Second World War."[16] Those who chose through the use of words to apprehend the assaults on their universe had to do so in trying circumstances, a fact insufficiently recognized by these harsher critics.

But the recording and preservation of experience became a matter of fierce moment to writers, artists, publishers, editors, and, not least, the British reading public, and the effects of the war on publishing were quickly evident. "The book trade," Lehmann recalled of the first days of the war, "was also motionless, stunned, dead to all appearance." An increase in book buying (to read during blackout nights) occurred in the spring of 1940 when "the series of devastating shocks followed one another without respite . . . [and] the realization that the full might of Nazi Germany faced us directly across the Channel was grim indeed."[17] Of course, this state of affairs registered its imprint on book publishing and reading. The beginning of the Blitz meant the dramatic reduction of paper supplies for printing books. Even worse, on the famous night of December 29, 1940, Paternoster Row, the publishers' warehouses situated near St. Paul's, sustained a hit, and at least five million books were reduced to ashes that one night—with lamentable and lasting consequences for authors, publishers, and readers.[18]

The scarcity of paper, one of the most pressing problems plaguing publishers, was mentioned repeatedly in their discussions with writers. Not only did the meager supply bother contemporary authors, it also significantly affected the reissue of the classics (so much in demand during the war). Henry James and Anthony Trollope, who had re-created entire universes of custom, manners, furniture, clothes, and large casts of characters in lavish detail, enjoyed a suddenly widened popularity.[19] In these dramas of the past wartime readers found comfort born of stability and certainty of expectation possible in ordered societies.[20] To those working to sustain creative life in wartime, rationing the material to make books posed an enormous obstacle. For Lehmann in his stewardship at the Hogarth Press "the chief trouble... during the war was buying paper."[21] During one of the darkest times of the war, the beginning of 1942, eighteen writers, including Bernard Shaw, H. G. Wells, and J. B. Priestley, wrote to *The Times,* protesting that "to save the book trade" would only take "a trifling number of key-workers... [and] less than 1 and 1/4 per cent of the total national consumption of paper." They pitched their appeal in terms of the great demand for books: "Unless action is taken... soon, ... to arrest the disintegration of the book trade, the public which is turning more and more to books for the help they give, will ask and get nothing."[22]

Books published in earlier times became attractive not just because they described a more familiar and agreeable world. Wartime editions published in accordance with the strict official standards laid down for publishing were of decidedly inferior quality in their paper and printing, as Waugh observed when he paid a visit to Nancy Mitford's book shop where he found "shabby little new books and sumptuous old ones."[23] Undoubtedly, some of the editions Waugh disparaged included the "Penguin Pockets," introduced by the Council on Books in Wartime (a group of publishers); given free to an estimated twelve million people, they were sized to fit into army shirt pockets.[24] Other titles, too lengthy or arcane to be published or reprinted in mass editions, drew much popular interest as well. Histories, in general, sold well. In fact, several "straight" histories published during the war, such as G. M. Trevelyan's *English Social History* (1944), Robert Graves's and Alan Hodge's *The Long Weekend* (1944), and Osbert Sitwell's *Left Hand, Right Hand! Volume 1* (1944), achieved unusual popularity.[25]

The vogue for reading about the past extended into the realm of autobiography, which became important to writers like Bowen during the war. As Anthony Powell remembers it, the war gave an "attraction to the prosiest aspects of the past."[26] Perhaps it was that the corroboration of the continuation of previous eras of human existence, both peaceful and violent, gave reassurance in a period that seemed only transient, at best. Such family sagas as Sir Hugh Walpole's *Rogue Herries* (1930), John Galsworthy's *Forsyte Saga* (1922), and Mazo de la Roche's *Whiteoak Chronicles* (collected in 1940), as well as favorites from childhood such as those by Rudyard Kipling and Arthur Ransome, enjoyed a huge vogue.[27]

With wartime conditions pinching, however, writers and readers were forced to think about alternative possibilities in publishing. Cyril Connolly put his mind to establishing a journal designed to keep creative expression alive during the war. During the autumn of 1939 Connolly began to negotiate the details of a contract with his friend, Victor William Watson—the scion of a margarine entrepreneur—and Stephen Spender.[28] These conversations led to an agreement to publish a monthly journal called *Horizon;* Watson "undertook to pay 23 pounds a month to subsidise 1,000 copies of the magazine." The first issue of the journal appeared at Christmastide of 1939.[29]

Almost from its start *Horizon* represented a cherished landmark of culture, civilization, and good taste to a significant group of writers and readers. Elizabeth Bowen, among many others, wrote steadily for it and celebrated it as a monument to the preservation of the writer's craft. Costing one shilling, the first issue attracted much attention. Virginia Woolf, who detested Connolly, commented acridly on his latest venture: "Horizon out; small; trivial, dull. So I think from not reading it."[30] Few readers shared her bias, and after only a few months it enjoyed a circulation of eight thousand. An impressive roster of writers contributed in the first six months: W. H. Auden, John Betjeman, William Empson, Louis MacNeice, Dylan Thomas, George Orwell, Herbert Read, Stephen Spender, H. E. Bates, Elizabeth Bowen, Julian Maclaren-Ross, and V. S. Pritchett.[31]

Horizon filled a void newly created with the cessation (in 1939) of such publications as *Cornhill, Criterion, London Mercury, New Verse,* and *Twentieth-Century Verse*.[32] Writers like Waugh, who had never liked Connolly in the first place, discerned something comical and effete about his self-conscious crusade to preserve the best of Western culture. However implausible it might have appeared to Connolly's critics, the idea for *Horizon* had been germinating in his mind for a long time. The magazine had begun with its founder's daydream in 1933 "to edit a monthly magazine entirely subsidized by self. No advertisements. Harmless title. Deleterious Contents." And what many satirized and found annoying in Connolly—his high-minded persistence, or self-appointment to the chancellorship of culture—kept the magazine going. Before he was through, he was soliciting help from such figures as Stephen Spender, who was a co-editor from 1939 to 1941; Connolly acknowledged with caution the importance of Spender's role: "It was due largely to him that we printed such good war poetry and such intelligent articles about war aims; on the other hand *Horizon* at that time manifested a tendency to become a Left-Wing 'School Magazine.'"[33] From Christmas, 1939, to New Year's Day, 1950, the total run of pages reached "some ten thousand." By the start of 1950 Connolly had grown bored with the magazine and weary of pushing for the survival of aesthetic values without the immediate crisis of war. In his Introduction to *The Golden Horizon,* Connolly made reference to the connection between literature and war in his literary journal: "[*Horizon's*] 'History of the War' illustrates those moments when literature seemed to follow life like a barge on a quiet canal towed by a madman on a motorcycle."[34]

A competitor to *Horizon* had appeared in the fall of 1940 in the guise of John Lehmann's *Penguin New Writing.* Lehmann wrote of its beginnings: "My bi-annual book magazine had, during the autumn of 1940, given birth to a vigorous foal in the stable of Allen Lane and his Penguin Books." He aimed for a different kind of contributor: the "younger writers who were being absorbed into the armed forces" as well as another audience.[35] According to Ronald Blythe, the distinction between the two was this: "To be published in *New Writing* was to have arrived ... [it] lacked [the] curious glamour of *Horizon.*"[36] Immediately very popular, the *Penguin New Writing* had large print orders, sometimes as many as one hundred thousand copies per issue; many of its readers were members of the military. *Penguin New Writing* spoke more frequently of the logistical and practical ramifications of war. The admittedly biased Lehmann claimed, "Enthusiasts for *Penguin New Writing* were to be found in every part of the world the war had penetrated, and in every class."[37] Statistically speaking, Lehmann's magazine had ten times as wide a circulation as that enjoyed by *Horizon*. While several of the contributors overlapped—George Orwell, V. S. Pritchett, Dylan Thomas, Graham Greene, Jean-Paul Sartre, Julian Maclaren-Ross, Henry Green, W. H. Auden, Louis MacNeice, and Cecil Day-Lewis, among others—the tone and timbre differed essentially.[38] As the regular production of these literary magazines suggests, the fight to preserve culture dominated the lives of many civilians and soldiers alike.

Despite, or perhaps because of, the fact that disorder became a daily companion in wartime, familiar landmarks became so scarce that Londoners determined to carry on as normally as possible. They readily adapted to wholly new vocabularies and regulations such as were necessitated by the blackout. Evelyn Waugh noted mischievously in his diary in October, 1939, that the blackout was "really formidable—all the gossip is of traffic casualties—the night watchman of the St. James's knocked down the club steps, Cyril Connolly's mistress lamed for life and Cyril obliged to return to his wife."[39] Virginia Woolf gave a more impressionistic view of the city in that same month: "Very few buses. Tubes closed. No children. No loitering. Everyone humped with a gas mask. Strain & grimness. At night is so verdurous & gloomy that one expects a badger or a fox to prowl along the pavement."[40] In John Lehmann's words, two cities, the daytime one and "the other London," became "the new, symbolic city of the black-out."[41] Death went on the prowl in the nighttime.

During the early weeks of the air raids cinemas stayed open double time, and the Savoy and the Dorchester hotels became swank centers for a certain enjoyably vulgar after-hours life. But when the ceaseless bombing of the Blitz pummeled London in the fall of 1940, people with nowhere else to go began to flock to the underground shelters of the tube stations for the night. On one occasion in late September of that year 177,000 people were thought to have spent the night on platforms in the tube where it was warm, crowded, and far from the noise of the bombs.[42] These were the scenes that moved Henry Moore to create the sculptures memorializing those citizens who endured interminable nights of darkness shared with strangers.

People clung to familiar rituals and even invented new expressions to confront the unimaginable. When a bomb hit people asked *not* where it landed but, rather, "where is the incident?"[43] Citizens learned to adapt by devising ways to screen out impending disaster from their consciousness. Vere Hodgson remembers being in the dentist's chair on a day in August, 1944, when the alert sounded; her dentist adroitly reached over and lowered the shade over the window and then continued his work.[44] Yet, despite such brave measures, the bombings left an indelible psychological mark on all who suffered them. Many described the terrible stench that bombs left behind and the plaster dust, which turned people white overnight, an observation the maid makes in Bowen's short story, "Oh, Madam..." (1940). Others wrote of the unmistakable noise of bombings, a noise that Lehmann characterized to Isherwood in the fall of 1940 as a "melancholy fading wail, like a dog in unutterable pain."[45] To Woolf, writing in the summer of 1940, "the siren—its [sic] now weeping willie in the papers—is as punctual as the vespers."[46] Later Evelyn Waugh complained about the "inconvenience" of being awake in the darkness of June, 1944, while he waited "for the sounds of the planes which are indistinguishable to an ear like mine from the noise of a motor car."[47]

Everyone developed idiosyncratic strategies for surviving the disruption and uncertainty. Virginia Woolf often imagined the coming of death: "It wd have been a peaceful matter of fact death to be popped off on the terrace playing bowls this very fine cool August evening."[48] Whatever the mechanisms invented for overcoming raw, nauseating fear, all who experienced the bombings could not fail to feel sometimes close to death. As Graham Greene, working as an air raid warden in London while waiting to be called up, explained: "one really thought that this was the end but it wasn't exactly frightening—one had ceased to believe in the possibility of surviving the night."[49] Perpetual danger became commonplace. As Vere Hodgson wrote of January 8, 1941, "a plane came very low as I was having lunch in the cafe—But my heart did not miss a beat! I never thought I should get used to having my lunch on a battlefield!" She added: "strange how at one time the Warning made my heart beat faster. Now it affects me no more than a dinner gong."[50]

Still, such brave fronts commonly weakened over time; Hodgson wrote in the winter of 1943, "We are all overtired with these years of Blackout and war and Anxiety and Domestic Difficulty."[51] Some like Lehmann, on the other hand, recalled the ceaseless activity of war as being invigorating in its own way: "danger to oneself and to everyone around one pumped some stimulating substance into one's veins, an adrenalin that tapped reserves of energy that otherwise would have lain dormant."[52] Because there could be, of course, no uniform reaction to these terrors, citizens resented being told *en masse* how to feel or respond. A widely hated Ministry of Information poster reproached British citizens: "*Your* courage, your cheerfulness, *your* resolution will bring us victory."[53]

For Cyril Connolly in his gloomier moods the war was a time "which dissipates energy and disperses friends, which lowers the standard of thinking and feeling, and which sends all those who walk near emotional, mental, or financial precipices toppling over." In his essay "Writers and Society, 1940–1943," he concluded that "the position of the artist today should occasion general concern were it not that the whole human race seems threatened by an interior urge to destruction." In contemplating Ireland's self-imposed distance from the war, he asked, "Are not the wisest people in the world those who have kept their calendar at 1938?"[54]

The first year of war, which featured jittery nerves and restless bouts of activity, became known as it progressed for long stale periods of waiting. After the debacle of Dunkirk at the end of May, which left England physically and figuratively wounded, as well as filled with pride for the improvised civilian "navy," it seemed that nothing would ever be the same again. The Battle of Britain began in the summer of 1940. The aerial dogfights over the Channel seized the national imagination as they presented a concrete and vivid manifestation of the larger ideological battle between good and evil which the war exemplified. Vere Hodgson describes these Channel battles as "wonderful fights" and says she has heard "there is tremendous betting on the stock exchange as to the numbers brought down."[55] Such statistics became part of the national vocabulary of war, and by gambling on them people attempted to control, or at least influence, their horrifyingly random destinies. John Lehmann gave a memorable picture of the skies over London, seen from a train in those days of late summer and early autumn: "A major air battle was taking place overhead in the cloudless blue sky, with sudden whining zooms, and the intermittent rattle of machine-gun fire clearly audible."[56] Soon, the summer drama of the heavens expanded into the larger, longer ordeal known as the Blitz.

Beginning in the evening hours of September 7, 1940, the Luftwaffe began to attack areas of dense populations rather than airfields. Intense and continual bombing over London marked this phase of the war, which lasted until the spring of 1941; in seventy-six consecutive nights only one was quiet because of poor weather. Although the population had been preparing itself for months for such an assault, carrying gas masks, evacuating children, digging shelters, and assembling emergency supplies, the merciless, ceaseless bombing still came as a shock. In that first of the real wartime Septembers alone, sixteen thousand people became casualties of the aerial assault on London, and seven thousand of them died.[57]

When the fall chilled into winter with dropping temperatures, spirits fell as the bombing worsened. The heavy raids continued, becoming quieter in early December, heavier in late December, extending into February, April, and May with a kind of grand finale occurring on May 10. By the close of this nine-month period, fifty thousand Londoners had been "seriously injured," over two million had been made homeless (one-sixth of all Londoners), and twenty thousand city dwellers had been killed.[58] Exhausted by the effort imposed by such horrors, Londoners wearily endeavored to accept the surreal since normal life seemed all but invisible.

Hitler's invasion of Russia in the spring of 1941 brought an easing of pressure for the British, and they sighed and wondered what would happen next. Lehmann, in looking back on the war as a whole, referred to those middle years as "that strange period in the life of wartime Londoners, the three-year breathing space." During the last two years of the war, whenever the raids resumed, Lehmann recalled what he termed a "hallucinatory fortress," which the mind constructed to give an illusion of safety and insulation.[59] Evelyn Waugh's diary entry for October 28, 1942, reflects a similar sense of security as a respite from terror. On this, his thirty-ninth birthday, he summed up the year for his personal record: "A good year. I have begotten a fine daughter, published a successful book [*Put Out More Flags*], drunk 300 bottles of wine and smoked 300 or more Havana cigars. I have gone back to soldiering among friends."[60] During the following spring, bombing became more intermittent in London because the Germans were directing their attention elsewhere; most notable were the famous "Baedeker Raids" launched at historically significant towns to avenge some of the British devastation of Germany. A year later, however, Waugh was depressed by the cumulative effects of war on the London scene: "London shabbier and shoddier in the sunlight than in shadow ... aimless, horrible groups of soldiers in shabby battledress.... Restaurants crowded; one is jostled by polyglot strangers."[61]

The winter of 1944 saw the beginning of what was known as the "little Blitz," and by June, V-bombs (known variously as "flying bombs," "buzz bombs," or "Doodle-Bugs") had arrived to provide fresh frights.[62] When the bombs recommenced, they fell on a changed city. Gone in large measure was the heroic spirit of the Blitz, for by now exhaustion had set in, and the war seemed to have lost its immediacy. As Lehmann recalled, "that winter had the peculiar terror of a recrudescence of struggle and uncertainty just when the worst had seemed to be over."[63] The flying bombs transformed the experience of an air raid, for there was no longer any definable sequence to expect. In the eerie silence that preceded their impact, already jangled nerves stretched tighter.

The rocket bombs presented these frayed Londoners with new, unwanted challenges. Their sound reminded Vera Brittain of "a mixture of an angry bee & a broken-down tug on the Thames."[64] That summer of 1944 began to appear to Lehmann as a moment when he belonged to a "civilization that had lost its way, a world out of control."[65] To make matters worse, in the fall of 1944 supersonic rockets, or V-2s, winged their way toward England.[66] These devices, which gave no warning, seemed to mock the long battle against machines that fell from the sky. Then, gradually, as the Allies began to add to their list more victories than stalemates or defeats, the quiet realization spread that the worst might already have happened. The locus of the war shifted but only after a spate of last desperate raids. By the beginning of April, 1945, Vera Brittain could write, "No bombs. Strange sense of relief, like convalescence after an illness; found myself still listening."[67] Her choice of this metaphor of recovery after sickness was a popular one; many people watching spring come to England could not believe that they might be well again, that the bombs might stop falling and they might be safe once more. As April quickened into May, peace shimmered as a dim mirage on the horizon. After six years of war its end seemed so long in coming that its celebration was bound to be anticlimactic.

Without a doubt, war had transformed every aspect of life it touched. Virginia Woolf tried an experiment of trying to see "exactly how the war" alters life—on Thursday, December 19, 1940, in Sussex:

> It changes when I order dinner.... Petrol changes the day too... we dont go hungry or cold. But luxury is nipped off and hospitality.... The post is the most obvious inconvenience perhaps.... I bicycle to Lewes instead of driving. Then the black out—thats half an hour daily drudgery... we dip into our great jars for pickled eggs & pretend that they don't taste differently. We are of course marooned here by the bombs in London... otherwise we draw breath as usual.[68]

Deprivation characterized existence on the home front most saliently—of clothes, food, fuel, light, security, and time. Getting through a day involved performing a series of Byzantine tasks generated by the blackout, the need for gas masks, food and clothing rationing, and travel restrictions. Makeshift attempts at normalcy resulted in such innovations as painting stocking seam lines with gravy browning on women's legs, a substitution that had its drawbacks: When it rained, "the dogs used to come round, sniffing your legs." Some of the wartime frugalities worked surprisingly well, notably the system of food rationing that, in its stringency, offered new taste thrills such as nettle tea. But many went hungry because of inefficiency and cheating. Always on the watch for those who tried to circumvent the regulations, the Ministry of Information labeled such miscreants "Squander Bug" or "Fuel Demon."[69]

Boredom, waiting, and *listening* became watchwords during the war. At once there seemed to be no time and nothing but time. Wardens and the antiaircraft crews endured long nights in tense waiting while suddenly a whole nation lived in an altered atmosphere, where hours sometimes passed slowly. The BBC responded with significant programming changes. In June, 1940, they began a sequence of programs called "music while you work," aimed at factory workers to increase their output and induce tranquillity. J. B. Priestley, in fact, titled a collection of wartime broadcasts to honor those factory workers who knew daylight only on Saturdays. His broadcasts were aired for fifteen minutes on Sunday nights after the nine o'clock news from June, 1940, with a break in winter, returning in January, 1941, continuing until March; they were "designed to stop the audience switching over promptly to Hamburg Radio and Lord Haw-Haw."[70] Such programs, and such acts of censorship, became a commonplace for those who survived war on the home front. Many found that creation, in spite of restrictions, made war more bearable.

Work kept Elizabeth Bowen going during the war. She explained in the fall of 1945 that she had existed throughout the war "both as a civilian and as a writer, with every pore open," while she had "lived so many lives." Although she had written "continually" during the war, she had poured much of her prodigious energy into war-related occupations; like several fellow writers, among them T. S. Eliot, she signed up to be an air raid warden, a responsibility that kept her more than busy.[71] In a BBC interview given after the war, she described her nights on duty: "You stump up and down the streets making a clatter with the boots you are wearing, knowing you can't prevent a bomb falling, but thinking, 'At any rate, I am taking part in this; I may be doing some good.'" Her job as a warden significantly widened her circle of acquaintances by exposing her to "types—so different that, but for the war, we would not have met at all."[72]

The tough balancing act that Bowen tried to sustain in her war work shuttling between Ireland and England took its toll. Its price can be seen in the emotional strain she projects onto the heroine of *The Heat of the Day,* Stella Rodney, who maintains an intense pace both in her job and in her private life. Like many of her fellow writers, Bowen described her creative impulses as under constant challenge. She was later to say that in wartime writing became simultaneously more essential and more difficult. The sheer intensity of life in London made the time, solitude, and money required for writing all the more elusive. Early in the war when she became an air raid warden, Bowen had joined the growing ranks of women who worked in civil defense, a number that rose to 375,000 in 1943, at which point women comprised one-quarter of the total number of workers in civil defense. This sudden influx of women into a province traditionally restricted to men did not happen without confusion. There was a general bewilderment about what to do with the women and how to treat them, and unfairness became manifest when the first women who were injured as civil defense workers were compensated or assessed at only two-thirds the amount allotted to men.[73]

The conscription of women, taking place in large numbers from 1942 on, perhaps the most "controversial" action of the government during the war, changed the contours of working life to an unimaginable degree. In March, 1941, Minister of Labour and National Service Ernest Bevin asked women "to go into essential war industries"; by December all unmarried women ages twenty to thirty were pressed into service.[74] When the call-up was enlarged to include women up to age fifty-one, a loud protest was raised. Despite the opposition, need overruled; by 1943, 7,258,000 women—46 percent of those between the ages of fourteen and fifty-nine—"were engaged in some form of National Service." Obviously, the ramifications of such sweeping alterations in the social scene rarely appeared immediately. But the costs of the burdens women undertook could neither be minimized nor overlooked: Of all the civilian adults seriously injured or killed in the war, 48 percent were women, adding significantly to the costs of war in human suffering.[75] Beyond the other upheavals imposed by war, women found themselves unclear about the rapid changes to the labels used to define them. Bowen dramatizes this struggle through several female characters of differing classes in her novel of wartime, *The Heat of the Day*.

Despite the expanded opportunities available (usually by necessity) to women, contradictions abounded. A barrage of disparate messages bombarded British women in wartime. While married women understood that they were to do as much war work as possible, they also were given "pronatalist" literature and told of "the prescription of a wife's destiny to that of a full-time mother."[76] For a multitude of reasons the changes that war necessitated marked a turning point in the lives of all who lived through it, men and women alike.

And looking back in 1945 Bowen summarized that sense when she remarked: "when you stand by to die every night, you see, if only in moments, what life was meant to be."[77] While she had carried on her familiar routines as much as possible, the sense of fragility in everyday life plagued her. Her life during the war would have met, in every particular, the rigorous standards Harold Nicolson described in a letter to his wife, Vita Sackville-West, in December, 1942: "I feel that this war is a test of our character and I rejoice that all those I love have come through it enhanced and not diminished."[78] Bowen had taken the war as a challenge to be faced and overcome, tamed and subdued.

One summer evening, while Bowen was serving coffee on the balcony of her Clarence Terrace house, an air raid forced the party inside. Reportedly, she diffused the terror of the moment by saying, "I feel I should apologise for the noise."[79] It may have been that evening Stephen Spender remembered when he related leaving a dinner party at No. 2 Clarence Terrace to go "walking out into the street afterwards to find it lit whiter than daylight."[80] Bowen also tried to maintain some levity in the sporadic letters she wrote to her cousin in Ireland: "I am getting quite nice and thin. Air raids are slightly constipating." A certain amount of this bravado must have been whistling in the dark, for after the war she characterized the previous years as a time of "*desiccation*" of "our day-to-day lives."[81] Yet Bowen succeeded for a time in keeping up appearances; Charles Ritchie had once described her residence as "the last house in London which still felt like a pre-war house."[82] First bombed in May, 1941, Bowen's house was repairable enough that she and her husband could continue to live there. In the summer of 1944 it withstood another bad raid, but then a second attack by a V-1 bomb drove the Camerons out for many months while they waited for restoration to begin. Not only had her home in London been badly damaged, but wartime restrictions had severely curtailed her visits to Bowen's Court.

Bowen did not confine her wartime work to her service as an air raid warden. The grumbling of publishers notwithstanding, the government was well aware of the value of the printed word. It established and deputized the Ministry of Information to convey information (carefully selected and organized) as well as to gather salient details about the life of the nation for its own use. And very soon the ministry became a magnet for those who wrote for their living—at various times during the war years it employed Graham Greene, Cecil Day Lewis, Laurie Lee, Elizabeth Bowen, John Betjeman, and John Lehmann, to name only a few.[83] Evelyn Waugh, in his novel *Put Out More Flags*, satirized the ministry, making sharp fun of its convoluted bureaucracy and sometimes ludicrous dissemination of unwanted and unnecessary information. Ambrose Silk, the irreverent and befuddled character in the novel, becomes "one of the many reforms introduced at the first of its many purges."[84]

But Bowen had reason to hold another view. Her position with the Ministry of Information made her visits to southern Ireland feasible. These journeys began in the summer of 1940 when she asked the ministry if she could do the kind of work she "felt was wanted in Ireland."[85] When Ireland had declared its neutrality at the start of the Second World War the act appeared to many Irish citizens as "the acid test of real independence."[86] The fact of neutrality took second place to what ensued, "proving to the world and itself its independence." The wartime Irish prime minister, Eamon de Valera, managed to link the mythos of Ireland's integrity with the decision to stay removed from the armed conflict.[87] To appreciate Bowen's unusual and ethically ambiguous role in her employment by the ministry, an understanding of Ireland's position in the war must be clear.

Yet the uncertain nature of neutrality carried with it many incongruities. As Trevor Salmon has shown in his study of neutrality in Ireland, this stance was only possible, in fact, because of the "protective umbrella" that was spread over the country during the war. If England had not, at least to a degree, made neutrality feasible, Ireland could not have survived, because the country had "no 'strategic reserve' to maintain the viability of such a situation." The British never officially recognized Ireland's stand, for doing so "would have been an anathema to British policy on Ireland."[88] Although some historians have argued that

Ireland's position in wartime "represented scarcely more of an experience of cultural isolation and deprivation than had any of the years that preceded them," the deliberate choice not to participate represented an articulation of will that led to desperate shortages at the same time that it signaled a vigorous independence.[89]

Certain practical considerations came into being to make this anomalous tactic work. De Valera's strong personality, political charisma, and determination gave him and his policies ubiquitous appeal among the majority of his fellow citizens. The second reason neutrality became possible was logistical: The "invasion of Ireland never became a vital interest for either belligerent." Had Ireland come to be regarded as a useful economic or strategic location for war, the tenuous declaration of independence would have been a much trickier problem. The most difficult test for neutrality occurred during the second half of 1940 when England wanted to use the Treaty ports as a much desired base to coordinate the sinking of German U-boats.[90]

Choosing neutrality, or in Salmon's terms nonparticipation, capped a long struggle in Ireland to act and to speak independently. By cutting itself off from the rest of the nations involved in this world war for four long years, southern Ireland created a separate space for itself, underscoring its geography as an island. In the face of much initial public outrage and some internal political opposition, de Valera stood his ground. The act of daring (or cowardice, as some have characterized it) certainly had long-lasting ramifications for residents of Ireland. For those Anglo-Irish like Bowen who inhabited the nebulous space between the two countries, neutrality unleashed a series of dilemmas involving commitment, allegiance, and responsibility. Cyril Connolly, always interested in writers outside England, devoted the January, 1942, issue of *Horizon* to literature in Ireland, expressing his concern for the doubts and regrets of the Anglo-Irish, who "feel that England is paying the price for its abandonment, after the last war, of the aristocratic qualities of the iron hand and personal honour."[91]

The split quality of Bowen's own Anglo-Irish vision enabled her to see Ireland simultaneously from within and without on the missions she undertook as an employee of the Ministry of Information. When Bowen first received permission to travel to Ireland, to make confidential reports to the ministry, her subterranean uncertainties surfaced, and just before she departed on her initial trip she wrote to Virginia Woolf: "Now it has come to the point I have rather a feeling of dismay and of not wanting to leave this country." After her arrival Bowen privately described the political atmosphere in Dublin to Woolf as "a craggy dangerous miniature world."[92]

In Dublin Bowen ensconced herself in a service flat in St. Stephen's Green; from there she made forays into the hermetic society that characterized the city in those years. By her own admission she worked discreetly, telling the people she met that she was taking a vacation, a rest from her work. To augment her anonymity, she used her married name, Mrs. Alan Cameron, which she usually reserved only for social occasions. One of her reports, dating from November 9, 1940, still exists in the state papers of Lord Halifax in the Foreign Office files at the Public Records Office in Kew. This one was probably meant to be destroyed, as the others may have been, but since it was rerouted from Lord Cranborne to Lord Halifax it got separated from the rest of the Foreign Office papers on the Irish situation. Of course, it contains some delicate information.[93] That such highly placed officials as Lord Cranborne read the reports Bowen wrote from Ireland strongly suggests that she was involved in some important undercover missions. Many years later, when these papers were opened in 1975, the *Irish Times* recounted that Cranborne had used Bowen's report of November 9 to "urge Churchill to wage an economic war to force Ireland to surrender the [Treaty] ports." The crucial timing of her report had deposited her in the midst of the heated and continuing argument between Eamon de Valera and Churchill about British use of these ports.[94]

Over tea and sherry Bowen met with a wide variety of figures in Dublin, a place she described to William Plomer as "a grand shell of an extinct capital city."[95] Sought out, she was warmly entertained and hence able to meet with students, politicians, and clerics. One evening she discussed the problem of unemployed university graduates with several young Trinity men. Surprised by their lack of interest in her comments on European affairs, she described them as reflecting the "claustrophobic" and "restless" temper of the Irish society as a whole. Through a good imperialist metaphor, she likened the prohibition of travel between England and Ireland to the "closing of the Burma Road" (PRO 257).[96] Unable to abandon her colonial training, Bowen found herself in the midst of a battle with institutions that echoed her own skirmishes with herself.

Several of the writers whose aid the ministry enlisted made their way to Ireland, such as John Betjeman, who was sent to Dublin in 1941 to be press attaché to the British representative in the city.[97] During the war, according to John Lehmann, Betjeman "acted as a two-way channel between the countries." He also managed to arrange a mutual exchange between Lehmann's *New Writing* and the *Bell,* a journal Seán O'Faoláin had started in 1940 to promote Irish culture and literature and which often published Bowen's short stories.[98]

Most of the observations Bowen made about Ireland in these years were conditioned by her fundamental and often-repeated understanding that, "while the rights of Eire's neutrality may be questioned, the conviction behind it must be believed."[99] By presenting herself as a translator between the Irish and the English, Bowen worked to arrive at a compromise between the factions warring within her. Her report to the ministry suggests the tone of someone undertaking to mediate between two differing and uncomprehending parties. In attempting to rationalize her activities as what one historian has termed an "allied agent," she assumed the role of an apparently impartial observer.[100] These efforts were limited not only by the biases implicit in her Anglo-Irish outlook but even more by her remove from Irish society, a gap symbolized by her inability to comprehend a word of Gaelic. She related, for example, that although there was a Gaelic Festival in full swing at the Dublin Mansion House in November, 1940, she could not read any of the Gaelic accounts of it. She had never had any interest in the Irish Revival of the 1890s or the Gaelic League, having only learned of these cultural celebrations when she was at school in England "about 1916" (*BC* 401).

After taking tea with the Fine Gael party's deputy leader James Dillon, whom Bowen discovered to be "less parochial in outlook than most Irishmen," she deduced that it was "wild" to think that he might be pro-German, although she regretted that he was probably a fascist. She also disliked what she perceived as his "morbid interest" in Hitler's personality (PRO 265). Her comments—amazing in view of the fact that Dillon was the "only outspoken public voice against both neutrality and Hitler in Eire"—demonstrate her own political naiveté.[101] When Dillon, a devout Catholic, resigned as deputy leader of the Fine Gael party in February, 1942, breaking with the party over the issue of neutrality, he was "virtually the sole voice in the *Dail* to denounce the fundamental evil of Nazi philosophy."[102] The party also could not countenance "his public and morally courageous repudiation of national policy" when they expelled him.[103] Dillon had no idea of Bowen's real purpose and was stunned when her report came to his attention in 1979.[104] Her abuse of the presumed confidentiality of their meeting profoundly disturbed and puzzled him.

Following her meeting with Joe Walsh, the Irish secretary of state for external affairs, she questioned his capacity for judgment, basing her doubts on what she deemed his "uncouth person" and the rumors she had heard of his "apparently sinister" past (PRO 266). Bowen also had a political agenda in her discussions with clerics. Not only did Britain mount "an economic pressure campaign against Ireland," but some members of the Foreign Office in London also had an "obsession . . . with the state of Catholic and clerical opinion in Dublin regarding the war and the efforts made to influence such opinion in a pro-allied direction."[105] Continuing a long pattern, the split between the two countries went beyond politics into the darker reaches of religious conflict. Well aware of this bitter history while writing her report, Bowen makes such apparently judicious comments as, "I wish that the English kept history in mind more, that the Irish kept it in mind less" (PRO 255). Perhaps some of these caveats were intended for herself as she vacillated about what she thought she believed.

The ministry valued the duality of outlook that gave Bowen the ability to navigate the political and emotional climate in Dublin, a place where she observed public opinion to be "almost dangerously fluid." She spoke her mind in view of her certain knowledge of the temperaments distinguishing each country: "The childishness and obtuseness of this country cannot fail to be irritating to the British mind." And she offered practical advice with an ear for what the British would want to hear and what the Irish would tolerate. At the same time she expressed uneasiness about the hard-headed quality of some portions of the British response: "I could wish some factions in England showed less anti-Irish feeling" (PRO 257, 252, 255). One of the ministry's plans, to send propaganda writers to Dublin, struck her as a foolish strategic error.

While proclaiming that Eire's neutrality should be viewed "positively" as "its first free assertion," Bowen challenged the ramifications of that decision: "it is typical of [Ireland's] intense and narrow view of herself that she cannot see that her attitude must appear to England an affair of blindness, egotism, escapism, or sheer funk." Yet, she cautioned her audience, "any hint of a violation of Eire may well be used to implement enemy propaganda and weaken the British case." Charged with suspicion and resentment, the atmosphere of Dublin in November, 1940, appeared unfortunately different from earlier months; she speculated that Ireland would consider opening its ports only if England were to offer to resume the treaty discussions. To answer the disapproval she feared her readers might spout, she insisted that Eire was not making what she termed a "fetish" out of its neutrality. She viewed the country's positive attitude toward neutrality as laudable. But she also concluded in her report that, if the Anglo-Irish could learn to be more flexible by "not so zealously represent[ing] themselves as England's stronghold here" by allying themselves to their interests with Eire's, they could begin to redress the historically painful situation. "The worst defeatism, on behalf of Britain," that she met in Ireland and tried to counter ". . . has been among the Protestant Anglo-Irish" (PRO 253, 263).

Her power to hold herself curiously apart from an emotionally charged situation, and thus to maintain a certain personal immunity, allowed Bowen to shape her own identity in asserting her differences from the predominantly Catholic country of her birth. With more than a hint of frustration the Protestant writer wrote to London, "one reason why one cannot deal with Ireland is that she has this vast super-rational element." Her suspicion of Catholicism runs as an undercurrent throughout the report. She became angered by what she noted as the "smugness," even "phariseeism" of the official "spirituality" she encountered. More than once she had heard the comment that "the bombing is a punishment of England for her materialism" (PRO 261, 259). Obviously troubled by the power of Catholicism, she was distressed even more by the anti-Semitism that she reported was on the rise in Dublin (particularly in the business sector).

Bowen related in this November, 1940, missive to the ministry that she was not convinced of the correctness of her interpretation of England's situation. Since she had been there she had "emphasized . . . (I hope rightly) that England has no wish that Eire should enter the war" (PRO 254). Her days in Dublin only served to confirm her insecurity about her tenuous personal, racial, and national position. She confessed to dubiety concerning the British government's expectations of her for this job that paid about one hundred pounds a year.[106] Later, in a funny but sad letter to Virginia Woolf, Bowen described her February, 1941, visit to Lord Cranborne at the Dominions Office. Apparently, she wanted to discuss matters relating to the Irish situation which she could not entrust to paper. After getting lost on her way to the office because neither she nor the taxi driver knew the address, she was challenged by bayonets at the entrance: "Inside there were forms to fill in, then the long passages that though very hot still smell of stone.... Unfortunately it was just as I had imagined... there were almost no surprises."[107] Although the government could not fully reconcile her conflicting expectations, it found her work of use. The report that survives so pleased Lord Cranborne when he read it at the Dominions Office that he sent it on to the British foreign secretary, Lord Halifax, with a note describing it as "sensible and well-balanced."[108]

As Bowen's experience indicates, closer relations with the government often proved to be an inescapable, if frustrating, aspect of wartime. For the British population as a whole, it was difficult to accept being told what to do, as the state transformed itself into what Charles Ritchie once described as a nanny or governess. Vere Hodgson gives a vivid instance of this changed circumstance when just after the end of the war in Europe, on May 16, 1945, she notes her amusement "at the rescinding of the bill against Gloom and Despondency, now it is not against the law to be gloomy or despondent.... Now we can be as unhappy as we please"; she added, ironically, "Freedom is returning."[109]

VE Day, the eighth of May, 1945, was anticlimactic to many, perhaps because of their misgivings about how long it might take to resume the life they had known or their doubt that this return could be possible. The events of the day itself followed a highly orchestrated plan: "Flags now everywhere; 'planes flying over crowds; bells ringing; mounted policemen moving back a throng which grew immense."[110] John Lehmann compared VE Day unfavorably to the close of war in 1918: "celebrations seemed to go off at half-cock, and there was none of that sudden wild relief from unendurable tension that I remembered from my boyhood in 1918."[111] Just before the approach of VE Day Bowen wrote to Ritchie that for her these hours were filled with "a sort of general paralysis and apprehension, and everyone wondering what they ought to do." On the long-awaited day, Bowen kept a full schedule, put out flags, and finally went to Westminster Abbey where, after her return to Clarence Terrace, she described the celebrations and bonfires as a "hilarious parody of war."[112]

Others chose their own private means of marking the passing of war in Europe. Anthony Powell, according to his wife, "was probably the only person in England at that moment lying in bed reading the *Cambridge History of English Literature.*"[113] The buildup to the celebrations gave other writers pause. Evelyn Waugh wrote in his diary on May 6, 1945, "all day there was expectation of VE Day and finally at 9 it was announced for tomorrow.... I thank God to find myself still a writer and at work on something as 'uncontemporary' as I am." Waugh was one who did not look optimistically to peace; on the last day of March he had expressed his doubts in his diary: "Everyone expects the end in a few weeks but without elation ... expect worse from the peace than they had in the war." He also hoped to be absent from the festivities proposed for VE Day, about which he had "Gloomy apprehensions." To combat his depression he threw himself into the novel he was then writing, *Brideshead Revisited*.[114]

That novel, a many-layered fantasy, looked to another time, another age, and responded to much the same impulse that had prompted Powell to cast a backward glance. Published on May 28, 1945, the book met with an enormously successful reception; Waugh noted in his diary on July 1, 1945, that it had "sold out in the first week and [was] still in continual demand."[115] The lavish but already anachronistic days he evoked in his portrayal of the country house in the 1920s—of wines, fine foods, jewels, and paintings—brought to mind a wealth of images for a people who were facing shortages of all necessities with little possibility of procuring anything fresh, clean, or new.[116] His search for the mythically glorious days before the catastrophes of this Second World War mirrors the journey Elizabeth Bowen undertook just before the beginning of the war. Then, she re-created the historical, social, political, and personal "living force" of her own ancestral country house (*BC* 32). For both writers faith in an imagined building brought grace and dignity to a troubled and uncertain age.

Chapter 7

Rifling the Past

War is not an accident: it is an outcome. One cannot look too far back to ask, of what?
—Elizabeth Bowen, *Bowen's Court*

During the 1930s a number of Elizabeth Bowen's friends, both English and Irish, had urged her to write about her family's history in Ireland. Since Bowen enjoyed cultivating her Irish side, she played up the mystique of her Big House to her English friends. Intrigued enough to make her first excursion to Ireland in April, 1934, Virginia Woolf encouraged her hostess to "remember the lives of the Bowens."[1] In a letter to Vanessa Bell, Woolf described her stay at Bowen's Court in less enthusiastic terms: "The remarkable thing about Ireland is that . . . There is no architecture of any kind . . . so Elizabeths home was merely a great stone box . . . however they insisted upon keeping up a ramshackle kind of state, dressing for dinner and so on."[2]

Woolf was even more detailed in her diary entry of the same April visit:

> There we spent one night . . . & it was all as it should be—pompous & pretentious & imitative & ruined—a great barrack of grey stone, 4 storeys & basements, like a town house, high empty rooms, . . . All the furniture clumsy solid cut out of single wood—the wake sofa, on wh. the dead lay—carpets shrunk in the great rooms, tattered farm girls waiting, . . . & then I talked to the cook, & she showed me the wheel for blowing the fire in the windy pompous kitchen, half underground— . . . no there was a fine turkey but everywhere desolation & pretention cracked grand pianos, faked old portraits, stained walls—& yet with character & charm.[3]

Woolf's account suggests the anomalous spirit of the place evoked in Bowen's description of the "long Room" at the top of the house. This huge expanse had been designed as a ballroom but never used for dances because the family feared the weight of the revelers would bring down the house. For Bowen, the concern that the house might tumble did not detract from its elegant beauty that was so foreign to her English friends.

Seán O'Faoláin had exclaimed in a 1937 letter to Bowen, "*Do* for God's sake write a book about Ireland."[4] Early in the summer of 1939 she heeded the advice of her friends and began the project she had been contemplating for a long time in her critical writings and elsewhere. In a 1938 book review, she had characterized the genre of memoir as "half way between aesthetics and pathology," and, like many of her contemporaries, she became absorbed in the philosophy informing the practice of autobiography.[5] As the world sped toward the nightmare of war she sought refuge in her private and her public past, which began "to matter" "more than ever" when "it loses false mystery" (*BC* 453). Writers such as John Lehmann, who saw in childhood "a strange insulated intensity, an hallucinatory effulgence," and J. B. Priestley, who referred to his first home as "the only solidly real place we ever know," struck responsive chords in Bowen.[6] Her autobiographical project affirmed her Burkean sensibilities as expressed in his essay on the French Revolution: "the long struggle in every individual to preserve possession of what he has found to belong to him and to distinguish him, is one of the securities against injustice and despotism implanted in our nature."[7]

Often writers who roamed the recesses of their pasts fastened upon their earliest years.[8] Sir Osbert Sitwell, whose four-volume autobiography appeared from 1944 to 1949, explained in his introduction: "since the whole of life and its background is being dissolved in chaos before our eyes, it is impossible—because our balance from day to day remains too precarious—to wrest a book from the future."[9] In the spring before the war Virginia Woolf had also turned her hand to writing some memoirs, which became known as "A Sketch of the Past" in *Moments of Being*.[10]

The popularity of stories written about the self began early in the war and continued throughout the conflict. For some writers, the desire to reminisce was immediate: Henry Green's *Pack My Bag* came out in 1939, and Louis MacNeice's *The Strings Are False* appeared in 1940. Vera Brittain gave a lecture on "Autobiographies" at St. George Chapel in Liverpool at the end of November, 1939, which, she smugly reported, attracted "the biggest audience they had [that] season."[11] Evidently, many members of the public were eager to hear and read about these personal histories, perhaps in the hope of finding some meanings in their own existences. By writing her family story, Bowen subscribed to the other side of the same impulse—to share the meaning she deduced from the history of her house with her readers—in the hopes they might find it as useful as she did.

In her autobiography she insists on the singularity of her estate: "There is no house like Bowen's Court, with its great Renaissance plainness set under near mountains among trees" (BC 108).[12] Particularly proud of the details Woolf had mentioned (such as the Italian plasterwork), Bowen argued that these ornaments underscored the differences between Irish and English decorative tastes and signified Ireland's long connection with the Continent.[13] The men who built the Big Houses turned to "the European idea—to seek what was humanistic, classic and disciplined."[14] Eighteenth-century Anglo-Irish architecture conferred integrity and responsibility upon its inhabitants in a way Bowen believed no English house could, and she continually makes this distinction in her fiction.

Farraways and the host of other fictional vulgar English houses such as Holme Dene in *The Heat of the Day* serve as transient and unsatisfactory alternatives to the Anglo-Irish Big House, Mt. Morris. In dedicating *Bowen's Court* to her father, Bowen took some of the first steps toward securing the immortality of the house. The threat of war impressed upon her the necessity of standing "more and more closely" by what a person "loved" while, at the same time, being "ready to sacrifice even this." The act of writing her autobiography enabled her to mediate between her ancestry and her future because, she believed, "when I write, I am re-creating what was created for me."[15]

By adopting the role of the "family story-teller," Bowen reexamined what it meant to be a member of "an imposed race" (BC 69, 36). Cognizant of the inherent dangers of becoming self-absorbed while immersing herself in the past, Bowen dramatized her belief in autobiography not as a "private document" but as "literature" in a 1945 BBC broadcast entitled "Anthony Trollope—A New Judgement." This radio play describes the story of a young soldier who takes a volume by Trollope from his uncle's bookshelves en route to battle. The boy's haste leads him to grab not a novel, as he had hoped, but Trollope's "mouldy old autobiography." Trollope comes back to life in Bowen's rendition to reassure the youth about the wisdom of his mistake: "May I say there's no book of mine I would rather see you take with you to the battle? Read it, will you?—and *then* go back to the novels. Maybe I wrote it for you. It's the truth—or as near the truth as man ever came."[16]

Like her vision of the nineteenth-century author, Bowen held to her conviction that the past, both individual and collective, could be instructive to an anxious present. In doing so, she echoed Burke's philosophy of enlightened conservation: "the idea of inheritance forms a sure principle of transmission; without at all excluding a principle of improvement." Her task called on the same qualities Burke had identified in his long essay as "a rigorous mind, steady preserving attention, various powers of comparison and combination, and the resources of an understanding."[17] While the earlier Anglo-Irish War had prompted the semi-autobiographical fiction, *The Last September,* the Second World War led Bowen to a much more direct and probing exercise of memory.

"With great excitement" Bowen read a draft of "The Leaning Tower," a lecture on autobiography given by Virginia Woolf in April, 1940, to the Brighton Women's Educational Association.[18] Woolf used this forum to examine the causes of the great rise in the popularity of autobiography from 1930 to 1940; she chose the metaphor of a tower to signify the artist's relationship to society. For the young men Woolf discusses—such as Day Lewis, Auden, and Spender—the tower was "raised above the rest of us . . . built first in his parents' station, then on his parents' gold," to form his "angle of vision." Woolf describes these writers as having begun life by sitting "upon a tower," but then recognizing that "even in England towers that were built of gold and stucco were never steady towers."[19] Calling her analysis "deadly accurate," Bowen enjoyed Woolf's attack on the limitations implicit in the selfishness of the young men's work.[20]

While Bowen admired Woolf's apt use of the metaphor of the flawed tower as "perfect," she especially praised what Woolf had to say about "family" and "books descending from books"; these thoughts confirmed her own instinct that "art ought to breed." She agreed with the conclusion Woolf drew that, although the "leaning tower people may be imitated (now) . . . they can breed nothing."[21] Woolf identified the combination of international uncertainty and narrow vision to explain the taste for autobiography: "When all faces are changing and obscured, the only face one can see clearly is one's own." As she wrote in "The Leaning Tower," "if you do not tell the truth about yourself, you cannot tell it about other people" ("Tower," 148). In the afterword to *Bowen's Court,* written in 1941, Bowen contemplated the contrast between these two attitudes; in wartime, by necessity, "all faces" had to "look outward upon the world." Paradoxically, she began this exercise by looking at the "self-centered" members of her own family (*BC* 454). Woolf understood the basis of this perspective.

In describing the genesis of her essay, Woolf had suggested in February, 1940, that, "the idea struck me that the Leaning Tower School is the school of auto-analysis after the suppression of the 19thc."[22] Earlier Bowen had linked the image of the tower with selfishness in her 1932 novel, *To the North;* the ineffectual Julian Tower is circumscribed by his extreme self-absorption. Solipsism and self-consciousness also paralyze Markie Linkwater, Emmeline's cruel boyfriend. To describe the precariousness of their relationship, he resorts to the image of a fragile edifice: "He had a frightening glimpse... of how very high a structure there was to come down. The tall tower, that rocked by some shock at its base or some flaw in its structure totters and snaps in the air, falls wide" (*TTN* 184). The weak young men Bowen portrays in these fictions, with their fear of falling buildings, typify the impotence and passivity of many of her male characters. In her family history, Bowen would examine with particular care the men who had ruled her estate for any signs of such moral flimsiness.

The tensions within Bowen's conflicting attitudes toward autobiography naturally influenced her reaction to Woolf's essay. Bowen hoped that the past would buttress her identity by recalling to her the places where she had felt secure, but at the same time she deeply feared simply escaping into those former days. Although she tried to make right her family's part in the struggle over nationality and autonomy in Ireland, she discovered on her journey that the past can be of only limited usefulness. Yet she remained deeply attached to this past, which she described in a review of *Uncle Silas* by Sheridan Le Fanu, another Anglo-Irish writer, as "the hermetic solitude and autocracy of the great country house, the demonic power of the family myth, fatalism, feudalism and the 'ascendancy' outlook."[23]

Bowen's Court reflects many of the same concerns that preoccupied its author in fiction, especially in the 1930s: the love of a house, or place; the past's bearing upon the present; the role of the Anglo-Irish; and the meaning of spiritual and financial inheritance. The autobiography interweaves the story of Bowen's ancestors, who came to Ireland under

Oliver Cromwell and began to build their Big House in 1775 (in the midst of the economic boom of that decade), with the saga of Ireland. Defying classification, the book combines history, family lore, imaginative reconstruction, and personal reflection as it examines the past in light of the wartime present. While Bowen recognizes the painful injustices associated with the conquering Anglo-Irish, she insists that the Bowens, and the house they built, have enriched the social and moral welfare of Ireland and, by extension, the world at large.

L. P. Hartley's review of *Bowen's Court* comments on the intensity of Bowen's pursuit as she "delves into the past with a subdued fury of intention that animates the whole book."[24] Freely admitting that she was, "evidently, not a historian," Bowen roamed widely through that past to write her wartime autobiography. She adopted a self-consciously individualistic position: "It has seemed to me more honest to leave my reactions to history their first freshness, rather than to attempt to evaluate" (*BC* 336, 452). She was still justifying her reluctance to discuss "raw history" in a later essay, "The Bend Back" (1950), calling it "unnerving."[25]

In November, 1939, when she was at work on her autobiography, Bowen wrote a review of the history of another Anglo-Irish family, *The Moores of Moore Hall* by Joseph Hone. She described the relation of this family to their adopted land: "Ireland broke each of the Moores in her oblique way. But being spirited people, they broke well."[26] During that trying first autumn of 1939 she was compelled to cement the foundation of her Anglo-Irish identity. The uncertain emotional climate surrounding her while she was beginning *Bowen's Court* strengthened the curious ambivalence underlying her characterizations of her race.

Bowen completed the first two chapters of her book before the outbreak of war. When she looked back on the summer of 1939, she referred to it as a time of reflection given to her by "God or Hitler" when "the cutting away of our dead wood could not have been more painful."[27] After she had finished a draft of *Bowen's Court* at Christmastide of 1941, she began to plumb the recesses of her imagination to rediscover the first seven years of her life. This journey resulted in the publication of *Seven Winters,* or a "fragment of autobiography," in 1942. In this second study of the self Bowen continued to grapple with such troubling questions as religion and race as she returned to the superficially more innocent world of her childhood. She recounted that she was startled to discover, in the company of her British governess, that

"Ireland was not the norm." This "time-lag" separating Anglo-Ireland and Ireland preoccupied her more fully during the Second World War when she forged an unbreakable link between herself and her past, "invest[ing]" her sense of being in memory.[28]

After the elaborate dance Bowen had choreographed to describe herself in the 1930s, she became more insistent on both her Irishness and her affection for the British royal family during the Second World War. She went further in exploring the geography of her identity in such wartime essays as "The Big House" (1940) and "Tipperary Woman" (1944).[29] A play entitled *Castle Anna,* which tells the story of a spinster who is infatuated with a fantasy of family life in an Irish country house, also dates from this period.[30] Her preoccupation with Ireland as a place, an idea, and a heritage came to dominate her wartime writings, as she tried to explain her feelings for England to herself as much as to others. She claimed to her interviewer at the *Bell* in 1942 that she viewed herself "as an Irish novelist" who had "never been influenced by any English writer, with the possible exception of Jane Austen" for the simple reason that "English novelists simply don't influence one." Declaring Ireland her own, she informed the *Bell* that it would be very difficult for anyone who was not Irish to write about the country because it "requires such an enormous amount of knowledge and experience" before "the foreigner begins to make an impression even on the rim of things."[31]

The war much hindered *Bowen's Court*'s appearance in print. Although she wrote the afterword between December, 1941, and January, 1942, the book did not come out until the following June. The reasons for the delay surface in the correspondence between Frank Morley and John Hayward. These letters illustrate a familiar story of wartime publishing, especially when the subject concerned Irish matters. John Hayward, a London literary figure and friend of T. S. Eliot, spent the war in Cambridge. His correspondent, Frank Morley, born in the United States of British parents, had helped in the establishment of the publishing house Faber and Faber in London, but in the autumn of 1939 Morley went to the United States to be editor-in-chief at Harcourt Brace. Paul Fussell claims that "Morley returned to the States at this time specifically to assist the covert work of British propaganda in wearing down American neutrality."[32]

Morley commissioned these letters describing conditions for writers in London ostensibly to keep up with the publishing situation across the Atlantic. Hayward, who was interested in Bowen's work, obliged by commenting extensively on her situation, as well as that of many other writers. According to him, Faber and Faber "(and particularly Tom [Eliot]) have long hoped to publish for her." Hayward encouraged Morley that the time was ripe for him to keep "a discreet eye and ear open" for Bowen, claiming an important place for her in England: "Since Virginia Woolf's death, she is coming more and more to be regarded as the outstanding woman novelist of her generation."[33] Hayward was, perhaps, one of the first to know that Bowen was writing her autobiography.

In September, 1939, he had heard some gossip that she was at work on a book "part fact, part fiction... about the Bowens of Bowen's Court." Keeping his ear to the ground, he reported in June, 1942, that he had learned of another rumor that Bowen had offered Macmillan a book, which he surmised was *Bowen's Court*. He then spent a day with Bowen, just after the book had been published; hence he relayed to New York another version of its creation:

> As so often happens in these days I was surprised to learn that her long-delayed book *Bowen's Court* had just been published by Longmans. One can never tell these days when the narrow "bottleneck" at the binders is going to let a new book slip out into the world. Elizabeth was as much surprised as I was, for there had been no preliminary announcement, either from her publishers or in the public prints. Longmans gave her a 350 pound advance for the book. At the time of the Blitz on London they left her free to place the ms. with another publisher, as they themselves could not guarantee publication. She offered it to Cape, who turned it down on the grounds that it contained too much controversial material about Anglo-Irish relations. She tells me that Jonathan [Cape] is becoming increasingly difficult and touchy in this respect and is inclined to exercise a tiresome personal censorship on anything that strikes him as "subversive"—Longmans, in due course, found themselves able to carry on with publication and the book has duly reappeared but she is not tied to them in any way.[34]

Not only did the production of *Bowen's Court* tell the story of the unexpected vagaries affecting wartime publishing, but it also illustrated the consequences of the dramatic shortages plaguing the publishing industry.

The tale that Bowen told had much to do with war. By investigating the story of Bowen's Court as a Big House, she necessarily involved herself in a discussion of the concept of possession—of land, of rights, of tradition, and of ideas. Perhaps she remembered Woolf's words in *Three Guineas* in 1938, just a year before the conflict erupted: "And are not force and possessiveness very closely connected with war?"[35] Convinced of the length of her lineage, Bowen adopted the plural pronoun *we* to describe events during the lives of her ancestors. She included herself among "we north-east County Cork gentry" who, indeed, "began rather roughly as settlers," in case any doubt remained about where she belonged, not only geographically but also by birth (*BC* 17).

Henry [Bowen] III, Bowen's great-great-great-grandfather (1723–88), built Bowen's Court, the "severely classical" house whose limestone facade shows "almost living changes of colour." Her detailed and admiring description of the stone shows a preoccupation with the physical relationship of the house to the land and, by metaphorical extension, with her ancestors' ties to their adopted country. She stressed that, although the house was "imposed on seized land, built in the ruler's ruling tradition," it "is, all the same, of the local rock, and sheds the same grey gleam you see over the countryside" (*BC* 22, 31). While she acknowledged that she was the daughter of a conquering family, during wartime she strained to believe in the Bowens' compatibility with the surrounding countryside.

Bowen's ancestral home occupied such a great part of her consciousness that in her autobiography it functions as the central character and the organizing principle.[36] The house kept her vision together during these otherwise unendurable years. By beginning and ending the book with an image of the building, Bowen illustrates the house's grasp upon her. Rarely did she break the rule she had set for her own narrative, and whenever she did wander she registered annoyance at being diverted (*BC* 392). Through her resurrection of the relevance of the Big House for all time, she fashioned a "biography" of her "Irish house" reminiscent of the house Yeats memorialized in "Coole and Ballylee" (1931).[37]

> A spot whereon the founders lived and died
> Seemed once more dear than life; ancestral trees
> Or gardens rich in memory glorified
> Marriages, alliances and families,
> And every bride's ambition satisfied.

A Merry Christmas
and a Happy New Year
to you, both.
most affectionately
from
Elizabeth
(my house)

Elizabeth Bowen's Christmas card to Alice Runnels James, ca. 1954, showing Bowen's Court. (By permission of the Houghton Library, Harvard University.)

> Where fashion or mere fantasy decrees
> Man shifts about—all that great glory spent—
> Like some poor Arab tribesman and his tent.[38]

In her prose elegy, Bowen subscribed to the poet's conviction that the house and its inhabitants bestowed a spiritual grace upon the world.[39]

Despite her adoration of the idea of the Big House, Bowen regarded the Irish estate itself as "something between a *raison d'être* and a predicament."[40] Although she described Bowen's Court, and houses like it, as "house-island[s]," she insisted upon them as symbolic of the tie between the Anglo-Irish and their country (*BC* 20). She bragged, in other wartime essays, that "the doors of the big houses stand open all day." Paradoxically, the children who emerged from these houses that were like "ships out at sea" were themselves "*farouches,* haughty, quite ignorant of the outside world." Called "big" in Ireland, the houses were not large by English standards: "But the houses that I know best, and write of, would be only called 'big' in Ireland—in England they would be 'country houses,' no more." Compensating for their comparatively small size, she defended the "true bigness" of the "manner in which these houses were conceived" ("Big House," 29, 27, 26).[41] And, indeed, under Bowen's direct and prideful gaze the Big House assumed mythical dimensions as it became "a symbolic hearth, a magnetic idea, the focus of generations of intense living" (*BC* 403).

The peculiar personal power of the house emerged in Bowen's evocation—in *Bowen's Court* and elsewhere—of its ability to affect the life within: "The great bold rooms" and "the high doors" imposed an order on the family's life. Enjoined by its architectural features, the family lived an existence characterized by "formality" and "steady behaviour." Bowen viewed the builder and the writer as artists who shared the ability to give life to a book or building in danger of becoming "academic." Henry III set "a pattern" for all future Bowens when he commissioned the house with all its idiosyncrasies. In fact, Bowen once said that, if she could not have been a writer, she would have liked to be an architect.[42]

The author's imagination reached full flight in her re-creation of the actual construction of the house in *Bowen's Court*. When the roof was installed, she wrote, with the self-consciousness and bravado often characteristic of the Anglo-Irish, "Anglo-Ireland knew her power and felt her spirit move."[43] Her romanticization of the scene strikes a sadly ironic note since, when she was writing the book, Anglo-Ireland had lost all significant political power. Obviously aware of her bias, she buries in her chronicle moments of reflection upon the danger of worshipping such symbols, which "tempt one to deflect narrative or misrepresent facts." Not to be deterred for long, however, Bowen dove into a retrospective reconstruction of Henry III's "state of creative nervosity" as he watched the "crowning act of his life," the completion of Bowen's Court (*BC* 161, 169).

Bowen rationalized the constraints on the design of the house necessitated by the poverty resulting from his overreaching temperament. According to the logic of this descendant, such cutbacks as the "halt" of the grand staircase "in full flight" only "make the scale of the first idea more strongly felt" (*BC* 31). Henry Bowen was not the only one with enormous ambition; although most Anglo-Irish builders began with noble ideas, too often they "died badly in debt and left their families saddled with mansions they could ill afford" ("Big House," 27). As she untangled her ancestors' grand and dense history, she concluded with conviction that, although "a Bowen made Bowen's Court, since then, with a rather alarming sureness, Bowen's Court has made all succeeding Bowens," including herself (*BC* 32).

In detail, Bowen examined the morally questionable builder of Bowen's Court, who, in her estimation, had left his children "no principle" because he was "a pre-eminently social figure" who moved in "a Philistine, snobbish, limited and on the whole pretty graceless society." Her harsh judgment does not make reference to the sentimental evocation of the Anglo-Irish that she had employed on other occasions. Henry III died surrounded by his children and the "esteem of what looked like a lasting order." Yet she used her exploration of his existence to make a bitterly comparative evaluation of her own time. Bad as it was, it was not 1939–42: "And to what did our fine feelings, our regard for the arts, our intimacies, our inspiring conversations, our wish to be clear of the bonds of sex and class and nationality, our wish to try to be fair to everyone bring us? To 1939" (*BC* 125).

She paid particular attention to defining the gentry's way of life, seen from the context of her wartime vision. The neighbors of her ancestor, John [Bowen] II (the builder Henry III's brother), were "that rather rare thing in Ireland, gentry content to live as gentry and nothing more." Bowen lamented the grandiosity of what she designated as the "Versailles fantasy," which took hold of so many of the Anglo-Irish. Eventually, she argued, their pathetic gestures at living opulently hastened their decline. Another neighbor by the name of Big George demonstrated his delusions, establishing his "rule by force of sheer fantasy," when he ordered the construction of the enormous Mitchelstown Castle (*BC* 103, 258). In the afterword to *Bowen's Court* she merged the individual and collective components of these dreams and condemned them both as having the same toxic danger of fantasy: "the private cruelty and the world war both have their start in the heated brain" (*BC* 454). Increasingly, the connection between the internal and the external, between insanity and war, became prevalent in her writing.

Bowen argued that by living in the past, the Anglo-Irish lost themselves in another land; she pinpointed the era of her great-grandfather, Henry V (1808–41), as the instant when "Anglo-Ireland began to claim and patent the ever-lasting Irish regret." If there were to be an elegiac dirge for Anglo-Ireland, then she wanted a member of her race to sing it, since "only dispossessed people know their land in the dark" (*BC* 258, 132). She failed to mention that the Anglo-Irish themselves dispossessed the Irish in some of their own battles over land. The sole hope for the survival of the Anglo-Irish lay, she wrote, in their foresight and responsibility in adapting to a changing present. It was, after all, the Naylors' rigidity and narrow-mindedness that doomed the fictional Danielstown to flames in *The Last September*.

The contemporary international preoccupation with race, class, and nationality heightened Bowen's ethnically based conception of the Anglo-Irish. She determined that the consolidation of their collective identity had occurred after 1760; before then it resembled "children playing in new gardens, now and then slinging pebbles over the fence" (*BC* 158).[44] By selecting such a figure of speech, Bowen defined her book as a story of a people as well as a history of her house and family. When she wrote that society could "only exist when people are sure of themselves and immune from fears," she echoed what Woolf had written in *Three Guineas*, that "a society is a conglomeration of people joined together for certain aims" (*BC* 258).[45]

While Bowen mourned the loss of the tightly woven fabric that had clothed her ancestors since their inception as a race and as a class, she conscientiously exposed the handicaps weakening the divided inheritance of the Anglo-Irish. Every detail of the autobiography bears the mark of having been written by someone with the peculiar vantage point of dual nationality. When she explained that "in Ireland we take . . . [ruins] as a part of life," she immediately added that the English viewed these relics with an "air of waste and nonchalance." As she articulated differences between Irish and English understandings of the world, she also interpreted the linguistic divergences dividing the two peoples: "English people also say 'park'; where we say 'demesne.'" The moral lives of the English squire and the Irish landowner both fell under Bowen's scrutiny: The squire believed in his duty "to teach the poor what is what"; the Irish estate owner, in contrast, displayed "an indifferent delicacy" mixed with laziness in his attitude toward the less fortunate (BC 11, 21, 125–26).

Although Bowen made many varying claims for the Anglo-Irish throughout her career, in *Bowen's Court* she was as tenacious in her defense as in her criticism of them. She included herself by her choice of the pronoun *we* and thus acknowledged her own responsibility: "We did believe we did something: we lived well, we circulated our money, we, consciously or unconsciously, set out to give life an ideal mould." When she analyzed the faults of the gentry she could show the same rigor she had applied to her critical view of the Naylors in *The Last September;* she deplored such darker moments as the Anglo-Irish show of "class temper" during the Doneraile Conspiracy of 1829 (BC 208, 266).

On the other hand, Bowen wrote that she could not discuss the Union of 1800, which "was a bad deal: and it is, or seems to be, a tragedy that puts uninformed comment quite out of countenance." The union with England had seemed to the Anglo-Irish, Bowen reported, "a vital shock to its self-respect.... If we *are* then, no more than England's creatures, let us cash in on her monied fun. A masochistic attraction towards England—too unwilling to be in love—in the Anglo-Irish began from now on, to be evident" (BC 219, 223).[46] The *we* here demarcates the extent of Bowen's own historical and racial investment in the struggles of the past; she further emphasizes the unhappy and self-destructive view the Anglo-Irish had held toward England for as long as she could perceive.

Despite her natural disavowal of self-exposure, in her personal history she took refuge from the inevitable losses of the war years while reconsidering the implications of the landed tradition.[47] Hermione Lee concludes that it was during World War II that Bowen's "idea of a spiritual inheritance became brutally palpable."[48] Then, she extolled the values of a generation against the threat of dispossession entailed in war. In pursuit of this certainty life inside the house became subject to Bowen's creative reconstruction. Without much substantial evidence the family myth took shape, a myth in which life was "lived at high pitch . . . in psychological closeness to one another" (*BC* 19).

To depict daily life in the past she invoked the inherited predilection for fantasy. Portraits of Henry II, her great-great-great-great-grandfather, who died in 1722, and his wife, Jane Cole, supplied Bowen with ready vignettes of their domestic routines: "Perhaps they strolled outdoors in the long Irish twilights or steely evenings after the rain—Jane holding the hem of her skirts clear of the damp." Other portraits, such as the one of her grandfather in 1881, "confront all time and the special threat of that year [the year of Gladstone's Land Act], with a glass-blue stare that shows the pressure behind" (*BC* 116, 117, 362). She derived from the house what Burke had glimpsed in the artifacts of the past, "its gallery of portraits, its monumental inscriptions, its records, its evidences, and titles."[49]

Reaching back into the past, she perceived that Bowen's Court had continued to enchant and entangle its residents, particularly Elizabeth's father Henry VI (1862–1930). Expected by his father, Robert (1830–88), to be a dutiful steward, Henry became instead an absentee landlord when he left full-time residence in Cork to practice law in Dublin. After he returned to the estate upon his retirement to belatedly fulfill the hopes of Robert, Henry found the life of the landed gentry tedious and oppressive. Robert's granddaughter, Elizabeth Bowen (an only child without offspring of her own), worried in print about maintaining her obligation to the tradition. About her father's tenancy she had asked: "the life not sufficient for Henry in his youth, had stayed on the steps of Bowen's Court waiting for him. But does vacuum fill the life one has not chosen to live?" Implicitly, Bowen posed the same question about her own choices: Would the house withstand all threats to its existence and wait for the return of the wandering daughter who had settled primarily in England? On her visits, she confided that the disrepair of her grandfather's farm implements left her feeling a "pang—on Robert's behalf" (*BC* 444, 376).

As she transposed her own position into her father's situation, the signs of decay sharpened her deepest fear that she could not keep the house alive. Entrusted with the guardianship of the house and its stories during her own uncertain era, she inverted the expected relation between language and its object by depicting the visitor's first view of Bowen's Court as having "the startling meaning and abstract clearness of a house in print." She conjoined the strength of the family with their possession of the building by insisting on her reciprocal relationship with that past: "the land outside Bowen's Court windows left prints on my ancestors' eyes that looked out. Perhaps their eyes left, also, prints on the scene. If so, those prints are part of the scene to me" (*BC* 20, 451). In Bowen's terms, that a member of the family still owned the house guaranteed its survival, at least in words.

Thoroughly, she re-created the moment when her great-grandfather, Henry V (1808–41), learned the house was his as a time when the "spiritual side" of "possession" announced itself. Careful to distinguish among differing kinds of ownership, she described her maternal grandmother, Mrs. Colley, not as "*possessive,* because that implies some assertion or fear or wish," but "*possessing.*" She attempted to separate the ideal of stewardship from the pain that often accompanied it. The proprietorship of Bowen's Court provided her with a spiritual and material anchor that proved ever more valuable as the Second World War spread over the world. After the deaths of her mother in 1912 and her father in 1930 the house had assumed another dimension by becoming her family. And, while she explained that she could not locate the appropriate word to convey her father's intricate relationship to the house, she had an even more difficult time deciphering her own. By referring to the furniture she and her mother had shipped from Bowen's Court to England in 1906 as "still in exile in my London house," she exposed her own inclinations. Bowen's Court was always home; Clarence Terrace, however beautiful, was not.

Bowen wrote in her autobiography that she hoped, by observing the patterns of existence demanded by the Big House, modern life could retain what the servant in *The Death of the Heart* had called "the ideal mode for living" where there is "always the religious element" (*DH* 245, 75). Bowen's Court contained both "character" and a long and proud history; thus, Bowen agreed it functioned as a universal symbol of home. The "spell" the Big House cast could be realized and preserved only if its value were appreciated. The echoes of the family's voices, or the "ghosts of the past . . . add something, a sort of order, a reason for living, to every minute and hour" (*DH* 28).

Character remained essential to the continuation of the race, and character preserved the Big House, even in disrepair. In Bowen's 1943 review of *The Desire to Please,* a family memoir written by Harold Nicolson, she recognized the same dilemmas that had buffeted her: the "suspicion of being implicated, the over-susceptibility to certain traits, the sense of guilt, the touches of harshness, ... the wary search for an ulterior motive."[50] Although her personal code of honor dictated that she revere her ancestors, her sense of justice demanded that she honestly face the family's foibles and faults. Her desire for the Bowens to be paragons conflicted with her avowed adherence to the importance of constructive criticism in shaping a better world. The Bowen characteristics—strong will, self-consciousness, "racial pride," faith in fantasy, desire for land—haunted her as she analyzed the damage the same beliefs had wrought in her lifetime.

Sharply criticizing the family predilection for illusion, she wrote: "Bowens have always been prone to avoid or balk at facts only to torment themselves with fantasies." While freely acknowledging her own preference for the imaginary, Bowen blamed many of the world's problems on a similar denial of reality. She argued that closely connected to the family tendency to retreat into fancy was the will, or the "force," she saw her father display "unimpaired by the Bowen weakness for self-regard." Even though she recognized that the survival of the line could be attributed to the family's collective determination, she held the same drive responsible for stubborn costly legal battles that were fueled by a fanatical desire for land. To prove her supposition, Bowen gives over much of *Bowen's Court* to a detailed discussion of the family history of litigation, which she based on the premise that "all Bowens want all land" (*BC* 100, 422, 118).

The very birth of the house could be credited to Henry [Bowen] III's (d. 1788) loss of the Kilbolane lawsuit, which, dragging on from 1759 until 1764, had its origins in an even earlier dispute over land adjacent to the Bowen property. Henry III's behavior over the legal battle he inherited, known as *Bowen v Evans,* confirmed some of his biographer's worst anxieties about the family character: "In full natures there is often this streak of fanaticism: war, religion, a phase of sexual love suddenly takes a man away from society and at once dehumanizes and superhumanizes him. With Henry Cole Bowen, litigation did this." Despite her disapproval of some of the excesses embedded within her family, on a visit to Kilbolane House, which had been built on the disputed land, she admitted that she had succumbed to the "vestigial stirrings of the family obsession." In tying herself to her family's history she proved her knowledge of their rituals: "The Bowens enter the churchyard near the top, through a narrow door of their own" (*BC* 149, 107, 254).

Throughout her memoir of the spirit animating her family, Bowen recalled her habit, first exhibited when she was a child, to see "life as a non-stop historical novel, disguised only thinly (in my day) by modern dress."[51] Her paradoxical tenets display the divided nature of a romantic and cynic, which she claimed for herself on occasion. The dreamer in Bowen made such sweeping assertions as "Ireland is a great country to die or be married in." She described her mother's (the former Florence Colley's) return from her honeymoon: When the new Mrs. Bowen came into view on the long carriage ride down a darkling avenue, the staff of the estate welcomed her with sparkling torches. The realist in Bowen took pride in the location of her father's funeral service; it was read outside St. Colman's church so that both Catholics and Protestants could attend, thereby preventing "an inhospitality that would have been Henry VI's first." As she recounted her father's funeral, she was recalling firsthand experiences with the English way of death, so much in contrast to the Irish practice of mourning in which "death makes no false or inhuman hush" (*BC* 393, 447).

From Bowen's vantage point the most difficult moments for her high-strung family must have involved departing from Bowen's Court, their stable center in uncertain surroundings. Henry IV, who gave his brother Robert (Bowen's great-great-grand-uncle [1769–1827]) a life lease on the house, had to face "a fact—which, as I have pointed out, few Bowens cared to do—it amounted to saying: 'I have gone away forever; I shall never come back.'" Poignantly, she invoked what she supposed to be Henry IV's emotions on the rainy day he left: He "sat well back from the windows [in the carriage], with no thoughts at all and a heavy heart" (*BC* 243, 237). She empathized closely with her ancestor at this juncture in his life. As the house became an increasingly eloquent symbol of all that she believed should be preserved, to imagine leaving it became ever more difficult.

War cut sharply across her worldview as Bowen was writing the last sections of her book, and, as she fully recognized, "in the savage and austere light of a burning world, details leap out with significance" (*BC* 453). While she was staying at Bowen's Court in January, 1941, after a mission to Dublin for the Ministry of Information, she described her progress on the autobiography to Virginia Woolf: "To be here is very nice, but I no longer like, as I used to, being here alone. I can't write letters, I can't make plans. The house is now very cold and empty, and very beautiful in a glassy sort of way.... I am doing the last chapter of the Bowen's Court book."[52]

Her letter alludes to what she expressed more completely in her afterword to *Bowen's Court*—the enormous emotional, intellectual, and physical difficulties associated with writing in wartime, when the disparity between what she was memorializing and the events occurring around her became paralyzing. She employed the afterword to bridge this disjunction in a moving treatment of all the previous wars she had witnessed. In this section, the most personally charged in the book, Bowen turned to Bowen's Court as an extension of her own identity, to gauge how it had survived previous conflicts.

Recalling Bowen's Court in earlier times of trouble gave Bowen courage; "the first time Ireland clashed with the house" in the 1798 uprising, the house survived handsomely. When the Republican army briefly occupied the house during the Civil War in the summer of 1922, the invaders "mined the lower avenue." Their wires "came through" the same corner of the library occupied by the "wireless," which later broadcast the news of the outbreak of the Second World War to Bowen and her housekeeper. During the spring of 1921, Bowen remembered, her father wrote to her in Italy where she was staying by Lake Como, warning her that Bowen's Court might not last through the Anglo-Irish War: "[looking into] the blue water, [I] taught myself to imagine Bowen's Court in flames. Perhaps that moment disinfected the future: realities of war I have seen since have been frightful; none of them have taken me by surprise" (*BC* 206, 441, 440).

Full possession of the house in her life and detailed depiction of it in her art made Bowen even less able to envision the consequences of relinquishing it. Only in fiction, such as *The Last September* or *The House in Paris,* where the Big House was burned in the Troubles, could she exorcise the demons of her imagination. During the Second World War the edifice became for her the mainstay of society: "From the point of view of the outside Irish world, does the Big House justify its existence? I believe it could now as never before." Relentlessly, she held to her belief that the Big House "has much to learn" in order to stay in tune with the world, and has "much to give" to that exchange ("Big House," 29, 30). It was as though, if she wrote these words often enough, she could make the protective powers of the magic hold.

The afterword treats painful issues with clarity and formality: "So,

Henry VI died, and I as his only child inherited Bowen's Court. I was the first woman heir: I had already changed my father's name for my husband's, and I have no children" (*BC* 448). Intimate emotions penetrate the flatness of such compressed sentences. When she summed up the loaded issues at stake—race, class, nationality, power, and possession—she reached a new directness of accountability: "My family got their position and drew their power from a situation that shows an inherent wrong.... England and Ireland each turned to the other a closed, harsh, distorted face." Neither country, she wrote, had accommodated the past; Ireland "dwells on" previous events, while England has not "enough recognized" past history. Bowen further explained that she had tried to "make the account fair" in weighing the balance of history. Finally, she acknowledged that above all she appreciated the dangers of the "power-hungry temperament" when it was "forced to operate in what is materially a void" (*BC* 453–55).

Obviously, she could not condemn entirely the heritage of her family. Although she recognized that the Bowens could be accused of appropriating authority, she explained with feeling that she did not believe she had to defend them: "you, on the other hand, may consider them indefensible." By resorting to her faith in the beneficial effects of character, she differentiated the conquering Bowens from the contemporary dictators and fascists who had also overridden native claims to land: The Bowens "found no facile solutions; they were not guilty of cant." Her ancestors showed "a virtuosity into which courage enters more than has been allowed... they have lived at their own expense" (*BC* 455–56). R. F. Foster notes a certain apt irony in Bowen's use of this phrase: "In a very Anglo-Irish mode, this judgement reverses economic fact to express something not far from psychological truth."[53]

Bowen commented extensively in the afterword on the influence the Second World War had exercised over *Bowen's Court*. She maintained that "the colour of [her] narration" was profoundly affected by war. While her values had remained unchanged in her eyes, she acknowledged they might have been "accentuated" by the destruction of war. Evidence of the present disaster could be seen everywhere; but Bowen located it particularly in her family's desire for possession, their denial of reality, and their stubbornness. She drew the lesson that the study of the past became ever more crucial: "Nothing that ever happened, nothing that was ever willed, planned or envisaged remains irrelevant to-day" (*BC* 453–54).

Bowen's autobiography draws force from her genius for holding two conflicting reactions to an event in her head. According to her, the "conservative experiment" practiced by Britain toward Anglo-Ireland in the 1890s "might be summarized as an attempt on the part of English gentlemen to treat the Irish as gentlemen." But she allowed that the Irish attitude toward the same policy held that it was "either bribery or admission of guilt." Applying the same duality of perspective close to home, she stressed her feeling of community with the Irish: "I can only say we could not have been better treated if we had been popular—(I only realize how much this is the case when I am in England, and feel lonely)" (BC 398, 278).

In dissecting her Irish self, Bowen defended the integrity of her family's behavior by claiming that she had "never heard . . . any remark about 'the Irish' prompted either by panic or the wish to insult." Her complementary vocation for definition and explanation affected her perception of the British view of the Irish: "the complete subjugation and the exploitation of Ireland became the object of the burgess class" in the wake of the flight of the earls in the seventeenth century. Yet, despite her admiration for objectivity, she could not disguise for long her Irish sympathies that she labored to hold in suspension during the war. When "the Englishmen looks at Ireland, something happens which is quite unbearable—the bottom drops out of his sense of right and wrong" (BC 278, 49, 263–64).[54]

Janus-like, Bowen elaborated upon the inherent misconceptions upon which her race had founded itself. She defended the Anglo-Irish choice to live in a land that did not accept them—"the grafting-on had been, at least where *they* were concerned, complete" (BC 160). While she usually protected her ancestors' reputations, she allowed that their sometimes foolish choices stemmed from the same pride, insecurity, rigidity, and egoism that she condemned where she found it in her life. Increasingly, Bowen confronted her family's and, consequently, her race's anomalous identity as her work on the book progressed and the war worsened. Although she had always voiced suspicions about the "narrowness" of "fantasy," which she portrayed in *The Death of the Heart,* as her reliance on the world of the imagination intensified, she began to question this phenomenon more probingly (DH 299). She admitted that during the long years of the war she reassured herself by the vision, or illusion, that holds *Bowen's Court* together:

> This illusion—peace at its most ecstatic—I may hold on to to sustain me throughout the war. I suppose that everyone, fighting or just enduring, now carries one private image—one peaceful scene—in his heart. Mine is Bowen's Court, war has made me this image out of a house built of anxious history (*BC* 457).

She had been so successful in collapsing the past and present into an eternal continuity that her private vision, made public in *Bowen's Court,* became independent of the house. The fact that she completed the book in London rather than in County Cork, as she had hoped, ceased to matter.

Her ability to preserve her heritage augmented her faith in "a family living in one place" forming "a continuous semi-physical dream," even though war encroached upon the sanctity of her belief by altering "the rhythm of habit in the house." Bowen insisted that life at Bowen's Court had not lost any of its "intensity" in war. To prove her point, she imagined herself lighting the traditional Christmas candle in the house in 1941. While the book appeared to be a consolation for immeasurable loss, Bowen cautioned herself not to retreat into an escapist fantasy. That December, when "the belt of fire has met right round the earth," she chided herself, "I must not think of the trees at Bowen's Court without thinking that upon an equal innocence on the part of nature, elsewhere, bombs fall" (*BC* 457).

Bowen wrote the last chapter of *Bowen's Court* against the backdrop of intermittent air attacks on London. In the mornings, "when the smoke and smell of raids still hung in the air," she returned to Clarence Terrace from a night in the shelter to complete the manuscript. To be prudent she sent copies of the drafts to various friends in the British countryside and the United States, while she carried the working versions of the afterword "in my overcoat pocket while we waited about on disturbed nights." Just as the vision of Bowen's Court in flames had "disinfected" the Irish Troubles for her, the indelible image of the house set in a serene landscape sustained her through the periods of bombing and her own work, "tied [her] in a double way to the house that Henry III built." By treating the house "as though it were everlasting," she ensured it would be in her own and in her readers' minds (*BC* 457, 440). In this work, she addressed her internal contradictions by transforming illusion into reality and the fact of material possession into a state of spiritual grace.

Chapter 8

"The Saving Hallucination"

Just as Elizabeth Bowen's autobiographical writings reflected the growing entanglement of her artistic interests with the history that she witnessed, so also do her short stories. Her naive complaint of boredom in 1923 that "when people discuss *weltpolitik*" she longed to talk of the "Short Story" seemed far removed from her attitude in 1940.[1] This genre, in fact, became the first place where her fiction showed the impress of political events. According to her retrospective analysis, "the art of the short story showed itself truly to *be* art in that it felt compulsions from the outside world." As she was to say in championing the genre in 1945, the "short story [was] the ideal *prose* medium for wartime creative writing."[2] Her stories reflect her talent for the form, a mastery most evident in time of war.

When Bowen later reflected upon her life during the war years she explained that she met life "both as a civilian and as a writer, with every pore open." She also noted that she had "lived so many lives"; many of these surfaced in the twenty compelling short stories she published during the Second World War.[3] During a 1959 BBC interview she said: "[throughout the war] I went on writing and writing away—not, I think, altogether wrongly, but feeling, 'Well this is the one thing I can do and what's the point of stopping it? If it's any good at any time, it's some good now.'"[4] The only times she put aside writing during the war for any significant period was when her Clarence Terrace house sustained serious bomb damage.[5]

In the concentrated period of wartime from 1939 to 1945 Bowen produced more short stories than at any other point in her career. The feverish pace of life in these years diverted her from the concentration necessary for a longer work of fiction. Although she had drafted five chapters of her wartime novel, *The Heat of the Day*, by 1945, she still had significant revisions ahead. The interval of eleven years between the publication of *The Death of the Heart* and *The Heat of the Day* represented the longest break between novels of her career.[6] As she engaged in what she termed "resistance writing," she frequently resorted to the world of the hallucinatory in her short stories to counter the psychic stress of war.[7] In honoring the conventions of the Celtic tradition of the ghost story, she often located these fictional fantasies in Ireland.

Beyond producing short stories commissioned by magazines throughout the war Bowen also put together two fine collections of stories. The first, *Look at All Those Roses,* which appeared in January, 1941, included only four stories written during the war. The second, published in England in October, 1945, as *The Demon Lover* and in the United States as *Ivy Gripped the Steps* the following spring, contained only stories dating from the war years. Her contemporary, the critic Henry Reed, concluded that *The Demon Lover* "most gave the feeling of wartime England." He determined that the "subtly degrading effects of war" hold the stories in *The Demon Lover* together: "that feeling of the deterioration of the spirit which, when the tumult, and the shouting, and the self-deception subside, is seen to be war's residue."[8] She was never to apply such concentration to the genre again, and in almost thirty years of writing after the war, she published only ten short stories.[9]

Bowen pursued the same pattern she had followed when she was at work on *Bowen's Court,* becoming involved in critical discussions of the form. The short story appealed to her for many reasons, not least its sheer brevity in days of limited paper supply and disrupted schedules. As Bowen pointed out, the expansion of publishing opportunities in journals such as *Horizon, English Story, Penguin New Writing, New Writing and Daylight,* and *Orion* gave evidence of its popularity ("Short Story," 7). She argued that the spiritual needs of these years also informed to the short story. When she reviewed V. S. Pritchett's *In My Good Books* for the *New Statesman* in 1942 she observed the attraction of the genre for the "reflective writer" who suffers in war "not so much of inhibition or dulling of his own feeling as an inability to obtain the focus necessary for art.... These years rebuff the imagination as much by being fragmentary as by being violent."[10]

The short story writer, she said in her 1945 essay on the state of the art, draws upon the "faculties of [the] poet" to discuss the large "significance of [a] little event" by the ability to "register the emotional colour of a moment." In a short story the writer can extrapolate and fabricate from such fragments as an overheard conversation on a train or a bus, which Bowen projected would take a novelist at least five years to assimilate ("Short Story," 7–8). She based her definition of the short story, "vision turned upon reason," on her conviction that it "is a matter of vision, rather than feeling."[11] In her introduction to the edition she prepared of *The Faber Book of Modern Stories,* she further argued that "the short story as an art has come into being through a disposition to see life in a certain way."[12]

While working on this collection, she explored the question of what a short story should possess, but some aspects of the task annoyed her. She complained in a cranky letter to William Plomer: "Yes, indeed, I am doing those abominable short stories (the collection, I mean)."[13] Dismayed by the poor quality of some of the submissions, she blamed their inadequacies on their creators' lack of vision, or perspective.

Taking into account the position of the short story as a relative newcomer to respectability in British literature, Bowen emphasized the distinctive challenge it posed to the novel: "the story, because of its real perks [sic] to poetry, because of its stress on language, is a very much greater imaginative test, is a very much higher trial of the artist behind it, than the novel, with its smoother surface, its more easy equilibrium."[14] Always appreciative of the poetic possibilities of short fiction, she announced in her introduction to the Faber volume 1936 that "the story should have the valid central emotion and inner spontaneity of the lyric; it should magnetize the imagination and give pleasure of however disturbing a kind."[15] The connection she draws between the short story and the lyric recalls the central tension present in all Bowen's work between the obfuscation of the self and the revelation of it. In a joint BBC interview in 1948 with Graham Greene and V. S. Pritchett she counted strife as "essential" for the writer who must possess "a hyperacute sense of every kind of conflict."[16] Years later, while teaching at Vassar in 1960, she told her class that the genre "lends itself" to the "invocation of feeling" not "the register of thoughts." Then, perhaps remembering her own wartime stories, she further noted that "form is the servant of subject" in the short story.[17]

She admired short story writers such as Guy de Maupassant, Anton Chekhov, D. H. Lawrence, Rudyard Kipling, Somerset Maugham, Aldous Huxley, James Joyce, William Plomer, Frank O'Connor, Liam O'Flaherty, and Seán O'Faoláin, who, she argued, used their visual talents. Her subscription to Gustave Flaubert's definition of style as "itself an absolute manner of seeing" contributed to her avowal that *Dubliners* was "the best book of stories ever written" ("Short Story," 4).[18] Two of her most successful wartime short stories, "Ivy Gripped the Steps" and "Mysterious Kôr," she said arose out of an "all but spell-binding beholding" of wartime London.[19]

There the conflict between wholesale destruction and the workings of individual destiny grew so daunting that Bowen sought refuge in the Irish tradition of the ghost story to supply the "saving hallucination" for her war-weary characters. Stories such as "The Demon Lover" (1941), "The Cheery Soul" (1942), "Pink May" (1942), "Green Holly" (1944), "The Happy Autumn Fields" (1944), "The Inherited Clock" (1944), "Mysterious Kôr" (1944), and "Ivy Gripped the Steps" (1945) resort to the ghostly province.[20] Sometimes the proximity of another world in these stories proves even more terrible than reality for the characters.[21] The fictions portray the dissolution of the distinctions between the living and the dead, the real and the imaginary. Long after the war Bowen felt compelled to defend these ghosts and phantoms: "I do not make use of the supernatural as a get-out; it is inseparable (whether or not it comes to the surface) from my sense of life. That I feel it unethical—for some reason?—to allow the supernatural into a novel may be one of my handicaps as a serious novelist."[22] Such stories as "The Demon Lover" force the reader to question the distinctions between reality and fantasy, which wartime life blurred. Bowen's friend Eudora Welty believed the ghostly realm was what allowed Bowen "to explore experience to its excruciating limits ... and enabled her to write as she did about World War Two."[23]

The speaker of "Pink May," published during the long middle period of the war in October, 1942, invents "the Puritan 'other' *presence*" to make the young female character's drab life seem more exciting to her friend. Later Bowen attributed this woman's vision to an opening up of the "susceptibilities, which are partly normal, partly those of our time."[24] "The Demon Lover," published in November, 1941, invokes a much more haunting ghost, an apparition that terrorizes a woman on a hot August day in London, than the phantom in "Pink May." After reading the story we become more convinced than ever of Bowen's assertion that ghosts "are the certainties" in the unsettled province of war. This earlier story gives credence to Bowen's belief that, for imagination in wartime, "the passive role is impossible."[25] Here she recalls the observation of Wallace Stevens, who wrote in his 1948 essay "Imagination as Value" that "the imagination is the power that enables us to perceive the normal in the abnormal, the opposite of chaos in chaos."[26]

Even the title of "The Demon Lover" suggests something ominous and threatening.[27] It evokes an English ballad by the same name which narrates the story of a woman who betrays her absent lover by marrying someone else. When the lover returns an enormously rich man, she abandons her husband and children for him, only to learn that he has become the devil himself.[28] Bowen's story describes the afternoon of a middle-aged woman, Mrs. Drover, who has come to London after a bombing to check on her shut-up house. Once inside the house the "dead air came to meet her," and she begins to do battle with monsters crouching in her own mind.[29]

The shock of what she encounters on her return catapults Mrs. Drover into a hallucination that conjures up the First World War. She returns to a mirage of August, 1916, when she was bidding farewell to her soldier-lover at the end of his leave. The piquancy of memory compels her to imagine that this man has written a letter to her, addressed to her London house, reminding her that he is still waiting for her. As she struggles to escape his hold on her, the reader realizes that what she is really trying to flee from are demons created by her own mind. She runs into the silent street to get a taxi before her lover arrives but recognizes the futility of escape. The only taxi waiting in the avenue is, of course, driven by the faceless lover of her nightmare. Climbing into the car, she screams in terror.

Her helpless surrender to this nameless demon suggests the impersonal power of the war to invade the depths of her inner life.[30] War is personified as a powerful masculine figure capable of abducting the innocent woman made captive by memory and desire. Like a character out of Wallace Stevens's vision, Mrs. Drover has employed her mind to fend off the forces of a violent world. As Stevens wrote, it "is a violence from within that protects us from a violence without. It is the imagination pressing back against the pressure of reality."[31] The unimaginable darkness drives Mrs. Drover to invent her own faceless devils. But she is not the only Bowen character who responds to the dislocations and shocks of the Second World War by reliving the enduring losses of the previous world war. By using a trick of consciousness that Bowen believed integral to the short story, "The Demon Lover" conveys the extremity of experience in wartime London.[32]

Bowen credited this expanded sensitivity to her eerie and unreal experiences as an air raid warden: "Walking in the darkness of the nights of six years (darkness which transformed a capital city into a network of inscrutable canyons) one developed new bare alert senses, with their own savage warnings and notations."[33] Her sensory awakening compelled her to take more risks with language. Of course, the experiments met with uneven results: The success of "The Demon Lover" has to be matched against the stilted quality of the dialogue in "Oh, Madam. . . ." Both stories display a broadened range and a heightened precision in Bowen's use of words. The "non-explanatory nature" of the short story freed her from what she called the burden of providing "the information desk of the novel."[34] Because she assumed less need to be consumed with plot (which is often her weak point), she concentrated on the moment, on her vision of "war-time—London blitzed, cosmopolitan, electric with expectations" ("Short Story," 8). Fifteen years after the end of the war, when she discussed the short story with her Vassar students, she emphasized that the "*isolated* 'violent' episode" did not suit the genre because violence needs "the before and after." She claimed that in Irwin Shaw's war stories, "the treatment of *war* in the *'action'* sense, [i.e.] reportage may be said to have driven the short-story writer off the field."[35] Since the war had grown too large for the domain of any one tale, she broke down its enormity into sections an individual could absorb.[36]

Apologizing that she only took what she called "disjected snapshots" in wartime, Bowen acknowledged that the difficulty with the pictures becomes one of perspective: They were taken too close, "in the middle of the *melee* of a battle."[37] She did not discuss the details of the deaths she must have witnessed as an air raid warden or the devastation represented by bomb sites, but instead portrayed the daily lives of ordinary people moving about in the midst of the "violent destruction of solid things." As she told her American audience in the preface to *Ivy Gripped the Steps,* she regretted that her stories do not give "more 'straight' pictures of the war-time scene." But she ascribed her choice of emphasis to her innate perception of war "more as a territory than as a page of history."[38]

Bowen explained that the short story writer must return to what allows "men and women [to] sustain themselves and keep their identities, throughout the cataclysm of world war." These she defines as "unchanging and stable things" such as home, affection, and childhood memories ("Short Story," 6). Viewed together the stories in this collection offer a unified panorama of the Bowen terrain in war. The individual characters whose stories she told were rooted in the landscape of war that she knew well: London in the Blitz and during the long spaces between air raids, neutral Ireland, the British south coast, and the countryside outside London. Her choice of settings underscores her lament that "war's everywhere—every place that you look."[39]

Consequently, the locations of the stories assume more importance than do the characters. Before the war, on the very day that *The House in Paris* came out in the summer of 1935, Bowen had mused about her travels in France in a letter to Virginia Woolf: "I believe I may only write novels for the pleasure of saying where people are. And the advantage of short stories is that it means a different place each time."[40] The elegantly proportioned Regency terraces Bowen had always placed "among the most civilized scenes on earth" stand at the hub of her wartime fictions. Her London stories refer to inhabitants of houses who reconcile themselves with the losses resulting from the bombings, both of their material possessions and of their spiritual lives. In her creative work, she tested the validity of her conviction that "undoubtedly bombing does something to you."[41]

Bowen wrote "In the Square" during "a hot, raid-less patch of 1941 summer, just after Germany had invaded Russia"; the story photographs the disturbing quality of life in a London terrace house after the Blitz.[42] Fixed specifically at nine o'clock on a "hot bright July evening," the fictional house seems stopped in time and season. Its reflection casts the "ghost of the glare of midday" when it recalls the quality of the light of an earlier, happier time. The first sentence of the story, which the author placed at the start of her collection *The Demon Lover,* draws us into a hallucinatory region. The atmosphere, always an index of the quality of life in her novels, as in *The Last September,* reminds us that we are in a bomb-damaged square on an unexpectedly stark day. Confined to the darkness of blacked-out nights and the hot glare of a dry summer, Bowen's characters live closer to the edge of existence. The initial paragraph of the story paints the "extinct" atmosphere of this summer in London with absent inhabitants, missing walls, and boarded-up windows.[43] The desolation of this terrace sounds eerily like Bowen's description of her own house in a letter written to Woolf in January, 1941: "Clarence Terrace is now perfectly empty, except for ourselves in No. 2, and one other, a house with a *reputation.*"[44]

An unlikely group of people inhabit this house in the square. Magdela, whose residence it is, has just returned after spending the preceding two years outside London. Her husband, Anthony, has also been away "since this all started," but Gina, his young secretary, has been staying in the house while working as an ambulance driver. Magdela's decadent nephew, Bennet, is visiting on his way to school. An independent couple, "only supposed to be caretakers," lives in the basement with their son who is employed as a policeman. This odd ménage has scrambled the usual domestic routine and, with grim resignation, Magdela now assumes that the house seems "to belong to everyone" ("In the Square," 611, 612). Stories such as this one record both the lessening of barriers among people and an awareness of loss that Bowen articulated when she admitted, during the war, "I felt one with, and just like, everyone else" as "the overcharged subconsciousness of everybody overflowed and merged."[45] Mollie Panter-Downes, the chronicler of wartime London life for the *New Yorker,* also remarked on the "un-English mateyness, which is one of the few pleasant things to come out of this war so far."[46] Although Bowen freely acknowledged this change in relations, she was quick to depict its darker side.

We only apprehend the alterations in the terrace of the story "In the Square" through the eyes of a visitor, Magdela's former lover Rupert, who is returning for the first time since the war began. On his arrival he "got a feeling of functional anarchy, of loose plumbing, of fittings shocked from their place" ("In the Square," 610). His observations emphasize the question that the war continually prompted: What does property, either emotional or material, mean? Throughout the story Rupert wonders why the railings have not been removed for scrap. For the historian A. J. P. Taylor, the removal of the railings marked "the brief period when the English people felt that they were a truly democratic community."[47] Bowen's character Rupert, on the other hand, regards these transformations as unsettling physical symbols of a decline in power and privacy.

During his visit to the house in the square Rupert is overcome by a strong memory of the essence of peacetime life. Anticipating his shock and disorientation, Magdela greets him with quiet surprise: "It's so curious to see you again, like this. Who would think that this was the same world?" ("In the Square," 611). The physical changes in the room mirror the transmutations in the emotional climate between Magdela and Rupert, who are unable to communicate their separate experiences to one another. The sound of the telephone bell punctuates the tension hanging between them and reminds Rupert of other, happier summer evenings when the bell rang all the time. Rupert is further dismayed when he realizes that Magdela is speaking to a new lover in the intimate whispers she used to save for him.

Life downstairs in the house parallels the reversal occurring in the drawing room as Gina waits for her new man to call. After beginning a romance with Magdela's husband, Anthony, Gina has now started another affair, leaving all parties unsatisfied. Bowen probes this young woman's perspective and in so doing offers a counterpoint to the scene between Magdela and Rupert. Gina's role testifies to the author's new openness in portraying lower-class characters whose fullness she had not often explored before the war. When Gina looks at the bomb-damaged square she thinks not of life before the war but of the fall of 1939 when she first came to the house. She sadly realizes, after trying to keep the several disjunctive strands of her life in order, that her feelings are "not at all fine" ("In the Square," 613). Each character who endures this hot London July is suffering through what Rosamond Lehmann called a "makeshift yet intense" existence.[48] Bowen herself frequently referred to the quickly shifting conditions of life in wartime.

At the christening of William Buchan's daughter in the winter of 1941 Bowen met Charles Ritchie, who was to become her lover for many years. The Canadian diplomat, stationed in London during the war, remembered their first meeting in detail: She was "well-dressed, intelligent, handsome face, watchful eyes. I had expected someone more Irish, more silent and brooding and at the same time more irresponsible." After Ritchie knew her better he confessed that "she looked more like a bridge-player than a poet" when he had first seen her.[49] Immediately, however, Bowen saw in him some intimations of herself when she sensed that Ritchie was similarly displaced from his origins. About them, she said, "I think we are curiously self-made creatures, carrying our personal worlds around with us like snails their shells, and at the same time adapting to wherever we are."[50]

Later in the autumn of 1941 Charles Ritchie recorded in his diary: "We have long since ceased to find the war thrilling. . . . The truth is that the war has become as much a part of our lives as the weather."[51] Often Bowen acknowledges this awareness in her fiction. Her story "In the Square" dramatizes two intimate turning points that punctuate a long anxious summer of waiting when both the contours of the personal and the individual seem indistinct. By closing the story with Magdela's question to Rupert—"Do you think we shall all see a great change?"—as

Bowen draws attention, as she does so commonly in her wartime stories, to the unsettled and unresolved quality of her characters' situations. Cut off from the past, they blunder through the present, fearful of their future: Magdela laments, "One has nothing except one's feelings" ("In the Square," 615).

In describing the Blitz, Bowen wrote, "Bombs only mark the material end of things. Their psychological end will be much more lastingly felt" ("Britain," 9). Her short stories assess the emotional and spiritual impact of the air raids. A story such as "In the Square," written after the Blitz, probes the longer-term consequences of the destruction. Other tales, like "Oh, Madam...," explore the more immediate effects of an air raid hit on the inhabitants of a London square. Bowen wrote this story, published in the *Listener* in early December, 1940, during the longest sustained stretch of the Blitz in London when she described the city "contract[ing] round her wounds." Her own usually happy associations with the season of harvest made the pain of the fall of 1940 all the more intense: "It is the hopeful start of the home year.... This year, leaves are swept up with a tinkle of glass in them. In Autumn, wherever you live most touches the heart—And it is the worst time not to live anywhere.... Home *looks* so safe, you cannot believe it is not" ("Britain," 4).

"Oh, Madam..." records one side of a conversation between a maid and her mistress on the morning after a night of heavy bombing; a departure in voice separates this work from earlier pieces. For the first time the sole speaking tone we hear belongs to a servant. Organized around the large pauses in the conversation that resemble the silences following direct hits, the maid responds to her mistress's implied comments. The gaps have an unsettling effect on the reader, who longs to uncover the feelings underlying the maid's ceaseless chatter about *things*. In the autumn of 1940 talk has become "a cheerful nervous release—it does not attempt to connect with deep-down things" ("Britain," 7). The two women obviously encounter a difference of opinion over their responses to the attack: The maid wants to keep the house going during the war, while her employer wants to close it down so that she can join the other "ladies" who have already fled to the country.

By experimenting in fiction with the new social atmosphere Bowen perceived abroad in London, she made concrete her pronouncement that, "For the first time, *we are* a democracy... we are almost a commune. It is true that what we see, from day to day, acts as a leveler" ("Britain,"

9). "Oh, Madam..." shows her discomfort with the use of the maid's voice. Although she portrays the woman's position sympathetically, Bowen's ear betrays her. In comparison with Gina, her counterpart in "In the Square," the maid's language sands implausible. This servant does not seem full-bodied, appearing more wooden and less fully realized than the earlier character.

When Bowen saw her stories together in a collection she noted the "rising tide of hallucination" which she perceived emanating from them. She situated the crest of this tide in the dreamscape of a full moon in London by placing "Mysterious Kôr" (first published in January, 1944) last. This story provides an alternate vision to the daylight demons of Mrs. Drover. Dreams on the moonlit night offer the illusion of safety rather than the blank terror instilled by the ghostly taxi driver. For Bowen, seeking her own personal landmarks, Kôr represented an eternal city in the midst of "weird moonlight over bomb-pitted London."[52]

By re-creating a mysterious terrain suggested by a book read in childhood, Bowen removed her wartime characters to another time, another place, and another country. The "Plain of Kôr," which the magical story evokes—where "the people whereof I speak built a mighty city on its bed, whereof naught but ruins and the name of Kôr remaineth"—resembles the way Bowen viewed London in the winter of 1944. Apparently, long ago and far away the people of Kôr had built caves into which the travelers described in the tale decide to venture. "Faintly illuminated with lamps, these caves seemed to me to stretch for almost an immeasurable distance, like the gas lights of an empty London street."[53] The real action of Bowen's story, however, takes place in the minds of the decidedly middle-class characters pondering what remains of London. Finding themselves struggling with the realization that "war's not just only war; it's years out of people's lives that they've never had before and won't have again," they look to illusions to save them.[54]

The powerful hallucination that infuses the story "The Happy Autumn Fields" supplies a bond between Bowen's two primary landscapes of war: bombed-out London and the neutral green expanses of County Cork. A woman, trapped in her London house during a bombing, dreams of a memory located in an "unshakably County Cork" landscape.[55] By the time Bowen created this story in August, 1944, her own London house had withstood two severe bombing attacks. In fact, she composed the story in a friend's flat, where she had gone after being driven from her own house when a "V1, landing across the road, blew 2 Clarence Terrace hollow inside, wrecking every room." She told Charles Ritchie about writing the story on a hot summer afternoon "in an excited way."[56] But even in the Irish landscape of "The Happy Autumn Fields" a "formless dread" hovers on the horizon as the young woman in the dream who walks across the fields "recognize[s] the colour of valediction."[57]

Ireland provided a respite from the bombings in London by allowing Bowen's characters to return to the "timelessness of an impermeably clouded late summer afternoon." In this particular story the dream remains imperfect because, when the survivor awakes, she learns that she cannot return; "the one way back to the fields was barred" ("Happy Autumn Fields," 683). The author explained in her preface to this collection of stories that the characters' recourse to memory, instead of offering the traditionally restorative qualities of the past, "counteracts fear by fear, stress by stress."[58] After living through the bomb blast the lone woman in the London terrace ponders the question that haunted so many of Bowen's characters in wartime: what will remain?

In a letter to Virginia Woolf after the bombing of Mecklenburgh and Tavistock squares Bowen asked: "When your flat went did that mean all the things in it too? All my life I have said, 'whatever happens there will always be tables and chairs.'"[59] Through a lifetime of emotional flux she had always counted on furniture as a symbol of continuity, but her wartime characters recognize the instability of these objects: "Everything pulverizes so easily because it is rot-dry." The decay extends beyond physical into emotional life in "The Happy Autumn Fields" as the characters argue over who will keep a box of photographs and memories capturing "a fragment torn out of a day" ("Happy Autumn Fields," 683). When war threatened the context provided by the past Bowen became more concerned with guarding the survival of her own ancestry. Drawn deeper into her heritage, she situated half of the ten stories she wrote between 1938 and 1945 in a specifically Irish setting. As she faced Eire's neutrality from the other side of the Irish sea, in her fiction she included her country of birth.

When she was in Dublin for an "activities" trip for the Ministry of Information during the fall of 1942 Bowen spoke with an interviewer at the *Bell* about her sympathies "as an Irish novelist. . . . As long as I can remember I've been extremely conscious of being Irish—even when I was writing about such very un-Irish things as suburban life in Paris or the English seaside."⁶⁰ Her repeated inclusion of her Irish stories in later volumes of her short stories acknowledges both her recognition of their superior literary qualities and their lasting hold on her heart. *A Day in the Dark and Other Stories* (1965), for example, contains such Irish stories as "The Happy Autumn Fields," "Summer Night," and "A Love Story: 1939."⁶¹ Set on a misty December evening in an Irish hotel, "A Love Story" renders opposing attitudes of the Irish and the English toward the war. Bowen builds an atmosphere suggestive of upheaval and suspension, greatly intensified by the war. Each individual in the story is away from home in one way or another, and each experiences failure in his or her ability to transform the hotel into a temporary home. Their transience disturbs them much more than it did the characters in *The Hotel*. Victims of the uncertainty and stasis engendered by Ireland's neutral position, some of the Irish in this later story express shame toward their country's position, one saying, "I wish I were proud of my country" ("A Love Story," 509). For Bowen, the stories that explored the intersection of nationality and geography remained among her favorites.

"Artistically," Bowen wrote that she had "been most nearly satisfied by some of [her] longer short stories," such as "Summer Night" and "Happy Autumn Fields." She explained that they gained from her ability to "analyze the locality from the inside."⁶² As V. S. Pritchett wrote, "I have come to think that, as with so many Irish writers, the essences she continually sought are more dramatically effective in her short stories. She was made for the drastic and nervous statement."⁶³ In Seán O'Faoláin's estimation, the genre allowed Bowen's "gift of emotional combustibility, a great gift of words, an eye of a hawk" to come forth.⁶⁴ Bowen justified her decision to include stories by Irish writers in the Faber collection she edited in 1936 by saying the tie between the countries, England and Ireland, "however irksome, has made some kind of affinity, however artificial."⁶⁵

Such powerful fictions set in Eire as "Sunday Afternoon" and "Summer Night" are among the best stories she ever wrote. Less successfully, she attempted propaganda in "Unwelcome Idea," written in the summer of 1940 when England viewed Eire's lack of participation as having a devastating effect on the war effort.⁶⁶ Published in August, 1940, around the time of Bowen's first intelligence trip to Ireland for the Ministry of Information, the story includes the observations she later took up in an essay entitled "Eire" for the *New Statesman*. There she wrote that life in Ireland, contrary to appearances, was "far from being the home of comfort and ease materially." "Unwelcome Idea" records a dull and unconvincing conversation between two female characters who adopt opposing positions toward daily life in Dublin. Neither character conveys any depth because each existed to demonstrate a truth Bowen only later acknowledged fully: "At present Eire suffers, in all senses, and while her deprivations are far less than Britain's, they have to be met without the heroic stimulus that comes from participation in war."[67] On her frequent trips to Ireland for the Ministry of Information Bowen became more attuned to the effect of the war on her own country. Stories such as "Summer Night" or "A Love Story: 1939" benefit from their origins in her "own material," as Louise Bogan has noted, rather than those like "Unwelcome Idea," which began in the "peculiar anecdote," or the too-close snapshot.[68]

Bowen's most successful Irish stories undertake to transfer the feeling of war to the neutral country. Those written after the Blitz, which was known in Dublin "only by bloated, uncertain and ghastly rumour," differ in tone from her earlier stories.[69] "Sunday Afternoon" gives a detailed portrait of Henry Russel's visit to his relatives in southern Ireland after he has lost his London apartment in the Blitz. An Anglo-Irishman, he is spending the war as a bureaucrat in a London ministry. While Henry suspects that his experiences of war in London have divided him from the life "secluded by glass" that he has left behind, he is startled to reencounter "the aesthetic of living" instilled in him as a child.[70] The assembled group on the lawn of the familiar Big House claims to be eager to hear the news from London. Yet, when he tries to tell them of his difficulties, he discovers that he cannot always trust their desire for information. As Bowen noted elsewhere, "Gratitude for exemption from the horrors mingled, in certain Irish people with a sensation of being side-tracked . . . fostered a listless irresponsibility."[71]

The afternoon's events reveal to Henry his inability to convey the essence of life in London during the Blitz to those cocooned in neutrality. The matriarch of the clan, Mrs. Vesey, qualifies her request for his reports: "But nothing dreadful: we are already feeling a little sad." Even in their questions the outsiders display their remove from Henry's experience. Belligerently, Ronald Cuffe inquires: "Are things there as shocking as they say—or are they more shocking?" Henry's faltering explanations trap him into a tense discussion over the ability of language to express the meaning of loss. Cuffe, who, as the brash young niece points out, has "always been safe," predicts that the war "will have no literature" ("Sunday," 616, 617, 618). As he attempts to translate his experiences, Henry's utterances reverberate with the perennial question for Bowen's characters: How can words communicate experiences that are, in truth, beyond the realm of human comprehension? Henry's interrogators claim to want to know if he lost everything when his flat was bombed.

Cautiously, Henry replies, "It's true that I lost my flat, and everything in my flat." Those Anglo-Irish who have spent the war in Eire concur it means the destruction of beautiful objects, while for Henry it signifies death. Yet the longer Henry spends with his relatives, the farther he feels from their concerns. After he says, "one cannot stay long away [from London]," he immediately realizes he has hurt them. "Their position was, he saw, more difficult than his own, and he could not have said a more cruel thing" ("Sunday," 619, 618). Just as the reader begins to empathize with Henry's viewpoint, Bowen raises the possibility that living outside the war can also be painful. And, to see both sides at once is to feel split at the core.

Maria Vesey, Henry's sharp-tongued niece, appears to be the only one who desires to escape from the constraints of the Big House. But although Henry might admire her pluckiness, her brashness offends him. The sparks between the two flare when he recognizes her defiance of the ethos he believes has shaped his character. In rebellion against the society of her elders, she represents a new "*outward* order of life—of brutality, of being without spirit." When she follows him down the avenue as he leaves, he finally tells her, "Maria, I can't like you. Everything you say is destructive and horrible" ("Sunday," 620, 621). She unnerves him by rejecting outright the values from his past that still matter to him.

Since Henry, like many fellow Anglo-Irish characters, is doubly "cast out," having been born between wartime generations, neither Maria nor her elders represents a world he can wholeheartedly embrace. When faced with the abrasive Maria, he becomes susceptible to the past, represented by the "charm of the afternoon." He fears that the alluring spell cast by the Big House may delay his trip to London by trapping him in passivity. The stoicism of the figures on the lawn causes him worry that his admiration for them may impede his return to London or the "zone of death." And in warning Maria that if she goes to London she will receive "an identity number, but no identity," he is also cautioning himself ("Sunday," 621, 622).

In another fine story, "Summer Night," Bowen dramatizes her sad conviction that there can be no escape from war, not even in neutral Ireland. She wrote the story, her longest one, at the request of her publisher, Victor Gollancz, who asked her to expand her volume *Look at All Those Roses*.[72] Always eager for Virginia Woolf's opinion, Bowen wrote to her on January 5, 1941, about "Summer Night" in *Look at All Those Roses:* "I should like very much to know what you think about it." The title echoes "A Summer Night," Auden's poem about the summer of 1933, which was published in 1934:

> After discharges of alarm
> All unpredicted let them calm
>   The pulse of nervous nations,
> Forgive the murderer in his glass,
> Tough in their patience to surpass
>   The tigress her swift motions.[73]

Bowen's story also resorts to animal metaphors to describe the inner state of the citizens of Eire. "Summer Night" portrays characters who suffer from the "national childishness" that Bowen isolates as one of the chief consequences of Eire's enforced separation from the rest of Europe.[74] The fictional men and women have become so locked in their nervous private worlds that they cannot connect honestly with one another. The Irish countryside on the July night when the story occurs appears a place that, although far from the war, remains deeply affected by it. The lonely spinster, staying with her relatives for the duration, looks out her window and pronounces: "Each moment is everywhere, it holds the war in its crystal; there is no elsewhere, no other place."[75]

Emotion rules "Summer Night" in a manner and intensity reminiscent of some of D. H. Lawrence's short stories. Explaining that she "constantly had [him] in mind" during wartime, Bowen wrote: "for six years of extinguished nights we moved towards, past, and alongside each other in the acute sightless awareness" of Lawrence's story of "The Blind Man."[76] "Summer Night" also unearths a core of Lawrencian sexuality that she rarely invokes in fiction. When the story opens Emma, the woman of the house, has hastily departed on a frantic drive to meet her married lover, Robinson.[77] She leaves in her wake her dull husband, the Major, two daughters, and the spinster, Aunt Fran. The charged and chaotic atmosphere of the house affects the children who, like Maria Vesey in "Sunday Afternoon," are close to the emotional raw edges of their surroundings. When the young girl, Vivie, cannot sleep, the narrator remarks, "One arbitrary line only divided this child from the animal." She prowls the house naked, discovering that in each room she enters "the human order seemed to have lapsed" ("Summer," 596). Her nocturnal journey describes her response to the chaos created by war.

War has disrupted the usual domestic routine of the household; Vivie even goes to the schoolroom at night to retrieve her chalks. Drawing colored snakes all over her body, she uses the mirror in her mother's room to "tattoo her behind." Compelled by the "anarchy" of the house, she jumps wildly on her mother's bed in a scene that echoes a similar female dance in Lawrence's novel *The Rainbow*. After soothing the frenzy of the young girl, Aunt Fran remembers the war and, looking out from her window, pronounces, "this is a threatened night" ("Summer," 597, 599). Vivie's bestiality has its counterparts in the social barbarisms that Robinson commits as he restlessly awaits Emma.

Impatient for her arrival, Robinson becomes sharp with his two guests, a deaf woman named Queenie and her brother Justin. The two men become embroiled in a debate that appears in a slightly varying form in each of Bowen's Irish stories: the argument over the moral justification for neutrality. Justin's comments illustrate the pain Eire's refusal to fight has caused him: "in the heart of the neutral Irishman indirect suffering pulled like a crooked knife." Robinson, presented as the more callous figure, exposes his limitations through his feeble responses to Justin's lament that the war is "an awful illumination" that has "destroyed our dark." Imprisoned in her deafness, Queenie mutely watches the discussion between the two men grow more heated. Since she cannot join the argument, she is doomed to observe, through the faulty filter of her senses, while Emma waits like a tigress, "crouching in her crouching car in the dark" ("Summer," 598, 590, 602).[78]

Bowen's story describes characters who fail to engage with one another and then must retreat into the confines of a private place. After the guests leave, Emma and Robinson walk in the gardens, where she recognizes that the difference in their moral codes matters ("Summer," 605). Unable to discuss the failure of the evening with her angry brother, Queenie withdraws into the memory of a July night twenty years before when she walked with her lover in the darkness of the same estate. She remembers the solitude and isolation that seemed to saturate that evening when her lover was afraid to touch her. Justin, still wounded, resorts to pen and paper and dashes off a heated note to Robinson declaring they must not meet in the future. Deep in the heart of southern Ireland, private worlds collide; Bowen's characters inhabit an atmosphere of emotional anarchy, the whole land clouded by the shadow of war. This shadow cast its darkness over many other tracts of land that Bowen held dear.

She found that in wartime her imagination reverted not only to Ireland but also to other scenes that figured prominently in her life, such as the garrisoned south coast of England. Blocked off for security reasons to civilian travel, the countryside where she had first lived outside Ireland with her mother represented another lost world. The several trips she made to this area for the Ministry of Information ensured its continued place in her consciousness. Two striking south coast short stories written after 1943, "The Inherited Clock" (1944) and "Ivy Gripped the Steps" (1945), show her affection for this place as they wind backwards from the present.[79] Unfortunately, the past cannot provide solace for the characters in either story; on the contrary, as Bowen explained, the recollection of earlier days "discharges its load of feeling into the anaesthetised and bewildered present" by mesmerizing the survivors.[80] "The Inherited Clock," as its title suggests, questions whether it was "impossible that the past should be able to injure the future irreparably."[81] The later story, "Ivy Gripped the Steps," locates the emotional frigidity of the protagonist, Gavin Doddington, in an early childhood disappointment.[82] According to Bowen, this story began in her vision of "an ivy-strangled house in a formerly suave residential avenue."[83]

Bowen overlays the memory of the apparently happy past on the devastated present of a deserted town in "Ivy Gripped the Steps." Beginning in September, 1944, when a glimpse of ivy pulls Gavin back into his idyllic Edwardian childhood summers spent in the town, the story recalls the structure of a romantic lyric poem. Just when he reaches the joyful pinnacle of his memory, the colorlessness of the present jostles him. The limbo of Gavin's emotions resembles the uncertainty that Henry Russel experiences in "Sunday Afternoon." Because he is "too young for the last war, too old for this," he also works for a ministry in London. Once in Southstone Gavin equates the "process of strangulation" symbolized by the ivy, with the war itself.[84] The past floods his thoughts as he suddenly sees, in his mind's eye, a long-ago hot June day on the cliffs.

Gavin remembers his hostess, the widowed Mrs. Nicholson, debating the possibility of war with her admirer, Admiral Concannon, on that glorious summer day. Refusing to be convinced by the admiral's dire predictions about the certainty of future war, she exposes her limitations in her responses: "I never even cared for history at school; I was glad when we came to the end of it" and realized "that it all ended happily" ("Ivy," 695, 696). A blissful and uninformed subscriber to the upward theory of history, Mrs. Nicholson pities the backward people of earlier times who could not see how nice the world would turn out to be.

Making use of her talent for bitter irony, Bowen pokes fun at the Mrs. Nicholsons of the world while she analyzes more seriously the attitudes that have prompted war. Simultaneously, she mocks and blames the widow's pathetically simpleminded imperialism: "Civilized countries are polite to each other, ... and uncivilized countries are put down." The young boy, listening to the conversation between his elders, begins to understand that he lived in a world where "history jerked itself painfully off the spool." Lyrically, Bowen evokes the myopic prewar scene that the Mrs. Nicholsons of the world have helped to foster: "along the Promenade, all day long, parasols, boater hats and light dresses flickered against the dense blue gauze backdrop that seldom let France be seen" ("Ivy," 696, 697, 703).

When the admiral arrives to fetch some cakes Mrs. Nicholson is donating to the local branch of the Awaken Britannia League (which the Concannons, predictably, are overseeing), Gavin overhears their conversation. The widow, countering the admiral's accusation that she has made "a ninnie of that unfortunate boy," explains that she has "no little dog. You would not like it, even, if I had a real little dog." Gavin's emotional core withers when Mrs. Nicholson destroys his childish trust through her revelation that she has only been using him as a diversion to make the admiral jealous. The pain of the memory stuns Gavin back to his present "tour of annihilation" as he returns to the scene of his first and most vividly recalled emotional wounding. As he stands outside the Concannons' house, now a shelter for the Auxiliary Territorial Service, a young girl sees his face "under an icy screen, of a whole stopped mechanism for feeling" that resembles a stopped clock ("Ivy," 707, 708, 711). Only in the middle of the annihilation of civilized values produced by the Second World War can characters such as Gavin identify, and hence understand, the source of their emotional aridity.

Bowen believed that in war "there was an element of chanciness and savageness about everything." She expresses this conviction in her depiction of soured relationships, disappearing houses, and "experts" tied to secret wartime drudgery. Stories such as "The Cheery Soul" (1942) and "Green Holly" (1944) mock the self-importance of bureaucrats, who invoke ghosts as "an unconscious, instinctive, saving resort" to stave off the dullness of their routine.[85] The depth of their entanglement in the war stimulates their overactive imaginations.

"Careless Talk," an earlier story, originally published in the *New Yorker* in 1941 under the title "Everything's Frightfully Interesting," describes a group of edgy Londoners meeting with a friend who has taken refuge in the country.[86] The fiction makes fun of the self-importance of men who see themselves doing top secret work at the War Office in what Henry Reed calls "a brilliantly literal interpretation of that official phrase."[87] The title of the story derives from the poster drawn by Fougasse (Cyril Kenneth Bird) and put out by the Ministry of Information, one of the twenty-five hundred that appeared in early 1940 as part of its "anti-gossip campaign." The cartoon depicted two men leaning across their armchairs to chat beneath a stylized, British portrait with the face of Hitler while one says to the other, "strictly between these four walls!"[88] The public was irritated by the condescending tone of the campaign, and three weeks after it had begun Churchill called it to a halt by noting its "innocuous desuetude."[89]

Very little that marked wartime life escaped Bowen's pencil, from altered bus schedules to the exhaustion that blanketed London at the end of the war. An unpublished story, "The Last Bus," dated November 29, 1944, tells the tale of an unlikely group of travelers stranded by the breakdown of the final country bus one evening.[90] It suggests the atmosphere of unexpected collegiality that grows up among the strangers, who, discovering themselves in startling proximity, begin to converse to allay their anxiety. Another story that was not published, "The Beginning of this Day," although undated, was probably written just after the war. It focuses on the uncertain days of the closing of the war, depicting the dilapidated garden that stands in the middle of bombed London. This story gives a sense of the faded quality of life in a city that was coming to the end of a long, exhausting war. The characters exclaim that to sit in this place is "to feel oneself a survivor from some vanished civilization."[91] Although the war dragged on, thoughts of the end of the hostilities began to appear like a mirage in some of Bowen's stories.

"......... but for Heaven's sake don't say I told you!"

CARELESS TALK COSTS LIVES

One of a series of cartoons aimed at stopping the spread of rumors in Britain during World War II, drawn by Fougasse [Cyril Kenneth Byrd]. (Courtesy of the Imperial War Museum, London.)

"Songs My Father Sang Me," published in November, 1944, portrays a World War One veteran explaining to his daughter that she should be able to see peace on the horizon as "an idea you have when there's a war on, to make you fight well. An idea that gets lost when there isn't a war."[92] Bowen's strongest postwar story, "I Hear You Say So," takes place the week after VE day and was published in *New Writing and Daylight* in September, 1945.[93] Here Bowen again displays the compression and talent for illumination evident in her other wartime stories. It also begins with a single moment, widening its scope to record the emotional touchstones anchoring a group of people's lives, until the camera narrows to scrutinize the emotions of a young widow.

The loveliness of the song of the nightingale in the park unifies the story by delighting its listeners. The cultural context of the nightingale had already been established by the very popular song "A Nightingale Sang in Berkeley Square":

> I may be right,
> I may be wrong,
> But I'm perfectly willing to swear,
> There were angels dining at the Ritz,
> And a nightingale sang in Berkeley Square.[94]

The beauty of the bird's song moves one woman to say it has come "much too soon, after a war like this. . . . They'd much better not feel at all till they feel normal." Her companion responds with the pressing question that plagues all Bowen's postwar characters: "But can people live without something they cannot have?" ("I Hear," 755, 756). Even the glory of the song seems dulled by the shakiness of the survivors, who are kept "puzzled and infantile" by this new experience. Neither the old nor the young are ready to believe in a peace, and, when a man explains that there were lots of nightingales in the last war in copses in France, a child misunderstands and hears the word *corpse*. The story achieves an uneasy coalition of reactions which emerge in a time when, as Mollie Panter-Downes wrote, "the deadly past was for most people only just under the surface of the beautiful, safe present."[95]

In the last years of the war, Bowen recorded a keen urgency to complete her collection of stories both so that she could receive the one hundred pound advance Cape had promised her and to get on with her novel. By November, 1944, she was running so short on money that she wrote to her bank to ask for an overdraft to finance repairs to Clarence Terrace.[96] She also requested an advance from Curtis Brown to pay her Irish income tax. Unable to fulfill her agreement to finish the volume by December, she delivered the collection to Cape on January 16, 1945.[97] The immediate success of the book demonstrated Bowen's mastery of the short story in its depiction of the sensations of wartime. After one month the publishers considered an increase of five thousand sheets for the volume, and in March the second impression was issued.[98] Her work had justified her opinion that, in her hands, the short story ideally captured the desperate illuminations sparked by war.

Bowen had cautioned in her 1945 essay on "The Short Story in England" that "we should not expect any *comprehensive* war novel until five, even ten years after hostilities cease" because, she explained, it would take that much time for longer fiction to digest and then recreate recent experiences ("Short Story," 7). Her own wartime novel, *The Heat of the Day*, did not appear until February, 1949, just halfway on the span of her prediction. After the war ended she devoted all of her energy to that novel. Although she had finished five chapters of it by 1945, she worked on it steadily for the next four years.[99] Protecting her time carefully, she repeatedly turned down requests for short stories with the explanation: "it is essential that I should finish my novel."[100] *The Heat of the Day*, which followed her most concentrated burst of short story writing, resembles a unified series of stories in its lyrical intensity.

Chapter 9

Fictional Silences

> War, if you come to think of it, hasn't started anything that wasn't already there.
> —Elizabeth Bowen, *The Heat of the Day*

The novel that emerged from Bowen's immersion in the Second World War epitomized "a state of living in which events assault the imagination." In *The Heat of the Day,* Bowen depicts the psychological ramifications of the changed landscape of war, as she had in the short stories which were "unconscious sketches" for this novel.[1] This fiction shows her tackling in a more sustained, and sometimes more agonized, manner the same questions she had addressed in her wartime short stories: the nature of betrayal, changing conceptions of class, the role of Ireland and the Anglo-Irish, and the ramifications of espionage work. Indeed, the novel reflects Bowen's ambition, as she announced it to Sir William Rothenstein after he congratulated her on *The Death of the Heart,* to "write that immense novel everyone wants to write" in accordance with her conviction "that themes, in novels especially, *should* be large."[2]

Montgomery's victory in Egypt, the Battle of El Alamein, and D day coincide with the important private moments of the novel. By juxtaposing each emotional turning point with a public one, Bowen realized her desire to write a "*present-day* historical novel" as she turned with "relief" to the larger world in "revulsion against psychological intricacies for their own sake."[3] This technique recalls the counterpointing she experimented with in *The Last September* where outside events endanger the internal lives of the characters. A world at war, in this later novel, invades and poisons the love affair between the central figures, Robert Kelway and Stella Rodney. Here, Bowen makes explicit her contention that "the relation of a man to society is an integral part of the concept of any novel."[4] In an article entitled "The Next Book," appearing in the autumn 1948 issue of *Now and Then,* she discussed this tension between "the individual self-absorption and the individual's awareness of the outside world. . . . But the trouble is, how am I to find a scene, characters, or plot which will be the ideal vehicle for my memory?" ("On Writing," 12).

Although Bowen recounted that writing the book had been an enormous struggle, when she looked back on it she called it her best novel to date.[5] While she had counseled, in her response to Cyril Connolly's questionnaire entitled "The Cost of Letters," that a writer's work should improve through contact with others, in composing *The Heat of the Day* she explained that "the diversion of energy is a danger."[6] Yet, her literary friends appreciated her efforts and praised her intention to present "the peculiar psychological climate" of wartime.[7] The novelist Elizabeth Taylor wrote to Bowen: "you rake up the dead leaves in our hearts and say many things which we did not know how to say ourselves—which we only very faintly perceived before."[8] Prone to hyperbole in the compliments she paid to Bowen's work, Rosamond Lehmann reported that she cried endlessly during her reading of the novel because of her close identification with Stella; for her the novel was "the unbearable recreation of war and London & our private lives and loves."[9] Charles Ritchie especially appreciated her distillation of the "hypnotic intensity of life in London" during the war years. On reflection he attributes her range of language to her wartime experience: "certainly the tension of those times brought all feeling closer to the surface and that seems to me to make her *writing* in *The Heat of the Day* and in her wartime short stories so markedly different from her books before and after."[10]

Bowen's novel also spoke to a wide circle beyond her own acquaintance; after its publication in February, 1949, it sold forty-five thousand copies almost immediately.[11] Critics had expressed trepidation during the war that the novel, which "will create a picture which cannot be effaced by tomorrow's newspaper," might not get written during time of war.[12] But *The Heat of the Day,* appearing after the conflict, answered these doubts by telling a story of war that people wanted to read. The wider canvas of the novel unifies London, the home counties, the south coast, and Ireland.[13] Bowen's compulsion to make these disparate elements cohere linguistically accounts for some of the weakness apparent in her technical constructions as she channeled the intensity of her short stories into the "calmer, stricter, more orthodox demands" of the novel.[14] By not allowing herself recourse to the world of the hallucinatory, she encountered even more obstacles to representing the "breaking down of immunity" she experienced in wartime (HD 93).

While the novels Bowen wrote before the war such as *The Death of the Heart* and *Friends and Relations* signal betrayal as "the end of the inner life" with attendant hurt and disappointment, in *The Heat of the Day* disloyalty could mean the end of a life.[15] Transformed though the lens of the war, scenes from prewar novels seemed to Bowen to fade into a lost past; as she wrote her wartime novel, she contemplated the wreckage of the once "gleaming terraces" reduced to "giant shells."[16] An indication of the stress placed on her by the additional burden of her divided loyalties during the war surfaced in an interview she gave the *Bell* in 1942, the year she began writing *The Heat of the Day* in earnest. Then, she described her own "strong feelings of nationality" as being "highly disturbing."[17]

As a result of Bowen's travel to Ireland on behalf of the Ministry of Information, conversations with Charles Ritchie about MI6, the British intelligence service, and her friendship with figures such as Goronwy Rees, she became more concerned with unmasking the meaning of loyalty and betrayal during a time of war.[18] Hovering on the edge of a wartime world of traitors and spies, she must have known how near she was to the edge of this shadowy land. Her friend Rosamond Lehmann, for example, was aware that their mutual friend, Goronwy Rees, had been invited by Guy Burgess to be a Soviet agent.[19] The critic Frank Kermode has speculated that Goronwy Rees as a young man might have been the model for the character of Eddy in *The Death of the Heart*.[20] Peter Quennell also believes Rees was the prototype for Eddy; apparently it was so successful a portrait that Rees threatened to sue Bowen after he read the book.[21]

Robert Kelway, whom Bowen referred to as "the problem character and the touchstone" of *The Heat of the Day*, spies on his own country and, thus, becomes its betrayer.[22] Curiously, Bowen made him a fascist, and he is unconvincing in part because we hear so little from him directly. Troubled by the question of Robert's political allegiance, Lehmann wrote to Bowen to ask why she had not made him a "communist thus pro-Russia and an ally?"[23] Robert shows himself to be a national traitor who is attracted to the orderliness of Hitler's Germany, because there he hopes to find an answer to the emptiness in his own life. Obviously cognizant of Robert's opaqueness, Bowen had supplied her indirect answer to Lehmann's query in her interview with the *Bell:* "The idea for a book usually comes to me in the shape of an abstract pattern. . . . Then the job is to construct characters to fit the situation. Characters have a way of growing of their own accord which means a great deal of re-writing."[24]

The ambiguities of Robert's character center on Bowen's hesitation about the distinction between being a traitor and a spy. In the effort to separate these two concepts (a task of particular immediacy for her) she struggled to fashion Robert into an abstraction. By making him a construct rather than a personality, she violates her own advice and has him do what a character never should, that is, he says things "which fit into situations intellectually conceived beforehand." As if to explain this irregularity, she declared after she had written *The Heat of the Day* that, in this book more than ever, the characters "took command" of her.[25] Robert's unevenness as a character reflects her own unsteady grasp of him (and echoes the perplexity of her own position in the employ of the Ministry of Information). He grows directly out of her Burkean investigation in *Bowen's Court* of the meaning of possession and heritage; she holds Robert's cold and empty English middle-class origins responsible for what some critics have called his "inability to conceive of his country emotionally." This, she argues, leads to his embrace of fascism.[26]

In Bowen's familiar blurring of the boundaries between politics and literature, Robert also suffers from his composite origins in fact and fiction. He is based, at least in part, on her lover Charles Ritchie, to whom she dedicated the novel.[27] He noted in a diary entry of January 20, 1942, that Bowen had told him she "would like to put me in her next novel."[28] But, recognizing that it was difficult to place "real people" in fiction, she said in a letter to William Plomer, about his book *Museum Pieces:* "And you have accomplished what I had always taken to be impossible—the bringing of 'real' people into the dimension of fiction."[29] An inherent contradiction, then, underlies her attitude toward the character who is at once the most despicable figure in the novel and a shadow of her own lover during wartime. During the course of the story, his complexity increases when he becomes a "mirror image" of the man who turns him in, Robert Harrison; significantly, both men share the name of Bowen's paternal grandfather.[30] Even near the end of her life Bowen was still trying to separate herself from this troubling character, Robert Kelway, with the untenable disclaimer that "no one of the characters in my novels has originated, as far as I know, in real life."[31]

John Hayward describes the autumn of 1942, the year the novel begins, as a time when "spiritually we are going through a bad patch, having lived too long on hopes which have been frustrated and sick of words as a substitute for deeds."[32] "The glaring ordeal of that mid-war period" tests the characters of *The Heat of the Day* in their relationships to one another during the "lightless middle of the tunnel" that was the fall of 1942 ("On Writing," 11).[33] The novel begins at an open-air concert in London's Regent's Park where Louie, a young woman whose husband is on duty with the army, meets Robert Harrison, who strikes her as odd. This counterspy is immediately made to appear suspect because he has neither an address nor an ascertainable past. An unpleasant, lugubrious figure, he begins the undoing of the love affair between Stella, a middle aged-divorcée who does "secret, exacting, not unimportant work" for a governmental bureaucracy, the Y.X.D., and Robert.

Harrison offers her a bargain—that she become sexually involved with him in exchange for his promise to protect Robert. Irreparably torn, Stella embarks upon an evasive life of deception. Her response to his dark threats—"your 'we' is my 'they,'"—signifies her membership in the culture described in the novel where everyone must take a side, however unwillingly (*HD* 40). Stella's ordeal begins that evening when Harrison's emotional blackmail forces her to consider whether she has misjudged Robert's character. Not coincidentally, Harrison approaches Stella at a time when war has made her vulnerable. Stella registers her shock on his first visit through the distortion of her syntax: "Up his sleeve he had something." During this meeting with Stella, Harrison, in a melodramatic but telling gesture, turns Robert's photograph to the wall. To Stella, in time, his eyes will become to her "black-blue, anarchical, foreign," as they come to reflect markers of his flawed soul. After her son, Roderick, arrives at Stella's flat, the memory of her meeting with Harrison becomes one of an "imperfect silence, mere resistance to sound" (*HD* 15, 198, 56).

Stella first responds to Harrison's allegations against Robert by scanning her memory for glimpses of the fall of 1940 when they had met: "Never had any season been more felt; one bought the poetic sense of it with the sense of death." She and Robert had begun their affair when he had come to London to work in the War Office after recovering from being wounded at Dunkirk. His leg never entirely healed, and his limp distinguishes him as a maimed man. But memories of the heroic excitement of earlier in the war had sustained the lovers through the tedium of 1942 when the Blitz had seemed "apocryphal, more far away than peace." They take sustenance from a different era when the soil of the city "seemed to generate more strength" and the dahlia leaves "against the sun blazoned out the idea of the finest hour" (*HD* 90, 92, 91). Each one of their meetings in that season had appeared to be a piece of unbelievably good luck against the high odds of the threat of sudden death. Their memories reflect some of Bowen's own experience of the Blitz, as remembered by Charles Ritchie: "what is extraordinary is her stamina and courage in going on with her writing—after hours of duty in the air raid wardens' shelter and after the bombings of her house."[34]

As she absorbs Harrison's warnings, Stella decides to ground Robert in his personal history. Simultaneously hoping and fearing what she will discover in his past, she joins him on a dismal visit to the tasteless Gothic villa his family calls home. Harrison greets her on her return from the excursion, and he applauds her instincts: "Today you did exactly what I should have done in your place . . . went to look at the first place the rot could start." Harrison has already guessed that Stella can never view Robert in the same light after the grim day she spends with his family, the Kelways. Appropriately, Holme Dene (meaning, literally, "Home of the Dane") is hidden behind a prominently displayed sign reading CAUTION: CONCEALED DRIVE (*HD* 131, 105).[35] Its inhabitants—Robert's mother, sister, niece, and nephew—seem as faceless and unwelcoming as the house itself. Bowen selects details that display the meanness of life at this house, where at tea each person greedily contemplates his or her measly butter ration. The ugly neo-Gothic structure, built around 1900, the year of Stella's birth, becomes immediately suspect in the Bowen terrain where such architecture represents all that is dark and evil in the world.[36] Not only has "time clogged" the ticking of the grandfather clock, freezing the house's relationship to the past, but the very emotions that hang ineffably in the "blackly furnished" drawing room feel stagnant (*HD* 108, 107).

It becomes clear that Robert's family has long since ceased to care about conversing with one another. As Stella studies his mother (who goes by "Muttikins"), she realizes with horror that the woman's "lack of wish for communication showed in her contemptuous use of words." Apparently, Robert has inherited his family's disregard for the currency of language. Like his mother who sits and stares out her windows at the "bewitched wood" surrounding her house, Robert has no conception of his own relationship to anyone or anything beyond himself, least of all his country. The Kelways give away their moral emptiness by speaking to one another "with difficulty, in the dead language" of a house filled with "repressions, doubts, fears, subterfuges, and fibs" (*HD* 109–10, 252, 256). Their words give only a small measure of the inadequacies implicit in their outlook on life. Robert's sister, Ernestine, remarks snidely, as Stella and Robert set out on their stroll, that "it took being shot in the leg to make Robert walk!" The children are not in any way immune to this vacancy; his niece and nephew are taught that England and Germany chiefly differ from one another because in Germany a guest would be forced to eat cake against his or her will. Stella, feeling "seedy" and "shady," watches the awful assemblage as though she were looking down a "darkening telescope" (*HD* 107, 111).[37]

Instead of maturing into a responsible adult under his family's roof, Robert came of age in a "man-eating house" with passages shaped liked "swastika-arms." Treason, he explains to Stella on his last night alive, had offered promise for him because it "bred my father out of me, gave me a new heredity." By being "born wounded," he had proved all the more susceptible to the falsity and betrayal embodied in his origins in "a class without a middle, a race without a country. Unwhole. Never earthed in" (*HD* 258, 257, 273, 272). The novelist's use of the word *race* to describe a class distinction conveys yet another instance of her belief in the breakdown of society along social and economic lines.

For Stella, Robert cannot be true to his word because a "man of faith has always a son somewhere" (*HD* 175). He appears the prototype of the failings of the English middle class, "suspended in the middle of nothing," meeting his death at the novel's climax, overcome by the denial of freedom and an inescapably paralyzing guilt. His guilt was inextricably entangled in his class; Bowen had avowed in a conversation with Charles Ritchie in October, 1941, that she saw guilt to be "specifically a middle-class complaint."[38] Because the Kelways do not properly understand the obligations and rights of possession as Bowen (or Burke) set them out, they keep Holme Dene perpetually on the market. Robert justifies this curious state of affairs on the grounds that he can make a distinction between the desirable situation of having a house like Holme Dene for sale and the unseemly circumstance of trying to rent it (*HD* 121).

The rottenness of the Kelways is thus established as originating in their lack of ethical appreciation for the graceful responsibility of ownership.[39] The "betrayed garden," overstuffed with a pergola, sundial, rock garden, dovecote, gnomes, and rusticated seats, horrifies Stella. Inside, features that are intended to appear antique are on closer inspection not even remotely authentic. Stella could not imagine who would want to buy the place. When, to their amazement, the Kelways do receive an offer on the house, they divide themselves into bitter camps. Robert, who never has seemed "to be living anywhere in particular," votes to sell immediately, while Ernestine refuses to part with this monument to her past, however crippling it might be (*HD* 121, 298).

During their visit to Holme Dene Robert takes Stella to see his "boyhood's den" in the attic that has been carefully arranged, as though he "were dead." The "sixty or seventy" photographs of Robert on display fascinate her. She sees a gallery of images of him, in tennis flannels, with his one-time fiancée, Decima (who perhaps decimated him), at school, and on vacation. Explaining why what he calls his "criminal record," or "his own lies," still hangs on the wall, he notes that his family "expect[s] me to be very fond of myself." Stella stares at the portraits intently, much as she often studies Robert's photograph in her flat, hoping that she can fashion a composite from the disconnected fragments of Robert's past. Frustrated in her attempts, she exclaims, "this room feels empty!" Robert confesses that when he returns to the room he also senses the vacuum of his identity. He feels uncomfortable with his pose: "What I think must have happened to him [his father] I cannot while we're in this house, say" (*HD* 117, 118). The tortured arrangement of his words indicates Robert's vehemence at being brought to face his damaged past.

Thrust into the claustrophobic atmosphere of Holme Dene, Stella longingly recalls her Anglo-Irish origins, which, like Bowen's, are those of the "hybrid." While she has once fantasized that she and Robert share the distinction of having come "loose" from their "moorings," after she sees his family she realizes that, while her past "dissolved behind her," his "was not to be denied" (*HD* 114, 115).[40] Only by summoning the memory of her heritage from "gentry till lately owning, still recollecting, land," does Stella escape the "consecration of the inside" that so disturbs her at Holme Dene (*HD* 110, 115). She contrasts the "handsome derelict gateway" that leads to Mt. Morris, her family's Big House in Ireland, with the hidden drive of Holme Dene, which turns away strangers.[41]

The Heat of the Day recaptures Stella's birthright as an Anglo-Irish woman in its invocation of Mt. Morris as a place where the past can enlighten rather than defile the present. By establishing a moral hierarchy of ownership, as Bowen had in her autobiography, the novel arrives at a definition of the meaning and obligation of possession. The Big House again becomes a character in this book as its destiny becomes closely linked with that of Stella's son, Roderick, who is serving in the British army. Roderick, who was conceived at Mt. Morris while Stella was on her honeymoon with her then-husband Victor (who had been wounded in the First World War), literally owes his existence to the house. And, although the marriage has failed, it left its mark on Stella through Roderick: "The time of her marriage had been a time after war; her own desire to find herself in some embrace from life had been universal, at work in the world" (*HD* 133).[42]

When Roderick's cousin Francis dies, he leaves Mt. Morris to Roderick, the son the Anglo-Irishman always wished to have. Just as in *Bowen's Court,* the issue of who will inherit the estate has been problematical. Since cousin Francis had no children (a fact which led to his wife's collapse), he has fastened on a favorite young relative, Roderick.[43] "Possessorship of Mount Morris affected Roderick strongly," giving him "what might be called a historic future" so that the house becomes "the hub of his imaginary life" and the inheritance of Mt. Morris changes him inalterably (*HD* 50).

Bored by the routine of his service in the army, Roderick turns for imaginative and spiritual sustenance to Mt. Morris, where "by geographically standing outside war it appeared also to be standing outside the present" (*HD* 50).[44] Roderick spends much time wondering about the estate; his letters to his mother ask: How many acres are under tillage? Is there a gun room? What are its contents? (*HD* 202). By showing himself to be trustworthy and optimistic, he makes real a dream of successfully perpetuating the tradition of the Big House. The characters align themselves morally by their ability to appreciate Roderick's Irish inheritance: Roderick and Stella welcome the bequest, while Harrison and Robert do not.

Roderick, eager to understand his inheritance, is puzzled by an ambiguous phrase in Cousin Francis's will: "in the hope . . . that he may care in his own way to carry on the old tradition." Stella warns him of what she has already discovered: "one must not be too much influenced by a dead person! After all, one must live how one can . . . and that often must mean disappointing the dead" (*HD* 72, 88). Roderick decides to follow his instincts about his responsibilities to the past by venturing to visit cousin Francis's widow at Wisteria Lodge in the British countryside. She has lived in this rest home for many years since suffering a breakdown over her inability to satisfy her husband's desire for an heir. Removed from the present, unaware of the war, she appears dazed and startled by the arrival of a young man in uniform. The nurses at the lodge warn the soldier not to upset her by discussing the past or the war, but it is the future that he wants to settle. And, in further pursuit of that hope, he obtains leave from the army so that he can become familiar with the Irish estate that is his "future." He becomes more enthusiastic on his acquaintance with the place; he then determines that "Mt. Morris has got to be my living," and he vows to set about the project scientifically and rationally: "One can't just go fluffing along as an amateur" (*HD* 313).

At the same time that the novel presents the possibility of reconciliation, rebirth, and continuity after the war—through an English soldier's inheritance of an Irish estate—*The Heat of the Day* also investigates the isolation implicit in neutrality.[45] Unlike the battered half-men who survive the First World War, Roderick can look to what lies ahead after his participation in this Second World War. Significantly, his prize rests outside the theater of war, in Ireland. Yet the characters have difficulty understanding the ramifications of war when they are in Ireland, a fact that is simultaneously positive and negative. Stella's fictional visit to Mt. Morris in November, 1942, coincides with the actual event of Field Marshal Montgomery's victory in Egypt when, as Harold Nicolson wrote, "the face of the war changed its entire expression."[46] Later Stella recalls that moment of joy when she glimpsed the "mirage of utter victory" and also the annoyance she encountered at the indifference of the Irish caretaker's daughter to the miraculous news (*HD* 178).

The Heat of the Day portrays what Bowen regarded as certain excesses and deficiencies in the Anglo-Irish position on the war. Cousin Francis took his loyalty to England and his consequent disappointment with Eire's neutrality to extreme measures, even hoping for a "German invasion." Before his death in May, 1942, he had prepared for this eventuality by digging tank traps in the avenues leading to Mt. Morris. Stella, who lives in England, sometimes displays insensitivity to the Irish attitude toward war. Her excitement at "being outside war" at Mt. Morris leads her to burn the caretakers' "light supplies for months ahead." They are too polite to tell her that, thanks to her thoughtlessness, they will go to bed in the dark for most of the winter months. By contrast, when Stella returns from Ireland she suffers Ernestine's British callousness toward the state of affairs in the neutral country. In Stella's eyes the stolid sister displays her moral bankruptcy by asking sarcastically: "And how was the Emerald Isle? Beef steak? Plenty of eggs and bacon?... Over *there,* I suppose, no one realized a war was on?" (*HD* 183). Ernestine's spiteful questioning displays one facet of what Bowen perceived as a common British attitude toward Ireland.

Stella's idyll in Ireland, and her renewed appreciation of her heritage (in contrast to her day at Holme Dene), gives her the strength to challenge Robert with the news of Harrison's accusations. Stella suddenly realizes on her return from Ireland that her time away has further separated her from Robert; when he asks her to marry him on that first night back in London she succumbs to a distant watchfulness. Robert bursts out in anger and frustration: "We have not then been really alone together for the last two months. You're two months gone with this." By comparing Stella's suspicions to the state of a woman pregnant with an unwanted child, Robert suggests the abortive future of their relationship. In Stella's last scene with him she maintains the metaphor in a reference to the flawed condition of their time as that of "a false pregnancy" (*HD* 191, 281).

The evening they endure after her trip to Ireland signals the onset of the final phase of their poisoned relationship. With the renewed confidence she has gathered from steeping herself in her ancestry, Stella allows herself to credit some truth to Harrison's accusations. The silence between Stella and Robert that she first noticed during her researches at Holme Dene grows increasingly intolerable. Their relationship, like the one between Lois and Gerald in *The Last September,* comes to stand for the long history of misunderstanding between Ireland and England which intensified and lengthened during the war. The fictional love affair deteriorates to resemble the state of relations between the two countries in the pre-treaty years when, as Bowen wrote, "each turned to the other a closed, harsh, distorted face" (*BC* 452).

In *The Heat of the Day* Bowen fashioned Stella and Robert into agents who might assist her in settling some of the ambiguities that continually plagued her consciousness. Stella turns upon Harrison as the serpent who has caused her to feel like a spy on herself: "Somehow you've distorted love. You may not feel what it feels like to be a spy; I do—ever since you came to me with that story." Stella suffers from the pangs of self-mistrust when she realizes that she is judging the man she thought she loved with a cold, objective eye. After she unequivocally accepts the fact of Robert's treason he answers her misgivings by hiding behind what he has learned so well from his family: "Don't you understand that all that language is dead currency?" (*HD* 142, 268).

Wearily, Robert describes the state of the world as he understands it: "There are no more countries left; nothing but names. What country have you and I outside this room: Exhausted shadows, dragging themselves out again to fight." He has lost his humanity because all capacity for communication is gone, and even words like *treason* and *country* signify nothing to him: "words, words like that, yes—what a terrific dust they can still raise in a mind, yours even. . . . What they once meant is gone" (*HD* 267, 268). Because Robert no longer subscribes to the power of language, he has become enamored of treason. Thus, he represents an intense manifestation of a declaration that Woolf had made earlier in *Three Guineas:* "a word without meaning is a dead word, a corrupt word."[47]

Unable to arrange his motives in a framework that Stella can accept, Robert rails against the war as "just so much bloody quibbling about some thing that's predecided itself," saying "I want the cackle cut." He reminds Stella that, unlike the First World War, the second one is "not a troubadours' war." When he looks at the "laughing photographs" of her handsome uniformed brothers who were killed at Flanders he remarks, "they took what they had with them: they were the finish." After Robert has left Stella's flat by way of the roof the language builds suspense by mirroring the emotional sequence the reader follows: "In the street below, not so much a step as the semi-stumble of someone after long-standing shifting his position could be, for the first time by her, heard" (*HD* 282, 276, 290).[48] After Stella's and Robert's charged conversation Robert jumps (or falls) to his death from the roof of Stella's flat in the same early morning hours of November [1942] that the Allies land in North Africa.[49] While the church bells peal in national celebration, Stella mourns his loss; she is finally forced to accept the consequences of his treason and her role in his demise.[50]

The author's use of the passive voice in this scene typifies its obfuscating presence throughout the novel. Through such linguistic inversions Bowen re-created for her readers the torpor and convolutions of the war years when words strained to represent the significant connection between historical events and individual dramas.[51] Daniel George, who read the novel for Cape, reported that the contorted language, the odd vocabulary, and the double negatives gave him trouble but he admired her efforts, saying that she had worked "miracles" by expressing "what's been 'inexpressible.'"[52]

Continually, Bowen's words recreated the tension between truth and belief that challenged her characters. She "put language to what for [her] was a totally new use," investigating the "actual pattern" of the cracked "surface" of civilization so evident in wartime ("On Writing," 11). The design she represented in *The Heat of the Day* was "a smashed-up" one "with its fragments invecting on one another."[53] The language of the novel is alive with what is not said, what is inherently inexpressible in the human experience of war. The plot turns on omissions: first Robert's silences, followed by Harrison's, then Stella's. Paul Fussell associates this quality with the poets of the Second World War whose "silence ranging from the embarrassed to the sullen" runs throughout their verse.[54] The most important moral decisions taken in *The Heat of the Day* hinge upon the choice between silence and speech. The crux of the plot follows from the silence that ensues when words have been betrayers and have thereby lost their ability to signify.

Harrison visits Stella in London for the first time since Robert's death during the little Blitz of February, 1944, when she is sitting in her flat, "reading, listening to the guns." Because his connection to Robert has "haunted" Stella, she is startled and, surprisingly, slightly relieved to see him; she even gets up the nerve to accuse him of having "killed Robert." Yet she repeats what she has once told Roderick—that "one never goes back. One never is where one was." And she tells Harrison of her future plans to marry a distant Anglo-Irish cousin, thus making a private peace between the past and the present. Harrison, on the other hand, appears to have made no firm decisions, a lapse he excuses by telling her that he specializes in "plans" rather than events. Against the backdrop of what Harrison calls "this dirty night," her sterile relationship with him fades away, just as "the guns, made fools of, died out again" (*HD* 315, 321, 319).

This figure of apparent evil, Harrison, provides the hinge figure in the secondary plot of the novel that tells the story of two lower-class women, Louie and Connie. By means of this parallel plot involving the stories of two women from different social strata, Bowen investigates many of the same dilemmas that Robert and Stella had encountered.

Although Connie and Louie initially seem very different from Stella, it soon becomes apparent that they share certain problems born of wartime. Bowen conveys dramatically how ancient social and economic distinctions were shrunk by the war, a phenomenon she had witnessed firsthand. In her only sustained portrayal of working-class characters who are not servants, Louie and Connie, "two diverse cases of the spiritual effects of social dislocation," represent the various stresses many women faced in wartime when they found themselves alone.[55]

While her husband, Tom, is abroad with the army Louie works in a factory. Although she dutifully lies to him in her letters, telling him that she looks at his picture every day, in her mind she sees the "face of a man already gone" (HD 158–59). Originally from the south coast, she has lost both her parents in a bomb blast early in the war. The more worldly-wise and cynical Connie, like Bowen, is an air raid warden. She befriends the guileless Louie and guides her through a newly found independence that daunts Louie. By giving a voice to characters outside her own province, Bowen lent authority, as she had in such stories as "In the Square," to her abstract observation that "the war on Britain was undergone by all types."[56]

Louie and Connie's language reflects a certain "livingness" that Bowen had admired, so much in contrast to the ghostly voice of the maid in "Oh, Madam . . ."[57] Her declaration in her review of the 1936 Royal Academy show, that "art makes us sympathize with the lower orders by showing them in market places and pubs," had been softened by a keener awareness of people, particularly women, beyond her usual circle.[58] The awkward dialect Bowen had created for Matchett, the servant in *The Death of the Heart,* has been replaced in *The Heat of the Day* by the more plausible voices of Connie and Louie. Connie never hesitates, for example, to expostulate against the stupidity of the general public who resent the air raid wardens for drawing pay in slow times: "the minute they stopped being pasted they became fresh" (HD 148).

The competent Connie anchors Louie, who is less surefooted. With her husband fighting in Egypt, Louie has been promiscuous, and a baby is due in the summer. Practical Connie, who appears "tough, cross, kind," with a "scissor-like stride in dark blue official slacks," sees no glamor in Louie's situation: "What do you think this makes you?— You're only one of many." Louie has been out on nights when the war "brought out something provocative in the step of most modest women," and she shares her predicament with many other women during this war (*HD* 147, 323, 145). All over Britain, illegitimacy and adultery increased.[59] This sexual pressure faced women of all classes; Stella has encountered her own ugly version of it from Harrison, but for many reasons she made different choices.

Because of Louie's friendship with Connie, the sheltered woman first begins to become a little more aware by reading the newspapers. She believes, as does Stella, that there is "much to be learned from the lessons of history," so she diligently reads whatever she can find. Catchy phrases intended to keep the British fighting spirit alive are made for Louie, who takes considerable comfort from platitudes such as "war now made us one big family" (*HD* 155, 152). She also falls prey to the dangers of the same appeals by trying to mold herself into whatever role the newspaper advertises that day. In contrast, Connie, who before the war sold newspapers at a kiosk, reads newspapers like a "tiger for information." She brusquely challenges the banalities Louie embraces but is wisely dubious about propagandist assertions that war could make anyone's character better.

Connie's differences with Louie about newspapers echo the larger conversation of the novel mourning the loss of the traditional linkage between the past and the future. Throughout the story Stella realizes that "the fateful course of her own fatalistic century seemed more and more her own." The apprehension of this truth accounts for the urgency of the historical debate among the characters of *The Heat of the Day* (especially Stella and Robert), who "are undergoing the test of their middle years" in the "testing extremes of their noonday"—that of the century, and that of the war (*HD* 134; "On Writing," 11). Stella, Connie, and Louie are all trying to apprehend their relevance to one another as well as to their ever-changing situations.

Initially, Connie's greater knowledge and competence overwhelm Louie. Over the course of their friendship, however, Louie's admiration "shift[ed] its ground: Decidedly Connie qualified by her nerve to be a saviour of the human race; at the same time she had a tongue like a file, so that you could not take her to be the race's lover" (*HD* 148). The novel displays Louie to be the more sympathetic character; Connie's misplaced moral zeal compels her to write a meddling missive to inform Tom of his wife's pregnancy. Before she can put the letter in the mail a telegram arrives, announcing Tom's death in action. Spared from confessing the truth, Louie decides to move back to the south coast with her newborn son. There, she will maintain the fiction of her son's paternity.⁶⁰ Her choice is set against the backdrop of the opening of the war's second front, which seemed like "a hallucination—something like the second coming or The End of The World."⁶¹ In returning to the south coast, Louie fulfills Bowen's dreamlike vision of it as a place where differing classes could meet and attain harmony. If not in life, then in art, she could resurrect the resolution that landscape had once brought.

Comforting his mother after Robert's death, Roderick invokes creation as "the only thing that can go on mattering once it has stopped hurting" (*HD* 300). The end of *The Heat of the Day* recalls the narrator in *The Death of the Heart*, who described art as the "emotion to which we remain faithful, after all" (*DH* 95). Bowen numbered herself among the creative writers, who were "the guardians and spokesmen of human values." Embracing fidelity to language as the means to shared experience, she increasingly emphasized her view of loyalty as the quality "essential to survival."⁶² Characters like Robert, who cannot believe in truth or the power of language to convey it, kill themselves.

Bowen returns to another familiar image from her prewar novel, *The Death of the Heart*, as she closes *The Heat of the Day*. Just before Portia Quayne departs for the south coast on a holiday, she sees Yeatsian swans on the lake in Regent's Park, "folded, dark-white cyphers on the white water in an immortal dream" (*DH* 130).⁶³ The swans still suggest artistic expression in this later novel, but they have acquired a public and historical significance beyond that of the private symbol. As Louie walks her baby, the young Tom, in Seale-on-Sea, she looks up at the sky and sees swans flying overhead. At that moment her internal vision merges with that of the birds' flight westward, as they follow the "homecoming bombers" (*HD* 329).⁶⁴

With this scene Bowen shows herself closer to a resolution about the war. Despite the expanse of the Second World War and its extinction of so much that mattered to Bowen, the paradox of her postwar novel about wartime lies in the hopeful moments she managed to interlace with its tragedies. In memorializing the psychological struggles of this conflict through art, Bowen remained somewhat optimistic. Presumably, Roderick will go on to refurbish Mt. Morris, Stella will contentedly marry a member of her race, and Louie will devote herself to bringing up a fine young son who may better the future.

Chapter 10

A Fantastical World

> Have we changed: Or is there no change at all? Dare one hope that? Can one pick up, now, here, from the point at which one left off? The marker waits in the half-read book—a blade of grass of the summer of 1939. Nothing undoes the years.
> —Elizabeth Bowen, "Opening Up the House"

After the success of *The Heat of the Day* marked the symbolic end of the war for Bowen, she worked to accommodate to what she called the "contaminating atmosphere—[of] aimlessness, sluggishness, voicelessness, moroseness" that characterized the postwar scene.[1] Her immediate reaction had led her to minimize war's effect. Since she claimed that she had had a "good war," she expressed impatience with the whining and handwringing she heard from others who had not suffered terribly. And, she did not succumb to the same sense of guilt she had experienced after the First World War because she did not believe that she "had a good war at anybody's expense."[2] Edmund Wilson remembered her boasting, in a lighthearted moment, that she had liked London better in wartime than in peace because it was quiet and all the people "one doesn't like" were away.[3] But, after her initial glibness a deeper realism about what she had witnessed set in, enabling her to admit some of her emotional scarring. On her first visit to New York City after the war she lamented rhetorically: "had not the world convulsed itself; did we not all, as a generation, carry the mark of new, awesome knowledge?"[4]

The postwar literary outlook in London was a discouraging one, made so in part by the bombing of publishers' stock, which had cut severely into authors' royalties. Books were scarce: Not only had they been destroyed in the Blitz but also many had been donated to the paper collection effort. A typical advertisement in a wartime edition of *Good*

Housekeeping in 1943 read: "Few books bear second reading—comb your bookcase for salvage."[5] Bowen complained to Sonia Chapter, of the foreign rights department at the Curtis Brown literary agency, in the spring of 1946: "hunting an author's works for needy authors could almost be a profession in itself these days."[6] Anthony Powell referred to the years immediately following the war as "a pause between the Acts. . . . The bomb-defaced weary squalid town, still suffering shortages of every sort, had to endure the grueling winter of 1946–1947."[7] Bowen's characters in stories such as "I Hear You Say So" (1945) realize that "all they had hoped of the future had been, really, a magic recapitulation of the past—the magic, dilatory past they had not had; their, really, irreparable loss."[8] Of course, as time passed, evaluations evolved. Evelyn Waugh, for one, wrote to Nancy Mitford in the 1950s: "my life ceased after the war."[9] People like Bowen, who was already straddling two countries, had to learn that altered conditions called for revised expectations.

Bowen began to say, in the midst of the "guarded relief" that characterized the end of the Second World War in London, that she would like to move to Ireland and take up the life "that has been enjoined upon one."[10] In an essay dating from August, 1945, "Opening up the House," she ruminated about the return that so many faced after the war: "whether the homecoming be wholly happy or troubling and overcast, it must be disturbing" since it is "accompanied by a whole rush of sensations against which we have no armour, by the breaking upon us of a great wave of memories we did not expect."[11] Her public and private writings of these years reveal that the political and social shape of postwar England brought out some of her worst snobbism coupled with her Burkean conservatism. As she expressed it in one instance to Plomer: "I can't stand all those little middle-class labour wets with their old L.S.E. [London School of Economics] ties and their women; scratch one of these cuties and you find the governess: or so I've always found."[12] Her tone suggests some of the antipathy she felt for the Kelways, who embodied what she hated most about the English middle class in *The Heat of the Day*.

While she had identified herself strongly with England during the war, to the point of "revering and poring over" pictures of royalty which Plomer sent her, when the Labour party came in and the defeated Churchill left office, she explained, it was time for her to depart. After she and Alan Cameron had journeyed to Bowen's Court at the end of the war, she wrote to Plomer: "Selfishly speaking I'd much rather live my life here. I've been coming gradually unstuck from England for a long time. I have adored England since 1940 because of the stylishness Mr. Churchill gave it, but I've always felt, when 'Mr. Churchill goes, I go.'"[13]

In "Folkestone," an essay she wrote in July, 1945, for the Ministry of Information, she had asked "*Can* the illusion [of life before the war] be coaxed back?"[14] The sight of holidaymakers wandering through the ruins of the amusement park caused her to question these platitudes. When Alan Cameron retired from the civil service because of poor health, he and Bowen chose to leave London and live permanently at Bowen's Court. But his unexpected death in August, 1952, shattered his wife's hopes for their life together in Ireland. Her long dependence on her husband became apparent while she remade the familiar contours of her life. Neither the practical nor the emotional reconstruction was easy.

Several months after her husband's death, in the winter of 1953, Bowen confessed that she had "been feeling jangled and astray" and "trying, as he would wish me to, to discover life again."[15] For solace she turned with renewed vigor to the cultivation of friendships, new and old, by entertaining frequently at Bowen's Court. Old standbys—John Lehmann and Cyril Connolly—returned, and newcomers such as Evelyn Waugh, Eudora Welty (who wrote to her in 1951 that she wished they'd "been related"), and Iris Murdoch were welcomed.[16] At the time Waugh was even toying with buying a house in Ireland because of his certainty that "England as a great power is done for."[17] A gregarious hostess, Bowen introduced her guests to the pattern of the life familiar to her in Ireland, often including them in such occasions as neighbors' weddings. After a solitary morning of writing she would invite her house guests to join her as she "motored like one possessed, mainly on the wrong side of the road."[18]

After the Second World War Bowen muted her identification with the Anglo-Irish, saying only that it "has had a certain effect on [her] writing" by giving her a "quickness of impressions" and taking from her the chance for "continuous absorbtion in any one region."[19] As she became more emphatically Irish, she grew more critical of the Anglo-Irish in the postwar years. She distinguished those good people who had been her family's neighbors when she was young from the Anglo-Irish who did nothing but run around, play in the countryside, and squander money in London.[20] Attempting to heal the divisions separating the Anglo-Irish and the Irish in a 1950 article on Bowen's Court, she spun out the fantasy that "the natural pulse of the country beats in its rooms" and beggars came to get bread at the door.[21]

When she had been living permanently in Ireland for two years Bowen described herself in 1953 as "Irish; my home is in County Cork." By the late 1950s and 1960s she associated her perspective entirely with her place of origin when she explained that "Ireland, being the country of my birth, may account, at times, for my manner of seeing things."[22] The most lasting aspect of Bowen's family history and national inheritance came in her ambivalence, which she described in 1956 as "a blend of impatience and evasiveness, a reluctance to be pinned down to a relationship—one which, all the same, nobody could have conceived of life without."[23] Her shifting attitudes toward her national—or, as she would have it, her racial—identity denote her consuming preoccupation with the task of self-definition in time and place. Even "Hand in Glove" (1952), one of the few postwar short stories she wrote with an Irish setting, describes a familiar scene with "an auspicious home," circa 1904, where "the neighborhood spun merrily round the military."[24]

These attempts to locate herself in Ireland accompanied her growing public stature, both national and international, which showed itself in such ventures as her membership in the writers' organization P.E.N., her coverage of the Paris Peace Conference for the *Cork Examiner,* and her undertaking of European lecture tours under the auspices of the British Council. She became known to a wider audience abroad as her books began to be translated into many different languages. But she remained, at least outwardly, self-deprecatory; after she had been awarded a C.B.E. (Commander of the British Empire) in 1948 she wrote to L. P. Hartley that it seemed "most unlike me to have the decoration—I have always seemed to myself such a seedy, ambiguous character." She displayed a similar lack of hubris in 1949 when she confessed that her greatest personal deficiency was "laziness."[25] Throughout her muttering she did not discount hard work, conveyed in her desire that young writers understand that the profession was "risky, ultra-exacting, lonely, dehumanizing, unlikely ever fully to be rewarded."[26]

Repeating a pattern she had followed at other critical junctures in her life, Bowen escaped from the demands creating fiction exacted into the more impersonal requirements imposed by nonfiction. In 1951 she returned to Ireland where she completed a history of the Shelbourne

Hotel in Dublin. This later book probes the social, political, and literary life surrounding a building, as had *Bowen's Court*. While the work lacks the power and range of her history of her own family, she again drew on her predilection for creating an unacademic version of history by interrelating architecture and behavior. In recounting the story of the hotel she also traces much Irish and Anglo-Irish history. Her tone here differs markedly from her earlier project, as she acknowledged: "Let us not in this book attempt to delve into rights and wrongs—enough to say, the existing trouble was rooted deep in the past." She confessed in *The Shelbourne Hotel* that she would like not to remember the entire time of the 1916 Easter Rising, the Anglo-Irish War, and the ensuing Civil War, and she cautioned, in discussing the First World War, that "in order to live through a great war it is necessary sometimes to forget it" (*SH* 149, 203, 184).

The completion of this book (with its rather lengthy British edition subtitle, *A Centre in Dublin Life for more than a Century*) freed Bowen to repossess Ireland in her fiction through a novel entitled *A World of Love* (1955), a reverberating response to *The Last September*. Set in Montefort, another fictional Anglo-Irish Big House in the south of Ireland, the story admits the diminished status of the Anglo-Irish in the postwar years of economic stagnation and political difficulties.[27] Montefort suggests Bowen's fear that, despite her ceaseless celebrations of the Big House, it might not be possible to discover a useful place for it in an altered world. In 1946 E. M. Forster had told Rosamond Lehmann that he could not write novels then because there were no houses; Lehmann's response was: "write a different kind of novel."[28] Bowen heeded her friend's advice; Montefort was the last fictional house to dominate a Bowen novel: *A World of Love* was the final novel she wrote while she still owned Bowen's Court. After she completed this work, she designed only gloomy castles and flimsy villas in her postwar fiction.

Bowen's distracted state of mind becomes evident in the lapse that occurred between her completion of *A World of Love* and her next book. She finished no single work in the five years between 1955 and 1960, when *A Time in Rome* came out. European travel, a novelty after the war, offered her a kind of provisional haven from the strains of creating fiction and personal sorrow. She recorded her new experiences of Rome in a work that intertwined her reactions to the capital with some history of the Catholic city. Less substantial than either *Bowen's Court* or *The Shelbourne Hotel,* the book drew from a similar impulse to conjoin her personal history with that of a larger (and in this case, eternal) universe. Her lifelong attraction to the essay as an art form, combined with the continuing pressure to earn more money, emerged in a collection of some of her earlier and best pieces of literary criticism into the 1962 volume, *Afterthought: Pieces about Writing* (in the United States a similar collection appeared earlier in the same year, *Seven Winters and Afterthoughts*). As the years passed, the imaginary realm again became the province where she could draw strength from the lost world of her childhood.

After the sale of Bowen's Court, Bowen voyaged to her earlier years in a novel entitled *The Little Girls*, published in 1964. It takes place on the south coast of England as she had known it as a child, the section of the country that she "love[d] best."[29] At this time in her career Bowen gravitated toward such sites of previous happiness as Oxford and the Kent coast. After a sojourn in the university town, where she had been awarded the degree of Doctor of Letters in 1957, she bought a small house in Hythe, the place she had drawn so affectionately in *The House in Paris*. But she did not remain long in any one locale; even after she had purchased the house she continued to travel throughout the 1960s.

Frequently Bowen drew on the lesson she had learned that the "heart and imagination" needed "to be fed, stabilized, treasured, taught" after a war of "excoriations, grinding impersonality, obliteration of so many tracks and landmarks." Initially, the past had drawn her in, but the specter of cowardice which might be associated with such a retreat haunted her: "Can this demand [for sustenance] be met only by recourse to life in the past? It at present seems so."[30] While remaining ambivalent about the past as a refuge, she cherished its potential riches. When properly understood, she argued, as she had earlier in *Bowen's Court*, former days could be an instructive and heartening tonic in later times of disillusion. A blind retreat into the reaches of earlier years, on the other hand, could result in emotional numbness and foolish vanity.

She warned against those who are mired in the past in a 1951 essay decrying the prevalence of "The Cult of Nostalgia": "there is something not very exhilarating about their company. They look, somehow, grey, middle-aged, rather mournfully middle class."[31] The figure of the governess was to appear again as a symbol of contempt and derision when she complained in 1960 that she was sick of her age's "governessy attitude towards the past": "You cannot do anything about it, other than try to see it does not recur."[32] Her condemnation of those who glorify former times recalls her disparaging description of the inhabitants of Holme Dene, who also had not been able to comprehend their relationship to their house, or to their history.

The discordance Bowen perceived between the values of days gone by and those of the present resembled the attitude described by so many after the First World War. Notwithstanding her attacks on those who donned blinders in their search for an idyllic prewar era, Bowen produced with increasing regularity autobiographical writings and memoirs that evoked the "most concrete, most personal" aspects of the "semi-mystical topography of childhood" ("Bend Back," 55; "Cult," 225). As she was to realize, the inner, private life of her youth could not entirely satisfy her adult quest to assure her identity. The Second World War had graphically demonstrated to her the perils of living only in a hermetically sealed, personal universe. In a 1951 essay for *Mademoiselle* entitled "First Writing," Bowen revealed her enduring fear "that [she] might fail to attain grown-up status." She wrote to William Plomer: The 1950s were the first time "in which I've enjoyed being 'grown-up' as much I expected to do when I was a child."[33] For *Vogue* she wrote a self-help article with the telling title "How to Be Yourself, But Not Eccentric" where she proffered her own hard-won advice: "it is infinitely rewarding to be oneself." By connecting this process of maturation to her country, she acknowledged that Ireland's stance during the war had made it "harder to be adult in Ireland."[34]

Her first postwar novel reflects a renewed fascination with the inhabitants she imagined occupying the land of the Anglo-Irish. In an article for the *New York Times Book Review* in 1949 Bowen described her next fictional project in terms of four long short stories that would each represent a season.[35] These sketches evolved into her 1955 novel, *A World of Love*. The book's tone draws from her technique in the short story—a compression of emotion and of event—during the passing of a few spring days on an estate in southern Ireland. To her it was an easy book to write, in part because of the "native naturalness of the setting."[36] Her only novel besides *The Last September* to be set exclusively in Ireland, *A World of Love* concerns itself with the changing function of the Big House and the Anglo-Irish in postwar Ireland.

Although her publishers at Cape "peevishly complain[ed]" that the book was too short, Bowen told L. P. Hartley that she liked it.[37] It portrays a place and people removed from war, but the consequences of that conflict continue, as in her earlier fiction, to guide her narrative. *A*

World of Love retreats from the public spaces and events that occupy *The Heat of the Day* into a closed, private territory of "a bourgeois country in search of a missing aristocracy."[38] *A World of Love* exhibits Bowen's talent, as Raymond Mortimer defined it in a letter to her, of lifting "the narrative from actuality into poetry."[39] Imitating some of the best of her short stories, such as "Ivy Gripped the Steps" and "The Inherited Clock," the novel patterns itself after the traditional lyric. Gerard Hopkins spoke of the distinctive structure of language in this novel "as music," not "in its sound, but its organization."[40] For Stephen Spender, the effect of the novel was "like a crystal through which one watches [the] characters."[41] And Rosamond Lehmann, always to be counted on for a favorable response, wrote effusively, "You have written something that I feel along my nerve-ends, as it were—that invades me like a climate."[42]

By means of a complex plot in *A World of Love,* Bowen investigates the inherent conflicts in the life of the romantic and intellectual, the apparent anachronisms of maintaining a Big House in the twentieth century, and the perpetual mismatch between the past and the present. The discovery of a packet of old love letters in the dilapidated country house throws a group of characters, bound to one another by family and sentiment, into anarchy.[43] Antonia, the willful and exotic owner of the house, has loaned it (for a price) to her illegitimate cousin, Fred, his faded wife, Lilia, and their two daughters, Jane and Maud. The inner lives of these characters resemble that of the poorly maintained mansion that exudes "an air of having gone down," or of possessing only "a ghost of style." Not only is the house in physical disrepair, but it has also lost its welcoming quality, that most important virtue of the Big House in Bowen's scheme. Unlike Stella Rodney's ancestors' house in *The Heat of the Day,* the passage of time has irreparably damaged Montefort. In distinct contrast to those who live in Danielstown in *The Last September* and love their house more dearly when it is attacked, those who dwell at Montefort are forever at odds with their surroundings, where the winters are long and the money is "short" and the calendar always shows the wrong date (*WL* 9, 103).

Taking a much less sentimental approach than she had employed in *The Heat of the Day,* Bowen reexamines the Anglo-Irish in postwar Ireland where, as historians of Ireland such as Seamus Deane argue, "a species of apartheid in Irish society" existed after partition.[44] The main characters in *A World of Love* have failed to understand the central principle of the race, that "inherent in this way of life, as in all others, is responsibility—the sense of one's debt to society."⁴⁵ Fred and Lilia enact their race's uncertain economic, political, and social status in their country through an equivocal relationship with the paternalistic Antonia: "They were not her tenants, for they paid no rent; neither were they her caretakers, for they drew no salary. Fred farmed the land, and paid across to Antonia a half share of such profits as could be made; he and his family lived in the house for nothing" (*WL* 13–14).

Bound to Antonia, Fred and Lilia keep the best room in the house in pristine readiness for her whimsical appearances, while they often grumble about their debt to her. Lilia, who came to live in Ireland only after her marriage to Fred, has never learned to be comfortable there: "These people do nothing but nose out money. And as I've always said to you, spies everywhere. No, I shall never trust this country" (*WL* 88). Antonia, responding to her uneasiness about earlier events, feels responsible for Lilia and Guy. The hidden letters reveal the source of her sense of obligation: She had had an affair with her cousin Guy, who at the time was engaged to Lilia. When Antonia learned that Guy had bequeathed nothing to Lilia after his death in the First World War, Antonia succumbed to eternal guilt.

Disenchanted with the dim and unrewarding nature of existence at Montefort, Lilia's daughter, Jane, is attracted to "the wreckage left by the past" when she finds a packet of Guy's love letters to Lilia in the attic of the house. Continually reliving the last moment she saw Guy when he departed for war, Lilia finds that the return of the much-worn past increases her dissatisfaction with the present. Guy becomes for Lilia another male "demon lover" like the fantastical man Mrs. Drover invents in Bowen's wartime story: the power of her memory "consumes the cells of the being if not the body" (*WL* 95).⁴⁶

Jane's discovery brings great pain to both Lilia and Antonia. Startled by her sudden power over the two women, Jane hesitates about how to handle the letters. She quickly decides to bury them, but they do not remain underground for long because her hateful younger sister, Maud, digs them up, thus opening old wounds.⁴⁷ Relentlessly wicked, Maud is first introduced as she sucks a raw egg. Reminiscent of Maria Vesey in "Sunday Afternoon," Maud epitomizes the ugly present and, as a testament to her wish to be contemporary, is "fanatical" in her insistence to hear Big Ben chime over the radio.

Guy's ghost, made manifest in the letters, manipulates and bewitches the residents of Montefort. For the first time since writing the stories collected in *The Demon Lover* and for the only time in a novel, in *A World of Love* Bowen utilizes the psychic realm that had been so valuable both artistically and personally to her during the war. Her renewed residence in Ireland had again involved her in the Irish tradition of the ghost story since, she acknowledged, "fiction is the ideal pacing-ground for the ghosts." She wrote two full-blown ghost stories in the 1950s which bore titles such as "Emergency in the Gothic Wing" and "The Claimant." And in 1952 she claimed in her introduction to *The Second Ghost Book,* edited by her friend Cynthia Asquith, that, "in our seeing of ghosts, each of us has exposed our susceptibilities, which are partly personal, partly those of our time. We are twentieth-century haunters of the haunted."[48]

A World of Love traverses two households that are connected by a single vision, that of Jane's perception of Guy. Not far from Montefort, stands the castle recently bought by the decadent Lady Latterly, whose name puns both Lady Chatterly and her futile efforts to purchase history through lavish decoration. "The costly fiasco of her herbaceous border, the delays, non-deliveries, breakages, leakages and general exploitation she had endured lost nothing in tellings except sympathy for her" (*WL* 57). The Anglo-Irish woman Antonia passes judgment on Lady Latterly as the essence of everything distasteful about "the *nouveau riche*" who have flocked to Ireland after the war. Jane, however, is excited by her invitation to dine at the castle. During Jane's evening there she has a vision of Guy emanating from an empty place at the table, sparked by her discovery of his letters. The appearance of this ghost is alternately enlightening and terrifying, underscoring the undeniable distance separating the present from the past. The two sisters, Maud and Jane, represent opposing attitudes prevalent among the new generation in Ireland. Jane, who buries herself in personal history, emerges at the end of the novel as someone ready for an adult love affair. Maud, in contrast, has learned nothing from her boisterous encounter with the specter of Guy and remains as obstreperous as ever. In fiction, as elsewhere, concern with the uneasy relation of the world after war to what had come before preoccupied Bowen.

She found herself moving around so much in the immediate postwar years that periodical writing absorbed much of her energy. Her more frequent trips to the United States in the 1950s brought her new contacts with the more lucrative American magazines—among them

Vogue, American Home, Glamour, House and Garden, McCall's, Women's Day, Mademoiselle, and *Holiday*.[49] She explained to William Plomer in May, 1958, "in New York I earn money as well as spend it."[50] Particularly, she enjoyed the energy and warmth she found in America, where she now had many close friends, including Charles Ritchie. Although he had married a distant cousin in 1948, Bowen maintained a close friendship with him until she died. She often stayed with the Ritchies when she was in America. Usually these were working vacations and she gave lecture tours, taught at academic institutions such as Vassar College and the University of Wisconsin, and wrote prolifically. This travel and money-making sapped the concentration she needed to write fiction. Although she managed to slip in some short stories from time to time, she could not muster the necessary concentration for longer fictions; she had written to L. P. Hartley in December, 1954, that she was still "writing some short stories": "it's so long since I did, and I do enjoy it."[51]

To close friends like Ritchie Bowen appeared curiously unsettled. He wrote in March, 1959, that, because Bowen was so worried about money herself, she was "more and more irritated by what she calls the Fortnum and Mason troubles of the rich."[52] For her contemporaries who regarded her as a wealthy woman this phase of her career was puzzling. It also has startled critics, who are surprised to find listed in a Bowen bibliography articles on Elizabeth II's coronation, the feminine shopper, the ideal Christmas, and "Enemies of Charm in Women, in Men." In this last article Bowen ventured that "into most women, as social creatures, the desire to be charming has been inculcated, and rightly. But charm, we must realize, has no mechanics; it can not be put consciously into action." Not unexpectedly, she targeted the rise of "aggressiveness" in women as "a most grievous enemy."[53]

Most of her writing in these articles reads as overblown and hyperbolic. Her report on Elizabeth II's coronation shows Bowen full of a grandiose royalism reflective of her high Tory outlook so evident in her fascination with the royal family during the Second World War: "Today we are not dealing in charming fairy tales: there is a spiritual sternness about her calling.... We behold ELIZABETH our undoubted queen."[54] While these articles can be easily misunderstood as frivolous diversions, they mark the phase in Bowen's career when earning money dominated all other concerns. As a widow, Bowen found it difficult to pay for her expensive life.

In these years she concentrated with renewed intensity on romantically optimistic pieces about Bowen's Court and the place of home, as if she were convincing herself of their existence. In an article entitled "Ireland Makes Irish," written for *Vogue,* she declared: "It is impossible, for any length of time, to be *in* this small vivid country and not *of* her."[55] And, she fantasized about the idea of family to an inordinate degree in her 1955 article entitled "Home for Christmas": "all that is dear, that is lasting, renews its hold on us: we are home again."[56] The perpetuation of the Anglo-Irish Big House began to consume her, an obsession expressed in such melodramatic echoes of a declaration as the one she had made in 1946: "I, who love these houses, would rather see the last of them razed to the ground" than believe them to be "fairy-tale retreats."[57] She demonstrated that she *did* think the Big House could accommodate a modern way of life when she used the proceeds from *The Heat of the Day* to install bathrooms in Bowen's Court, much to the relief of her friend and publisher, Blanche Knopf.[58] The happy resolution Bowen had forced upon Roderick at Mt. Morris in *The Heat of the Day* also became her own particular postwar dream: "I believe it is possible to bring these beautiful legacies of the old world into line with the more arduous ideas (or ideals) of the new."[59]

But her optimism that she could reconcile past and present by updating Bowen's Court could not fill all the cracks exposed in the harsh light cast by postwar realities. The clearer it became that she would have to part with the house, which was "built for a family and so it makes one," the more impassioned her writings about it became.[60] Even in her short stories such as "The Light in the Dark," published in *Vogue* in 1950, she had made such statements as "at Christmas no house is childless."[61] The Big House became more than ever the ideal house, or, as she put it, a "merger of Shaw's Heartbreak House and Horseback Hall," where all those with discordant views could come together. She further embellished the fantasy by describing her Big House as a writer's haven, where such figures as Eudora Welty, Evelyn Waugh, David Cecil, Cyril Connolly, and Virginia Woolf gathered happily. By the late 1950s she was maintaining that it was the perfect environment for writing, a place "crowded by images," where "it takes practically nothing to make one feel that the twentieth century is, after all, a fiction."[62] The building's growing distance from the present contributed to its tenuousness. Bowen had faced that recognition in *A World of Love,* which had plainly sketched the onerous dimensions of the upkeep of a large house.

By degrees, the realization that she had failed the Bowen tradition began to wash over her; for all the sustained energy she had poured into the effort, the dream of earning sufficient money to cover the draining expenses of Bowen's Court was illusory. Since her cousin Charles Bowen did not want to take on the estate, she was forced to sell the house in 1959. Her own childlessness ensured there would be no heir to carry on the tradition embodied in the house. After the house and its property had passed into a neighbor's hands, she lost her center—the building that had been home to her family since 1775. And, although she had said in 1949 that she believed one of her strongest traits was her ability to "cut her losses," relinquishing the property tested these inner resources to the extreme.[63] The neighbor who bought the house demolished it for timber, and she found the total disappearance of this physical legacy very difficult to accept.

Perhaps as compensation, *Bowen's Court* was reissued in 1964 at the suggestion of her publishers, Alfred and Blanche Knopf. In this edition Bowen purged herself of her sorrow by writing an addition to the afterword she had first completed in 1941; she told her story of the 1950s: "For seven years I tried to do what was impossible" while the anxiety "slowed down my power to write."[64] The tone alternates between bravado and pathos, but Bowen's sense that she has disappointed the expectations of the past suffuses her prose, and she notes the shame attendant on letting her family down.[65] Even out of this sorrow, however, she forces herself to take small comfort: "It was a clean end. Bowen's Court never lived to be a ruin."[66] For her ruins meant war, and she drew peace of mind from the knowledge that Bowen's Court had always been able to stand apart from the strife and controversy surrounding it.

Ironically, the same image that had carried Bowen through three wars sustained her even as the source of this illusion came apart piece by piece. Her early and intensive training of her imagination served her well when she wrote "Loss has not been entire. When I think of Bowen's Court, there it is." She argued that, because she held the picture in her mind's eye, she kept the introductory chapter in present tense, to keep the house still standing. While she accepted the truth of its loss, she refused to admit that "the space is empty."[67]

In her return to fiction after the loss of her house Bowen played out her own earlier prophecy, in *Bowen's Court*, that "we have everything to dread from the dispossessed."[68] Like Edmund Burke, she viewed those without land as being dangerous to a social or moral order. The characters who figure in her last two novels, *The Little Girls* (1964) and *Eva Trout* (1968), distinguish themselves by being unable to ground themselves in any particular landscape. The actors in the earlier novel compensate for their rootlessness by compulsively searching through their memories. Similarly, the wandering Eva Trout in Bowen's final novel cannot prevent herself from ruining her own life because she has no sense of context or of history. Moreover, she has no connection to the landed gentry; her family has made its money from stocks and bonds.[69]

The central question of *The Little Girls*, as Bowen had put it to herself, was: "*should* one let sleeping dogs lie?"[70] Following a familiar route, the book begins in the present, explores earlier days, and then rejoins the era where it began. The journey starts when an older woman, who goes by the name of Dinah, places an advertisement to find two of her schoolmates from the boarding school she attended before the First World War. Bowen vehemently denied to her friend William Plomer that the novel is implicitly about herself: "*The Little Girls*, as I feel that you saw, though others may not, is not autobiographical.... But it is what Americans would call 'a recall of sensory experience' book."[71] One of her least successful novels, it is filled with stiff characters who shuffle through a narrow plot.

When Dinah rounds up her schoolmates, Clare and Sheila, it becomes clear that for the instigator, memory, in this case enhanced by imagination, serves as the motivating force: "It's by picturing things that one lives" (*LG* 48).[72] Dinah leads a limited and unhappy life because the events of the past obscure her adult existence. While she is the most vividly drawn of the three, none of these shrill and overgrown children exists as a complete and satisfying character. They differ markedly from the rest of Bowen's creations because, as she explained, she had tried to present them from the outside.[73]

Time, in this novel, "opens and shuts ... like a fan," as she had said elsewhere of her chronological predilections. The three women contemplate the childhood games they played at St. Agatha's School in Southstone—based on the Folkestone landscape, which Bowen told Plomer she had "taken liberties with" in her fictional re-creation.[74] War determines the divisions of *The Little Girls*. The first part of the novel closes with Sheila's shocking revelation to her friends that St. Agatha's had "copped it" during the German bombings of the Second World War. The middle section memorializes days past as Dinah, in her flashback, runs on the beach at a birthday party held there on July 23, 1914. Clare concludes the book with her revisionist dreams of what might have been.[75] The central portion handsomely depicts the beach party, echoing some of the scenes of life before the First World War that Bowen recreated in "Ivy Gripped the Steps." Even the small details of the story, such as the victory wreath placed atop the gaily decorated cake, intimate that a war approaches. In their adult journey into their youth the characters focus on a box they buried once at school. The long-forgotten treasure becomes their gauge to determine where the years have taken them because, according to Clare, "nothing has gone for nothing but the days between" (*LG* 56).

Like Jane in *A World of Love,* the children in *The Little Girls* seek out former days for comparison with their postwar world. On their nostalgic ventures they encounter the same questions about the passage of time that have preoccupied so many other Bowen characters: "mistakes have histories, but no beginning—*like,* I suppose, history?" (*LG* 230). Ultimately, the women's wish to unearth the box becomes a manifestation of their desire to find a continuation of their childhood. Unfortunately, the rediscovery of their girlhood exploits proves unsettling rather than comforting. When the characters set off on a pilgrimage to Southstone in search of the box, Dinah remarks to Clare, "Places evaporate, don't they? . . . The poor harmless things." Predictably, when they discover the long-buried carton it has nothing in it. For Dinah the emptiness comes as a particularly nasty surprise; to console herself she wonders whether "it might be better to have pictures of places which are gone. Let them go completely." The women realize that the journey of remembrance can be a painful enterprise: "And then the war came, showing one nothing was too bad to be true" (*LG* 153, 169, 222). It seems too much to ask that anyone can own more than memory, memory that is left alone.

Bowen weaves modern idiom and syntax into her reconstitution of the complexity, as well as the hunt for earlier selves.[76] Perhaps to emphasize that this departure in her method was intentional, she based her approach in her "horror of anachronisms, real or apparent."[77] *The Little Girls* shows the author engaging in a personally loaded questioning of the meaning and worth of memory. As she trained herself to live in a world without Bowen's Court, she withstood much of the same confusion and loneliness that torment her characters. Having explored their former lives to the limits of their mind's eye, they concede that, since the past cannot help them, they must embrace their present, however unsatisfactory it may be. In her last two novels Bowen scrutinized the relation that might exist between women and what they inherited, particularly as they reconciled unsettling realities of their postwar lives with the forces of memory.

As she had done with *The Heat of the Day,* Bowen dedicated her final novel, *Eva Trout, or Changing Scenes* (1968), to Charles Ritchie. Winner of the prestigious James Tait Black Memorial Prize, this broad and disjointed novel departs most extremely from all of her previous work. Its difference reflects Bowen's attempts to settle into the new climate in which she lived and wrote. She used slang and dialect and experimented with a less opaque language to describe her exotic characters. In *To the North* Emmeline writes a letter to her boyfriend, Markie, which she never shows him: "Perhaps some day words will be different or there will be others" (*TTN* 125). Bowen had expressed her attitude toward the linguistic changes abroad in a postwar lecture, where she argued that losses in style, vocabulary, and proportion had accompanied the recent democratization of language, including the adoption of the "new expressive world."[78] By means of this renewed vigor of language, Bowen examined dispossession, dislocation, and loss without recourse to the reassuring illusions provided by earlier times.

Eva deviates from earlier Bowen protagonists in both her independence and her determination to take life under her own control. In the novel, Bowen stranded her characters in a society where loyalty, rootedness, possession, and language have all become unmoored. Her only postwar book to be set entirely in the contemporary world, it begins in 1959 then flashes ahead to what was then the present, 1967. Although many readers have either not enjoyed or been puzzled by this unusual book, *Eva Trout* represents Bowen's final response to the upheavals and shocks she endured in the aftermath of the Second World War.[79] By 1968, in large part because of her efforts with *The Little Girls,* Bowen had reiterated the dangers and dissatisfactions offered by resorting to the past as a guide to the future. She had begun to allow her characters to accept the necessity of confronting the world as it was, not as they thought it might have been or hoped it could be.

A painful heritage haunts rather than sustains Eva. When her parents died she, as an only child, had been left in the care of a hateful guardian, Constantine, who had once been Eva's father's lover.[80] For Eva, the process of becoming an adult entails acting out the tension between imagining and remembering, just like the characters in *The Little Girls*, who engaged in a similar Proustian metaphysical exercise. Although Eva is apparently oblivious to much of her earlier life, she threatens Constantine with the chilling warning that "much fades from human memory. Not all, though." Because of her inability to see herself in any single, sustained context, she exists on "demented fantasies and invented memories," which, "inside Eva's mind, lay about like various pieces of a fragmented picture" (*ET* 99, 39). The only way she can begin to discover herself involves making a "game" out of discerning colors and patterns in the fractured past.

Eva Trout fashions a corrupt and malevolent world where people readily manipulate and destroy one another. Not only has Bowen expanded her temporal province here, but she has also widened her field of characters by more explicitly including homosexuals, lesbians, and alcoholics among a restlessly wealthy cast. A member of that dangerous group, the "rootless rich" (prefigured by Lady Latterly and Antonia in *A World of Love*), Eva spends money instead of words, drives a Jaguar, and wears a "para-military" coat made of ocelot fur. When she appears in this garment, she "[brings] to mind Russian troops that were said to have passed through England in the summer of 1914, leaving snow in the trains" (*ET* 72). She comes across as all the more contemptible because her money derives from the interest made on other money—what Burke called that "extensive discontented monied interest"—rather than from the land.[81] When she travels to the new world, Chicago, she learns of the "filthy" roots of her family's money in "exploitation" (*ET* 140). Apparently, the Trouts had made their fortune by what Burke (and by extension, Bowen herself) termed "the spirit of money-jobbing and speculation," which "violatized" the "mass of land."[82] Eva has been ruined by the unscrupulousness of her ancestors, who eschewed the land as a source for preserving their fortune.

Tall and angular, Eva represents a larger-than-life figure out of a postwar nightmare: Her "capacity for making trouble, attracting trouble, strewing trouble around her, is quite endless." Even her name connotes her archetypal but peculiar nature as the combination of the original Biblical woman and a common fish. One of the few adults who takes an interest in her as a child, an English teacher named Iseult Smith (whose name implies both the romantic and the ordinary), sees Eva as a predator who possesses "the patient, abiding, encircling will of a monster" (*ET* 37, 88). Born during the Second World War, Eva owes her origins to that brutal time when humanity ripped itself apart. She suggests an extreme version of the harsher female figures in Bowen's wartime short stories, such as Maria Vesey in "Sunday Afternoon" and Emma in "Summer Night." "Chronically romantic," Eva exists on whims and wild flights of fancy, without regard for anyone else's feelings.[83] Either unwilling or unable to become a mother biologically (Bowen does not make this distinction clear), she "begets trouble" by making an elaborately selfish project out of adopting Jeremy, a deaf and mute child, who, says Eva, "was to be everything I shall not be" (*ET* 37, 202).

No matter how hard she tries, Eva never appears at home in her surroundings, whatever they may be. Her first schooling takes place in a preposterous castle, or a "home for afflicted children," bought by her father; he had purchased the place to give Ken, his rival for Constantine's affections, something to do. The dungeons and dark corridors indicate a dilapidation so severe the students worry that the walls will tumble down and suffocate them. The building becomes a pathetic pastiche of some of Bowen's earlier renditions of the Big House, closer to Lady Latterly's castle in *A World of Love* than to Bowen's Court. Although the founders of the place had desired, in their enlightenment, to enroll students of all races and classes, ironically, the ones who did matriculate at the school "were coloured only by having rushed about naked on private beaches—the race experiment having, so far, aborted. So had the one with class: young proletarians made one peevish by being difficult to get hold of." Despite Eva's unhappiness at this chateau, she insistently remembers it as the first place where she begins to know what it "meant to be herself." Having passed her early life in so much flight she had no room to be homesick "—for, sick for where?" (*ET* 43, 44).

In her wanderings Eva prowls a gloomy postwar landscape where "morality has come to seem . . . a luxury the characters cannot even imagine."[84] After she departs from the castle she travels around the world with her father until his untimely death. When she lands at another boarding school in the south of England, Iseult Smith offers to tutor her since the girl is too afraid to read or write. Eva eventually finds herself with nowhere to live, so Miss Smith (now Mrs. Arble by virtue of her marriage to a farmer turned garage mechanic) takes her into her home. With her typical insouciance, Eva descends into the midst of their barren marriage where Eric retreats behind the evening paper and Iseult defers her creative talents to earn extra money as a translator. Quickly, the combination of the manipulative Eva and the malcontent Arbles becomes disastrous.

Growing restless at the Arbles', the suddenly adult Eva abruptly decides to flee them and purchase her own house. In her wake she leaves a welter of discord and suspicion about her relations with Mr. Arble. Eventually, the Arbles' already shaky marriage dissolves thanks to Eva's lies and innuendos. Like her fictional predecessors, Louie and Dinah, Eva returns to a familiar town overlooking the Channel on the south coast of England. With the money she has inherited and the help of the feeble estate agent she hires, Mr. Denge, whom Eva instructs that she "want[s] to go home," she purchases a large villa with the incongruous name of Cathay. The romantic voyage suggested by the house's appellation is completely corrupting (*ET* 73).

In the end, Cathay proves to be one of Bowen's most unstable houses. It cannot protect Eva or offer her security; she does not even know how to boil water in the kitchen. Mr. Denge's deliberate euphemism for its poor condition, "a house of character," becomes a cruel parody of Bowen's use of the term in *Bowen's Court*. Built in 1908 and modernized in the 1920s, this villa had been badly damaged by the war. Like Holme Dene in *The Heat of the Day*, Cathay also compromises its integrity with fake features, such as the oak woodwork in the entrance hall, which is "just too black to be old." But this "knocked about dollhouse" demonstrates the limits to what Eva can acquire with her tainted money (*ET* 73, 75).

Eva Trout confirms the truth of the dire prophecies Bowen had voiced in *Bowen's Court,* particularly the belief that a calculating appetite for possession for its own sake underlies much of the evil in the modern world. Eva's renovation of Cathay more and more removes from it any resemblance to the Big House. After Eva buys the place she goes on a spending spree to satisfy her taste for communications devices. She orders the entire house to be rewired to accommodate a "large-screen television set, sonorous-looking radio, radio-gramophone in a teak coffin, other gramophone with attendant stereo cabinets, 16-millimetre projector with screen ready, a recording instrument of B.B.C. proportions . . . a superb typewriter, . . . a cash register . . . and an intercom" (*ET* 116). For someone who has as much trouble as Eva does in speaking with others these acquisitions ironically substitute for human intercourse.

Even after Eva has spent lots of money on "improving" Cathay, still restless, she is driven to travel. The subtitle of the novel, *Changing Scenes*, reflects Eva's almost frenetic movement—even as far as America where she adopts her son, Jeremy. When Eva suddenly becomes tired of foreign hotels and airports she decides that Jeremy needs a home, and she sweeps him off with her to Cathay. On their return it becomes obvious that this place, where "unmeaningness reigned," cannot function as their home, and it seems to be a case "of an absence which had been fatal." The disappointment of being unable to make England home leads to Eva's desolate postwar cry: "Where, then, was to be the promised land, the abiding city?" (*ET* 164, 141, 165).

Eva's voicelessness results directly from her inability to create a home and a household for herself and Jeremy. Since she cannot talk of love, she also cannot build a house where love can grow. No one in the novel really communicates with any other person. The characters continually misread one another; letters cross in the mail or do not reach their destination. Words fail, and promises are broken. Iseult characterizes Eva's way of speaking as "pompous," "unnatural-sounding," "wooden," "deadly," "hopeless," "shutting-off," and "misbegotten" (*ET* 59). Jeremy, who neither reads nor writes but only copies, represents a dark view of the future of language. When he peers at the inscription on the memorial stones in Westminster Abbey on a tour with Iseult, his only response is to trace the letter with his fingers.

While in her earlier postwar novels, such as *The Heat of the Day* and even *A World of Love,* Bowen had relied upon written language to offer insight into meaning and salvation, in *Eva Trout* she alluded to the anxious status of the novelist or artist in this postwar world. Clare had warned her friends in *The Little Girls* that by living in the past: "You'd put more than half the world out of business, including novelists" (*LG* 168). When Iseult pays a visit to Broadstairs, the house where Charles Dickens wrote *Bleak House,* she asks: "what, now one came to think of it, *had* James, that Dickens really had not?" Like Dickens, Bowen plays with the possibilities of naming in this novel, as she tended toward more literal and more obviously baroque labels. Self-conscious references to the British literary tradition abound. Iseult likes reading another favorite of Bowen's, D. H. Lawrence, while Constantine is described as "on the verge of Henry James country." Even Eva offers a mighty challenge to Bowen's predecessors: "It took Dickens not to be eclipsed by Eva" (*ET* 110, 27, 111). The allusions do not confine themselves to prose; one of the young men this strong woman tries to seduce describes her as the reverse of Browning's Pippa because she does not leave lives "unscathed." Yet this concern with the world of the writer indicates Bowen's own preoccupation with her stance in relation to the past and her fear about the meaning of creative work.

By her adoption of a deaf-mute child, Eva dramatically calls into question the assumption governing *The Heat of the Day*, that language can heal the mutilations wrought by the two world wars. Perhaps some wounds run too deep to mend. Even Bonnard, the doctor who has "been a figure in the Resistance," cannot cure Jeremy. But Eva's intimacy with her son is rooted in this very malaise, in "her mistrust of or objection to verbal intercourse." Together, they achieve a "cinematographic existence, with no sound-track," which makes "them near as twins in a womb." Such a silence has its circumscriptions; over the course of the novel, Eva begins to doubt the value of an exclusively visual existence. But when she sends Jeremy to a sculptor in the hope he will learn to express himself by forming shapes, the artist explains to Eva that for her "words do not connect"; she is "visual purely." For Eva, the conclusion that she reaches on a frantic afternoon at the National Portrait Gallery is more dispiriting. The images on the canvases cannot answer her urgent question, "What is a person?" (*ET* 228, 191, 201, 196). The universe she has fashioned for herself and Jeremy self-destructs when Eva realizes the value, and hence absence, of other forms of communication in her life.

Jeremy also senses this vacuum when he gets hold of a gun, which enables him to resort to the only action of which he is fully capable: a violent one. In the most melodramatic ending Bowen ever imagined, Jeremy shoots Eva dead as she is about to depart on yet another staged honeymoon.[85] Eva's son becomes a pathological extension of "the fatal child" in *The House in Paris* and the menacing Maud in *A World of Love*. Art cannot save this child or this mother. The swans of Regent's Park in *The Death of the Heart* and the birds on the south coast in *The Heat of the Day* have fled Bowen's world (*ET* 235). But she could not let this vision stand; in an essay in *Pictures and Conversations,* Bowen's final autobiographical work, she wrote: "in the long run, art is realer than life."[86] Not all the characters in her last novel give in to homicidal gloom. Bonnard, the doctor who recognizes his inability to give Jeremy speech, wisely ruminates to Eva: "One need not be frightened of growing old; to the last, there will always be something new" (*ET* 228). To the end, Bowen hoped for the rewards the gift of art could bring.

Although in the early 1970s a series of respiratory infections resulting from lung cancer weakened Bowen, she continued to write, and she again lit upon her earliest years as the magical kingdom offering unpredictable delights of memory. Despite her illness, she carried on with her work, in accordance with her gallant credo that "the main thing is to keep the show on the road."[87] At the time of her death in February, 1973, she was shaping a collection of autobiographical essays, which she wished to be published posthumously, as well as *The Move-In,* a fragmentary novel set in a dilapidated house in southern Ireland. Fittingly, Bowen had asked to be buried near her family in the Protestant churchyard outside St. Colman's, adjoining the land where Bowen's Court had stood. Her choice represented the final resolution of a lifelong search to place herself. After the Second World War it grew easier to admit what she had first discovered in early childhood—that, for her, Ireland was home.

Her friend and literary executor, Spencer Curtis Brown, followed Bowen's instructions to publish the partial and impressionistic autobiography, *Pictures and Conversations,* in 1975. The book, which she insisted should follow no standard time sequence nor make any claims to being "all-inclusive," is fragmentary and impressionistic.[88] She did not adhere to any of the usual conventions in this book, having once written to William Plomer that she hadn't "cared very much for most of [her] contemporaries' autobiographies."[89] Throughout her life she had examined the distinction between interior and exterior. In 1957 she had told Charles Ritchie that she did "not want to write a subjective autobiography"; rather "it comes more naturally . . . to invent"—which is what she had been doing all her life.[90]

"Our century," Elizabeth Bowen wrote in 1953, "as it takes its frantic course, seems barely habitable by humans: we have to learn how to survive while we write. And *to* write, we must draw on every resource; to express, we need a widened vocabulary, not only as to words, but as to ideas."[91] Her wartime and postwar fictions bear the mark of the continuing transformations she had undergone, both in her life and in her art, simply to survive. Through her use of language she demonstrated brilliantly that there is always something that can be "beheld for the first time," even when she scrutinized people and places she had seen before.[92]

The perspectives imposed by war caused Bowen to take many more risks than she might otherwise have done, both in choice of subject and style. In realizing the broadened social possibilities for women, she reminds us of what Virginia Woolf had declared in *A Room of One's Own*. After the Crimean war had "let Florence Nightingale out of the drawing-room," the First World War had "opened the doors to the average woman."[93] Emboldened by the experience of several more wars, Bowen ventured forth from the confines of the salon and, instead, constructed characters who actively questioned the validity of what their mothers and daughters—as well as their husbands, fathers, and sons—had fought to preserve on the battlefield and on the home front. The shifting and uncertain civilization she had inherited impelled her to paint her reactions on a far larger canvas than had she lived in a time of peace.

Abbreviations

BC	*Bowen's Court*
DH	*The Death of the Heart*
ET	*Eva Trout, or Changing Scenes*
H	*The Hotel*
HD	*The Heat of the Day*
HP	*The House in Paris*
LG	*The Little Girls*
LS	*The Last September*
SH	*The Shelbourne Hotel*
TTN	*To the North*
WL	*A World of Love*

Notes

Preface

1. Peter de Vries, "Touch and Go (with a low bow to Elizabeth Bowen)," *New Yorker,* January 26, 1952, 32.
2. Although the Bowens remained generally detached from the conflict, one of Bowen's distant paternal relatives was implicated in the death of a pacifist, Francis Sheehy Skeffington, in 1916. See Janet Egleson Dunleavy, "Elizabeth Bowen," in *Dictionary of Literary Biography,* vol. 15, ed. Bernard Oldsey (Detroit: Gale, 1983), 35.
3. Elizabeth Bowen, *The Heat of the Day* (1949; reprint, Harmondsworth, Middlesex: Penguin, 1985), 25.
4. Elizabeth Bowen to Virginia Woolf, University of Sussex, reprinted in *The Mulberry Tree,* ed. Hermione Lee (London: Virago Press, 1986), 218.
5. Elizabeth Bowen, "Herbert Place," reprinted in *Seven Winters and Afterthoughts* (New York: Alfred A. Knopf, 1962), 4–5.
6. Elizabeth Bowen, Foreword to *Seven Winters,* vii.
7. Victoria Glendinning, *Elizabeth Bowen: Portrait of a Writer* (New York: Penguin, 1985), 21.
8. Elizabeth Bowen, *Bowen's Court* (New York: Alfred A. Knopf, 1942), 417. (I quote from two different editions of *Bowen's Court:* the first, cited above, and a second, which was published with a new afterword in 1964 by Ecco Press. I differentiate between the two by using *BC* and *BC* 1964.)
9. F. S. L. Lyons, *Culture and Anarchy in Ireland, 1890–1939* (Oxford: Clarendon, 1979), 22.
10. Howard Moss, "Interior Children," *New Yorker,* February 5, 1979, 128; Lyons, *Culture and Anarchy,* 18.
11. Seamus Deane, *A Short History of Irish Literature* (London: Hutchinson, 1986), suggests using the admittedly imperfect term *Irish Literature,* 7.
12. James C. Beckett, *The Anglo-Irish Tradition* (Ithaca: Cornell University Press, 1976), 11; R. F. Foster, *Modern Ireland, 1600–1972* (London: Allen Lane/Penguin, 1988), 194.
13. *Webster's New Twentieth Century Dictionary of the English Language* (New York: Publishers' Guild, 1961), 1484.

14. Deane, *Short History*, 94.
15. Elizabeth Bowen, "Miss Bowen on Miss Bowen," *New York Times Book Review*, March 6, 1949, 33.
16. For more on this experience, see Elizabeth Bowen, "Downe House" (1957), reprinted in *The Mulberry Tree*, 16, 17.
17. Elizabeth Bowen, "First Writing," *Mademoiselle*, January, 1951, 119.
18. Elizabeth Bowen, "Coming to London" (1956), reprinted in *The Mulberry Tree*, 88.
19. Elizabeth Bowen, "Autobiographical Note" (October 11, 1948), 2, Harry Ransom Humanities Research Center. Hereafter this collection will be referred to in the notes as HRHRC.
20. V. S. Pritchett to Elizabeth Bowen (July 8, 1947), HRHRC.
21. Elizabeth Bowen, "Miss Bowen on Miss Bowen," 33.
22. Elizabeth Bowen to Alan Cameron (Wednesday [February or March] 14 [1923]), quoted in *The Mulberry Tree*, 195.
23. Elizabeth Bowen, March 11, 1957, as a guest on the British Broadcasting Corporation (BBC) program "Desert Island Disks," reprinted in *The Mulberry Tree*, 233.
24. Glendinning, *Elizabeth Bowen*, 72.
25. Charles Ritchie, in his diary entry of January 19, 1957, so characterized her outlook in *Diplomatic Passport* (Toronto: Macmillan of Canada, 1981), 125.
26. Seán O'Faoláin, "A Reading and Remembrance of Elizabeth Bowen," *London Review of Books*, March 4–17, 1982, 16. The best work on Bowen has been done by Hermione Lee, in *Elizabeth Bowen: An Estimation* (London and Totowa, N.J.: Vision/Barnes and Noble, 1981), as well as by Victoria Glendinning in *Elizabeth Bowen*, who refers to Bowen as "what happened after Bloomsbury; she is the link which connects Virginia Woolf with Iris Murdoch and Muriel Spark" (1). As Robert Coles has noted in *Irony in the Mind's Life* (Charlottesville: University Press of Virginia, 1973), "for a number of critics of combined political and literary sensibility she has been a vexing writer to face" (108). Elizabeth Hardwick, for one, was put off by Bowen's politics and mannerisms; in her review of *The Heat of the Day* she wrote, "nothing is more difficult to track down than Miss Bowen's true reputation" ("Elizabeth Bowen's Fiction," *Partisan Review* [November 16, 1949], 1118). Howard Moss perceived that she "was always noted, but not always for the right reasons" ("Interior Children," *New Yorker*, February 5, 1979, 121). He places her in the "great tradition of English moral comedy" as one of the "natural masters of English prose" who has been "wrongly thought of as a 'woman's writer,' all heartthrob and fuzz" ("Elizabeth Bowen," [Obituary] *New York Times Book Review* [April 8, 1973], 2).
27. Elizabeth Bowen, Foreword to *Collected Impressions* (New York: Longmans, Green, 1950), v.
28. Elizabeth Bowen, Interview with John K. Hutchens, *New York Herald Tribune Book Review*, March 26, 1950, 3; Foreword to *Seven Winters*, vii–viii.

29. Elizabeth Bowen, "Places," in *Pictures and Conversations* (London: Allen Lane, 1975), 62.

30. Elizabeth Bowen, Interview with Charles Monaghan, "Portrait of a Woman Reading: Elizabeth Bowen," *Chicago Tribune Book World*, November 10, 1968, 6.

31. Elizabeth Bowen, quoted in Glendinning, *Elizabeth Bowen*, 91.

32. Elizabeth Bowen, "Strength of Mind—Do Women Think Like Men?" *Listener* 26 (October, 1941): 593.

33. Elizabeth Bowen, "Notes on Writing a Novel" (1945), reprinted in *Pictures and Conversations*, 185.

34. Elizabeth Bowen, "Notes on Writing a Novel" (1945), reprinted in *Pictures and Conversations*, 185.

35. Elizabeth Bowen, "This Freedom," *New Statesman*, October, 31, 1936. She further declared that women are now "free to do what they ought, what they can, what they have it in them to do: they have no excuse for not doing it" (678).

36. Elizabeth Bowen, "Women's Place in the Affairs of Men," 2, HRHRC.

37. Elizabeth Bowen, *To the North* (1932; reprint, New York: Alfred A. Knopf, 1950), 13. Hereafter this title will be cited in the text as *TTN*.

38. Elizabeth Bowen, "Disloyalties" (1950), reprinted in *Seven Winters*, 67.

39. Elizabeth Bowen, *The Last September* (1929; reprint, New York: Avon Books, 1979), 122. Hereafter this title will be cited in the text as *LS*.

40. Julian Moynahan, "Elizabeth Bowen, Anglo-Irish Post-Mortem," *Raritan* 10 (Fall 1989): 69.

Chapter 1

1. Elizabeth Bowen, "Horse Show" (1942), reprinted in *Seven Winters*, 25.

2. Hermione Lee argues that Bowen's "attitude to the civilization she inhabited was confirmed by the war. . . . [It] intensified her sense that the century she had grown up with was inimical to faith, hope, and love" (*Elizabeth Bowen*, 156).

3. Virginia Woolf, "The Leaning Tower" (1940), reprinted in *The Moment and Other Essays* (New York: Harcourt Brace Jovanovich, 1974), 164, 163.

4. Elizabeth Bowen, "Contemporary," Review of *In My Good Books*, by V. S. Pritchett, reprinted in *The Mulberry Tree*, 160; the review originally appeared in the *New Statesman*, May 23, 1942.

5. Elizabeth Bowen, Interview with Charles Monaghan, "Elizabeth Bowen," 6.

6. Elizabeth Bowen, Preface to *Ivy Gripped the Steps and Other Stories* (New York: Alfred A. Knopf, 1946), viii.

7. Elizabeth Bowen, *Why Do I Write?* (part of a three-way correspondence with Graham Greene and V. S. Pritchett, 1948), reprinted in *The Mulberry Tree*, 224, 223.

8. Elizabeth Bowen, "Mainie Jellet" (n.d.), 2, HRHRC.

9. Elizabeth Bowen, "Books in General," review of *Mr. Beluncle*, by V. S. Pritchett, *New Statesman*, October 20, 1951, 438.
10. V. S. Pritchett, "Bowen's Inner Lives," *Vogue*, March, 1981, 362.
11. H. R. Ellis Davidson, *Myths and Symbols in Pagan Europe: Early Scandinavian and Celtic Religions* (Syracuse, N.Y.: Syracuse University Press, 1988), 92, 97.
12. Denise Riley, "Some Peculiarities of Social Policy concerning Women in Wartime and Postwar Britain," in *Behind the Lines: Gender and the Two World Wars*, ed. Margaret Randolph Higonnet, Jane Jenson, Sonya Michel, and Margaret Collins Weitz (New Haven, Conn.: Yale University Press, 1987), 260.
13. Virginia Woolf, *The Diary of Virginia Woolf*, vol. 5, ed. Anne Olivier Bell (May 15, 1940) (London: Hogarth Press, 1984), 285.
14. Virginia Woolf, *Three Guineas* (1938; reprint, London: Hogarth Press, 1952), 18, 15, 27, 60.
15. Introduction to Higonnet et al., *Behind the Lines*, 5.
16. For more on Woolf's attitude about the term *feminist*, see Alex Zwerdling, *Virginia Woolf and the Real World* (Berkeley: University of California Press, 1986), 210.
17. Jane Marcus, "The Asylums of Antaeus. Women, War and Madness: Is There a Feminist Fetishism?" in *The Difference Within: Feminism and Critical Theory*, ed. Elizabeth Meese and Alice Parker (Philadelphia: John Benjamin, 1989), 62.
18. Deidre Beddoe, *Back to Home and Duty: Women between the Wars, 1918–1939* (London: Pandora, 1989), 16.
19. Margaret Goldsmith, *Women at War* (London: Lindsay Brummond, 1943), 218, 120, 126, 129–31.
20. Goldsmith, *Women at War*, 127.
21. Elizabeth Bowen, *The House in Paris* (1935; reprint, New York: Alfred A. Knopf, 1936), 219. Hereafter this title will be cited in the text as *HP*.
22. John Hildebidle has written that Bowen's relation to the century "was a radically unsettling condition" (*Five Irish Writers: The Errand of Keeping Alive* [Cambridge: Harvard University Press, 1989], 92, 93).
23. Virginia Woolf, *Diary*, vol. 5 (March 16, 1936), 18. Woolf's idiosyncratic spelling and punctuation have been retained in quotations from her works throughout.
24. Virginia Woolf, *Diary*, vol. 5 (June 27, 1940), 299. Bowen had visited the Woolfs on June 25 and 26, 1940.
25. Cyril Connolly, *Cyril Connolly: Journal and Memoir*, ed. David Pryce-Jones (London: William Collins, 1983), 263.
26. "Even before 1914 the ruins were everywhere, though the systematic burnings belong mainly to the period 1917–1923." See T. R. Henn, "Yeats and the Poetry of War," in *Last Essays: Mainly on Anglo-Irish Literature* (New York: Barnes and Noble, 1976), 84.
27. Virginia Woolf, *Roger Fry: A Biography* (1940; reprint, New York: Harcourt Brace Jovanovich, 1968), 200.
28. Woolf, *Diary*, vol. 5 (September 14, 1938), 170.

29. Robert Wohl, *The Generation of 1914* (Cambridge: Harvard University Press, 1979), 211–12.

30. Wohl, *Generation of 1914*, 121.

31. L. P. Hartley, "Three Wars," in *Promise of Greatness: The War of 1914–1918*, ed. George A. Panichas (London: Cassell, 1968), 254.

32. Peter Conrad, "Tons of Fear," Review of *A Pacifist's War*, by Francis Partridge, *New Statesman*, July, 28, 1978, 124.

33. Paul Fussell, *Wartime: Understanding and Behavior in the Second World War* (New York: Oxford University Press, 1989), 115.

34. Cyril Connolly, "Writers and Society, 1940–1943," reprinted in *The Selected Essays of Cyril Connolly*, ed. Peter Quennell (New York: Stanley Moss/Persea Books, 1984), 135.

35. Sebastian D. G. Knowles, *A Purgatorial Flame: Seven British Writers and the Second World War* (Philadelphia: University of Pennsylvania Press, 1990), xiv; he has argued effectively that "the Second World War did not mark a hiatus in British literature; the progress of literary thought [especially modernism] continued through into the forties." See also Robert Hewison, *Under Siege: Literary Life in London, 1939–1945* (New York: Oxford University Press, 1977).

36. Paul Fussell, "Writing in Wartime: The Uses of Innocence," in *Thank God for the Atom Bomb and Other Essays* (New York: Summit Books, 1988), 131, 78.

37. Hartley, "Three Wars," 258.

38. Fussell, *Wartime*, 132.

39. David Craig and Michael Egan, *Extreme Situations: Literature and Crisis from the Great War to the Atom Bomb* (London: Macmillan, 1979), 1.

40. Matthew Arnold, "Irish Catholicism and British Liberalism," *Mixed Essays* (New York: Macmillan, 1883), 127.

41. In discussing Anglo-Irish literature T. R. Henn asks, "Is this whole corpus of literature in a sense illegitimate, or at least deserving of some other title: because it should have been written in Irish? Or is it basically defective because the members of the 'Ascendancy' must be *ex hypothesi*, ignorant of the innermost soul of Ireland?" ("The Weasel's Tooth," in *Last Essays*, 28).

42. Cyril Connolly, *Memoirs*, 254.

43. Elizabeth Bowen, *The Hotel* (1927; reprint, New York: Viking Penguin, 1984), 104. Hereafter this title will be cited in the text as *H*.

44. Henn, "Weasel's Tooth," 36; "Yeats and the Poetry of War," 85.

45. Seán O'Faoláin, *The Irish: A Character Study* (New York: Devin-Adair, 1949), 175.

46. Woolf, *Diary*, vol. 5 (December 2, 1939), 248.

47. Richard Cobb, "Survivors of the Home Front," Review of *The Other Garden*, by Francis Wyndham, *Times Literary Supplement*, October 2–8, 1987, 1073.

48. Ronald Blythe, ed. *Components of the Scene: Stories, Poems, and Essays of the Second World War* (Harmondsworth, Middlesex: Penguin, 1966), 25.

49. See Blythe, *Components*, table of contents.

50. Walter Allen, quoted in Blythe, *Components*, 21.

51. T. S. Eliot, section 2, "Little Gidding," *Four Quartets,* in *The Complete Poems and Plays, 1909–1950* (New York: Harcourt Brace Jovanovich, 1971), 140.

52. Elizabeth Bowen to John Hayward, from Bowen's Court (September 25, 1936), King's College Library, Cambridge.

Chapter 2

1. Elizabeth Bowen, *A Year I Remember—1918,* BBC third program, March 10, 1949, 8, HRHRC.

2. Elizabeth Bowen, interview with Charles Monaghan, "Elizabeth Bowen," 6. Some contemporary feminist critics argue that women seemed to succumb to the "guilt" of the female survivor at the same time that they felt themselves more powerful. See Sandra Gilbert, "Soldier's Heart: Literary Men, Literary Women, and the Great War," in Higonnet et al., *Behind the Lines,* 201, 200.

3. Elizabeth Bowen, "The Bend Back," first published as "Once Upon a Yesterday," *Saturday Review* 33 (May, 1950), reprinted in *The Mulberry Tree,* 54. In *The Great War and Modern Memory* (New York: Oxford University Press, 1975), Paul Fussell writes that the First World War was the "last to be conceived as taking place within a seamless, purposeful 'history' involving a coherent stream of time running from past through present to future" (21). Alfred McDowell makes the point that Bowen, along with Wharton and Cather, believed that "since World War One the world has been socially and morally out of joint"; see "*The Death of the Heart* and the Human Dilemma," *Modern Language Studies* 8 (1979): 15.

4. Hartley, "Three Wars," 251.

5. Elizabeth Bowen, *The Shelbourne Hotel* (New York: Alfred A. Knopf, 1951), 201. Hereafter this title will be cited in the text as *SH.*

6. Elizabeth Bowen, review of *Anne Douglas Sedgwick: A Portrait in Letters,* ed. Basil de Selincourt, reprinted in *Collected Impressions* (1936; reprint, New York: Longmans, Green, 1950), 94. Bowen included Sedgwick in the generation that had "faced the indictment of 1914 without a tremor" (94).

7. Elizabeth Bowen, "Firelight in the Flat," in *The Collected Stories of Elizabeth Bowen* (New York: Vintage Books, 1981), 435.

8. Elizabeth Bowen, *The Last September,* 92. Although the novel was first published in 1929, it was reissued with a preface in 1952.

9. Elizabeth Bowen, "Aunt Tatty" (1926) in *Collected Stories,* 267.

10. Elizabeth Bowen, *Friends and Relations* (1931; reprint, Harmondsworth, Middlesex: Penguin, 1984), 18.

11. Elizabeth Bowen, *The Death of the Heart* (1938; reprint, New York: Vintage Books, n.d.), 93–94, 276. Hereafter this novel will be referred to in the text as *DH.*

12. W. J. McCormack has written of the eclipse of the Anglo-Irish as occurring when "the hyphen which had existed as an equation became first a minus sign and then a cancellation" (*Ascendancy and Tradition in Anglo-Irish Literary History, 1789–1939* [Oxford: Clarendon Press, 1985], 47–48).

13. "In the context of Empire which so many of them served [the] essence of their tragedy was that the Empire was now about to repudiate them" (F. S. L. Lyons, *Culture and Anarchy in Ireland, 1890–1939* [Oxford: Clarendon Press, 1979], 102).

14. Christopher Isherwood, *Lions and Shadows: An Education in the Twenties* (London: Methuen, 1938), 74–76. See Andrew Rutherford, *The Literature of War: Five Studies in Heroic Virtue* (New York: Barnes and Nobles, 1979), 114.

15. Claire Tylee, *The Great War and Women's Consciousness: Images of Militarism and Womanhood in Women's Writings, 1914–1964* (London: Macmillan, 1990), 218, 245.

16. On myth, see Bernard Bergonzi, *Heroes' Twilight: A Study of the Literature of the Great War* (London: Macmillan, 1980), 198, 17, 31.

17. Gail Braybon, *Women Workers in the First World War* (Totowa, N.J.: Barnes and Noble, 1981), 154.

18. Bergonzi, *Heroes' Twilight*, 31.

19. Tylee, *The Great War*, 75

20. Because they shared in "the cultural myths and the behavioural inhibitions of their society," they also fell prey to the pain of war; see Tylee, *The Great War*, 187.

21. Bernard Bergonzi only mentions Virginia Woolf's *Mrs. Dalloway* once, although he devotes a whole chapter of *Heroes' Twilight* to civilian experience (223). The study of men's and women's literature of the war has also tended to follow gender lines. In his book on fiction of the First World War, George Parfitt reveals his reluctance to discuss women's war literature: "There are a number of novels about the war which were written by women, and these also have been largely ignored here. Vera Brittain's *Honourable Estate* ([London:] Gollancz, 1936) and Rose Macaulay's *Noncombatants and Others* ([London:] Hodder and Stoughton, 1916) have more to say about unease over the war than most male novels, but I do not feel sure of my grasp of either book. A woman should, however, make a study of these and other war novels by women." *Fiction of the First World War: A Study* ([London: Faber and Faber, 1988], 136).

22. Virginia Woolf to Margaret Llewelyn Davies, letter no. 740 (January 23, 1916), in *The Letters of Virginia Woolf*, vol. 2, ed. Nigel Nicholson (New York: Harcourt Brace Jovanovich, 1976), 76.

23. Tylee, *The Great War*, 256.

24. Wohl, *Generation of 1914*, 111.

25. Vera Brittain, *Testament of Youth* (London: Gollancz, 1933), 77.

26. Arthur Marwick, *Women at War* (London: Fontana, 1977), 163. By the end of the First World War the "number of working women had increased by almost fifty percent; 700,000 women employed had directly replaced men in the work force" (Gilbert, in Higonnet et. al, *Behind the Lines*, 205).

27. Marwick, *Women at War*, 163.

28. "While the Great War in some sense inverted the relationship of men, trapped and sacrificed in the trenches, to women, on the Home Front, it also reinscribed their differences" (Margaret Higonnet and Patrice L.-R. Higonnet, "The Double Helix," in Higonnet et al., *Behind the Lines*, 42).

29. Gilbert, in Higonnet et al., *Behind the Lines,* 209. See also Anne Summers, *Angels and Citizens: British Women as Military Nurses 1854–1914* (London: Routledge and Kegan Paul, 1988), for a discussion of the history of the contradictions implied in this icon (9).

30. Bergonzi, *Heroes' Twilight,* 146, 171.

31. Wohl, *Generation of 1914,* 106.

32. Elizabeth Bowen, "The Disinherited," in *Collected Stories.* See Lee, *Elizabeth Bowen,* for a strong discussion of the story. See J'nan M. Sellery and William O. Harris, *Elizabeth Bowen: A Bibliography* (Austin: Humanities Research Center, University of Texas at Austin, 1981), 217, item E35; the story is undated but Sellery and Harris date it from July 6, 1934; it was first published in *The Cat Jumps* (see 36, item A8).

33. Elizabeth Bowen, "The Last Night in the Old Home" (1934) in *Collected Stories,* 371.

34. Elizabeth Bowen, "Tears, Idle Tears" (1936), in *Collected Stories,* 483. For a bibliographic footnote on "Tears," see Sellery and Harris, *Elizabeth Bowen,* 131, item C31. The story was first published in the *Listener* 16 (September, 1936): 447–49.

35. Elizabeth Bowen, "The Tommy Crans" (1930), in *Collected Stories,* 349. For bibliographic information, see Sellery and Harris, *Elizabeth Bowen,* 129, item C12. The story was first published in *The Broadsheet Press* (London) (February, 1930).

36. Elizabeth Bowen, "Charity," in *Collected Stories.* The story was originally published in *Ann Lee's and Other Stories* (London: Sidgwick and Jackson, 1926).

37. In 1918, the war had left 8.5 million European men dead and 37.5 million casualties. These tragedies were not isolated individual occurrences, sparking private griefs. The toll of death severely altered the postwar landscape, especially affecting the relations between the sexes. England, having "lost 600,000 of its younger men" not even counting "the substantial proportion of the 1.6 million who were gravely mutilated" had seen the last of "9 per cent of all men under 55" (Marwick, *Women at War,* 162).

38. Elaine Showalter, "Rivers and Sassoon: The Inscription of Male Gender Anxieties," in Higonnet et al., *Behind the Lines,* 63. Ten years following World War I, 48 mental hospitals held sixty-five thousand shell-shock victims in England (Tylee, *The Great War,* 248–49).

Chapter 3

1. Elizabeth Bowen to Alan Cameron (January 19 [1923]), quoted in *The Mulberry Tree,* 143.

2. Elizabeth Bowen to Alan Cameron ([February or March] 12 [1923]), quoted in *The Mulberry Tree,* 194.

3. Peter Quennell, *Customs and Characters: Contemporary Portraits* (London: Weidenfeld and Nicolson, 1982), 88.

4. Elizabeth Bowen and Glyn Jones, "How I Write," BBC broadcast (May 10, 1950), 6, HRHRC.

5. C. M. Bowra, *Memories, 1898–1939* (Cambridge: Harvard University Press, 1967), 191.
6. Bowen to Alice Runnells James (April 26, 1953), Houghton Library, Harvard University.
7. Elizabeth Bowen, Revised Preface to 1949 reissue of *Encounters* (1923; reprint, London: Ace Books, 1961), 7–8, 9.
8. Bowen, "Stories by Elizabeth Bowen," in *Seven Winters*, 178.
9. Bowen, "Coming Home," in *Encounters*, 119.
10. Bowen, Preface to 1952 reissue of *The Last September*, x.
11. Elizabeth Bowen, "Daffodils" (1923), in *Collected Stories*, 23, 27.
12. Elizabeth Bowen, "Mrs. Windemere" (1923), in *Collected Stories*, 71, 73, 74.
13. For more on this topic, see Lee, *Elizabeth Bowen*, 100; and Hildebidle, *Five Irish Writers*, 92.
14. See Valentine Cunningham, *British Writers of the Thirties* (Oxford: Oxford University Press, 1989), for his discussion of zoos, 86–90.
15. Elizabeth Bowen, "Recent Photograph" (1926), in *Collected Stories*, 211.
16. See Sellery and Harris, *Elizabeth Bowen*, 101, item B1.
17. Elizabeth Bowen, "Telling" (1927), in *Collected Stories*, 326.
18. Elizabeth Bowen, "The Working Party" (1929), in *Collected Stories*, 287.
19. Elizabeth Bowen, "Foothold" (1929), in *Collected Stories*, 298.
20. Elizabeth Bowen, "Requiescat" (1923), in *Collected Stories*, 46.
21. Elizabeth Bowen, "Joining Charles" (published in 1926 as "The White House"), in *Collected Stories*; see Sellery and Harris, *Elizabeth Bowen*, 129, item C6.
22. The story was originally published in *Everybody's Magazine*, April, 1925, 135–42; see Sellery and Harris, *Elizabeth Bowen*, 129, item C6.
23. Carol Dyhouse, *Girls Growing Up in Late Victorian and Edwardian England* (London: Routledge and Kegan Paul, 1981), 150.
24. Elizabeth Bowen, "Shoes" (1929), in *Collected Stories*, 246.
25. See also Bowen, *Friends and Relations*, 129.
26. Elizabeth Bowen to Alan Cameron (Saturday 28 [April, 1923]), quoted in *The Mulberry Tree*, 196.
27. Elizabeth Bowen, "Human Habitation" (circa 1926), in *Collected Stories*, 148.
28. Elizabeth Bowen, "The Back Drawing-Room" (1926), in *Collected Stories*, 203, 204. The story first appeared in *Ann Lee's and Other Stories*; see Sellery and Harris, *Elizabeth Bowen*, 21, item A2.
29. Seán O'Faoláin, *The Irish*, 108.
30. Elizabeth Bowen, "The New House" (1923), in *Collected Stories*, 53.

Chapter 4

1. Bowen, Preface to *The Last September*, viii. Critical responses to *The Last September* have differed particularly on the novel's relationship to politics.

Hermione Lee believes, I think rightly, that the connection between politics and the story is less awkward in this novel than in *The Heat of the Day* (*Elizabeth Bowen*, 175). Others have noted the "hazy" aspect of war in the novel; see William Heath, *Elizabeth Bowen: An Introduction to Her Novels* (Madison: University of Wisconsin Press, 1961), 103; Richard Gill, "The Country House in a Time of Troubles," in *Elizabeth Bowen*, ed. Harold Bloom (New York: Chelsea House, 1987), 53. See also Phyllis Lassner, "The Past is a Burning Pattern: *The Last September*," in *Eire* 21 (Spring 1986). Gary T. Davenport argues in his article "Elizabeth Bowen and the Big House" that the book portrays the Irish Revolution as "the modern world's supreme trial of Anglo-Irish civilization" (*Southern Humanities Review* 8 [Winter 1974]: 32).

2. Terence Brown, *Ireland: A Social and Cultural History, 1922–1979* (London: Fontana, 1981), 110, 133 n. 5. The list reported in the *Morning Post* of April 9, 1923, is probably not even complete. See also Deane, *A Short History*, 207.

3. Brown, *Ireland*, 116: cf. Edith Somerville and Martin Ross, *The Big House of Inver* (London: Heinemann, 1925) and the 1926 play by Lennox Robinson, *The Big House* (London: Macmillan, 1926).

4. Brown, *Ireland*, 116.

5. Elizabeth Bowen to William Plomer (194[?]), Durham University Library.

6. Davenport maintains that the "real villainy" of the Anglo-Irish emerges in "Lady Naylor's betrayal of what Miss Bowen saw as the true character of the Anglo-Irish" ("Elizabeth Bowen," 31).

7. See Roger McHugh and Maurice Harmon, *A Short History of Anglo-Irish Literature* (Dublin: Wolfhound Press, 1982), 272.

8. William Butler Yeats, "Easter, 1916," in *The Poems: A New Edition*, ed. Richard J. Finneran (New York: Macmillan, 1983), 180.

9. For a further discussion of the Big House in *The Last September*, see Deirdre Laigle, "Images of the Big House in Elizabeth Bowen: *The Last September*," *Cahiers du Centre d'Etudes Irlandaises* 9 (1984): 61–80. Laigle describes Bowen as portraying the "Anglo-Irish as being clearly unaware that they represented not a power in themselves but a battleground between two opposing forces, and that the usual fate of battlegrounds was about to befall them" (77).

Chapter 5

1. The Burkean ideal of "a powerful and renovated traditionalism" informed her landowning project at Bowen's Court, according to Deane, *A Short History*, 35. Hermione Lee sees Bowen's inheritance from Burke as fourfold: From him she gleaned her ideas about the moral effects of property, the belief in benevolent imperialism, the reverence for tradition, and, finally, the primacy of private ownership (*Elizabeth Bowen*, 26).

2. Mark Bence-Jones, *Twilight of the Ascendancy* (London: Constable, 1987), 260.

3. Elizabeth Bowen, "Ireland Makes Irish," *Vogue*, August, 1946, 214.

4. Deane, *A Short History*, 204.

5. Although historians usually disagree over the exact instant that it occurred, they often identify the mid-to-late eighteenth century as the moment when the racial and class consciousness of the Anglo-Irish coalesced. See R. F. Foster, *Modern Ireland, 1600–1972* (London: Allen Lane/Penguin, 1988), 170. W. J. McCormack, in *Ascendancy and Tradition* dates it to the early 1790s; see introduction, 1–17.

6. Foster, *Modern Ireland*, 194.

7. Alfred Corn, "An Anglo-Irish Novelist," in *Elizabeth Bowen*, ed. Harold Bloom, 155. Virginia Woolf to Elizabeth Bowen, in *Recollections of Virginia Woolf*, ed. Joan Russell Noble (London: Peter Owen, 1972), 51.

8. Seán O'Faoláin, *The Vanishing Hero: Studies in Novelists of the Twenties* (Boston: Little, Brown, 1956), 147; "A Reading and Remembrance of Elizabeth Bowen," *London Review of Books* 4 (March, 1982): 15.

9. Elizabeth Bowen to Virginia Woolf, quoted in Quennell (London: Weidenfeld and Nicolson, 1982), 97.

10. Virginia Woolf, quoted in Elizabeth Bowen, BBC movie on Virginia Woolf, published in *Recollections of Virginia Woolf*, 48.

11. William Plomer to Elizabeth Bowen (October 6, 1938), 3, HRHRC.

12. Virginia Woolf, *The Diary of Virginia Woolf*, vol. 4 (1931–1935), ed. Anne Olivier Bell (March 24, 1932) (New York: Harcourt Brace Jovanovich, 1982), 187.

13. Woolf to Bowen, (Sunday [March 1939]), HRHRC.

14. Elizabeth Bowen, "Manners," review of book on the subject by Viola Tree, *New Statesman*, November 6, 1937, 728.

15. Anthony Powell, *To Keep the Ball Rolling: The Memoirs of Anthony Powell, Faces in My Time*, vol. 3 (London: Heinemann, 1980), 27.

16. Bowen, BBC broadcast, interview with John Bowen, William Craig, and W. N. Emer (September 11, 1959), 2, HRHRC.

17. Elizabeth Bowen, "Royal Academy" (1936), in *Collected Impressions*, 210; first printed in the *New Statesman*, May 9, 1936.

18. Elizabeth Bowen, "Sundays" (1942), reprinted in *Seven Winters*, 49.

19. Elizabeth Bowen, "Ireland" (post-April, 1948), 3, HRHRC.

20. Bowen to William Plomer (December 29, [no year given]), Durham University Library.

21. Bowen to William Plomer (June 5 [1930s]), Durham University Library.

22. Bowen, "Origins" (first published posthumously in 1975), in *Pictures and Conversations*, 23.

23. Bowen, "Ireland," 2.

24. Virginia Woolf, "The Artist and Politics" (1936), originally published as "Why Art To-Day Follows Politics" in the *Daily Worker*, reprinted in *The Moment and Other Essays*, 225.

25. See Hildebidle, *Five Irish Writers*, 96 and n. 5. He discusses Bowen's characters in the interwar years by applying Fussell's standards of judgment to them.

26. See Lee's excellent analysis of this story, "The Disinherited," in *Elizabeth Bowen*, 136–38, 147–49.

27. Elizabeth Bowen, "Maria" (1928), in *Collected Stories*, 408.

28. Powell writes in *Faces in My Time* that "1936 was indeed the last of the routine Intourist visits then in operation" (32).

29. A. Kingsley Weatherhead, in "Elizabeth Bowen: Writer in Residence" (*CEA Critic* 50 [Winter 1987–Summer 1988]), discusses the appropriateness of the name for the house as Emmeline's childhood home (38).

30. Cecilia, who is twenty-nine, Naomi thirty-nine, Ray thirty-six, and Julian thirty-five are all more or less Bowen's contemporaries.

31. Elizabeth Bowen, "A Walk in the Woods" (1937), in *Collected Stories*, 489; Elizabeth Bowen, "Attractive Modern Homes" (1936), in *Collected Stories*, 523, 521.

32. Elizabeth Bowen, "The Last Night in the Old Home" (1934), in *Collected Stories*.

33. See Sellery and Harris, *Elizabeth Bowen*, 135, item C81, on this change. The story was then reprinted in *Look at All Those Roses*.

34. Elizabeth Bowen, review of *Between the Acts*, by Virginia Woolf, *New Statesman and Nation* 22 (July, 1941): 63.

35. See Zwerdling, *Virginia Woolf and the Real World*, for a discussion of Woolf's connections of the inner and outer worlds (25, 174–175) and also on the composition of *Between the Acts* (302); Virginia Woolf, *Between the Acts* (1941; reprint, New York: Harcourt Brace Jovanovich, 1969), 19.

36. Woolf, *Between the Acts*, 176, 178.

37. "Sunday Afternoon," a wartime short story, records the lament of a character who complains that in London everyone has a number instead of an identity.

38. Elizabeth Bowen, "Autobiographical Note," 4, HRHRC.

Chapter 6

1. John Lehmann, *In My Own Time* (1955; reprint, Boston: Little, Brown, 1969), 233; Connolly, *Journal and Memoir*, 288.

2. Woolf, *Diary*, vol. 5 (September 30, 1938), 177; (January 29, 1939), 202; (August 28, 1939), 231.

3. Elizabeth Bowen, quoted in Glendinning, *Elizabeth Bowen*, 128.

4. Vere Hodgson, *Few Eggs and No Oranges* (May 11, 1941) (London: Dennis Dobson, 1976), 151.

5. Lehmann, *In My Own Time*, 227; *Thrown to the Woolfs* (London: Weidenfeld and Nicolson, 1978), 81.

6. Woolf, *Diary*, vol. 5 (September 6, 1939), 235.

7. Evelyn Waugh, *The Diaries of Evelyn Waugh*, ed. Michael Davie (All Saints Day, 1939) (Boston: Little, Brown, and Co., 1976), 448–49.

8. Woolf, *Diary*, vol. 5 (August 31, 1940), 313–14.

9. Lehmann, *In My Own Time* (September 3, 1940), 265; quoting his own letter to Isherwood, written in the fall of 1940, in *Thrown to the Woolfs* (85).

10. Hodgson, *Few Eggs* (May 21, 1941), 154; (June 15, 1941), 159.

11. Lehmann, *In My Own Time*, 343, 391.

12. Woolf, "The Artist and Politics," 225–28.
13. Waugh, *Diaries* (August 29, 1943), 548.
14. W. J. Bate, *The Burden of the Past and the English Poet* (Cambridge: Harvard Belknap Press, 1970), viii.
15. Connolly, "Writers and Society, 1940–1943," 131.
16. Fussell, *Wartime*, 132.
17. Lehmann, *Thrown to the Woolfs*, 81, 90.
18. In 1937, 17,137 books appeared; by 1939 that number had dropped to 14,094. In 1945, however, only 6,747 books came out. By December of 1941 the publishers' paper quota was only 31.5 percent of their prewar consumption. The losses of books as a direct result of the bombings were even more dramatic; by October, 1941, attacks had ruined twenty million volumes of publishers' stocks (see Hewison, *Under Siege*, 177–78). See also Alan Munton, *English Fiction of the Second World War* (London: Faber and Faber, 1989); Fussell, *Wartime*, 214–15.
19. Fussell, *Wartime*, 228–29; he writes that James and Trollope provided "counterweights to wartime utilitarianism and vulgarity of mind." Fussell also concludes that "some readers went in search of past eccentric personalities as a way of opposing anonymity and uniformity, as well as offsetting the obedient, goody-goody character the war had proposed as desirable" (229–30). This assessment can also be applied to the readers of *Bowen's Court* and other such autobiographies.
20. Norman Longmate, *How We Lived Then: A History of Everyday Life during the Second World War* (London: Hutchinson and Co., 1971), 442–47; Fussell, *Wartime*, 229.
21. Lehmann, *Thrown to the Woolfs*, 85.
22. Longmate, *How We Lived Then*, 447.
23. Waugh, *Diaries* (September 23, 1943), 549.
24. Fussell, *Wartime*, 239–42.
25. Longmate, *How We Lived Then*, 442.
26. Powell, *Faces in My Time*, 147.
27. Longmate, *How We Lived Then*, 447.
28. Connolly, *Journal and Memoir*, 287; Michael Shelden, *Friends of Promise: Cyril Connolly and the World of Horizon* (London: Hamish Hamilton, 1989), 2.
29. David Pryce-Jones, ed. *Evelyn Waugh and His World* (London: Weidenfeld and Nicolson, 1973), 287; Fussell, *Wartime*, 210.
30. Woolf, *Diary*, vol. 5 (December 16, 1939), 251.
31. To read its tables of contents (120 issues were published until January, 1950) is to scan the lists of some of the greatest intellectual and artistic figures of the age, such as Hesse, Russell, Gide, Sartre, Koestler, Huxley, Forster, Eliot, Wells, Greene, O'Faolain, MacNeice, Day Lewis, and Bowen. For more on this, see Fussell, *Wartime*, 216–18; see also Shelden, *Friends of Promise*, 1.
32. Shelden, *Friends of Promise*, 1.
33. Connolly, Introduction to *The Golden Horizon*, ed. Cyril Connolly (London: Weidenfeld and Nicolson, 1953), xiii, ix.
34. Fussell, in *Wartime*, surmises that "when peace came . . . *Hori-*

zon's . . . compensations [were] no longer so desperately needed" (219); Connolly, Introduction to *Golden Horizon*, x.

35. Lehmann, *Thrown to the Woolfs*, 95, 96.
36. Ronald Blythe, Introduction to *Components of the Scene*, 20.
37. Lehmann, *Thrown to the Woolfs*, 126.
38. "Compared with *Horizon* which could seem precious, remote, and merely aesthetic, *Penguin New Writing* appeared 'committed'—to the reality of the active life, to the necessity of politics in all its vulgarity, and to the redemption of postwar life by new imperatives of fairness and decency" (Fussell, *Wartime*, 244).
39. Waugh, *Diaries* (October 17, 1939), 446.
40. Woolf, *Diary*, vol. 5 (October 22, 1939), 242.
41. Lehmann, *In My Own Time*, 235.
42. Peter Lewis, *A People's War* (London: Thames Methuen, 1986), 55.
43. Fussell, *Wartime*, 148.
44. Hodgson, *Few Eggs*, 421.
45. Lehmann, *Thrown to the Woolfs*, 84.
46. Woolf, *Diary*, vol. 5 (August 28, 1940), 313.
47. Waugh, *Diaries* (June 24, 1944), 568.
48. Woolf, *Diary*, vol. 5 (August 28, 1940), 313.
49. Greene's journal entry is quoted in Humphrey Carpenter, *The Brideshead Generation* (Boston: Houghton Mifflin, 1990), 338.
50. Hodgson, *Few Eggs* (January 8, 1941), 105; (January 19, 1941), 109.
51. Hodgson, *Few Eggs* (February 22, 1943), 248.
52. Lehmann, *Thrown to the Woolfs*, 129.
53. Lewis, *A People's War*, 20.
54. Connolly, "Writers and Society," 123–51, 131, 123; *Horizon* 5 (January, 1942): 11.
55. Hodgson, *Few Eggs* (August 14, 1940), 45.
56. Lehmann, *Thrown to the Woolfs*, 91.
57. Lewis, *A People's War*, 49, 65.
58. Lewis, *A People's War*, 105, 107.
59. Lehmann, *In My Own Time*, 300, 366.
60. Waugh, *Diaries* (October 28, 1942), 530.
61. Waugh, *Diaries* (May 15, 1943), 536.
62. Lewis, *A People's War*, 215.
63. Lehmann, *In My Own Time*, 385.
64. Vera Brittain, *Diary, 1939–1945: Wartime Chronicle*, ed. Alan Bishop and Y. Aleksandra Bennett (June 23, 1944) (London: Gollancz, 1989), 251.
65. Lehmann, *In My Own Time* (Summer 1944), 376.
66. Lewis, *A People's War*, 219.
67. Brittain, *Wartime Chronicle* (April 3, 1945), 261.
68. Woolf, *Diaries*, vol. 5 (December 19, 1940), 344–45.
69. Lewis, *A People's War*, 168, 158.
70. Lewis, *A People's War*, 123, 178–80.

71. Bowen, Preface to *Ivy Gripped the Steps,* viii; "Autobiographical Note," 4, HRHRC.

72. Bowen, Introduction to *Pictures and Conversations,* xviii. See Angus Calder, *The People's War* (New York: Pantheon, 1969), for the job description of an air raid warden. One-sixth of them were women (226–27). By 1943 almost no woman under forty could avoid war work unless she had pressing family obligations (383). Bowen, "Autobiographical Note," 2, HRHRC.

73. Lewis, *A People's War,* 140, 141.

74. Lewis, *A People's War,* 116, 113; Munton, *English Fiction,* 28–29.

75. Harold C. Smith, "The Effect of War on the Status of Women," in *War and Social Change* (Manchester, England: Manchester University Press, 1986). To clarify further, Smith notes that "virtually all able-bodied single women between the ages of eighteen and forty (90%), as well as 80% of those in this age group who were married but had no children, were involved in the war effort" (211, 209).

76. Penny Summerfield, "Women, War, and Social Change: Women in Britain in World War Two," in *Total War and Social Change,* ed. Arthur Marwick (London: Macmillan, 1988), 110. See also Denise Riley, *War in the Nursery: Theories of the Child and the Mother* (London: Virago Press, 1982).

77. Elizabeth Bowen, "Britain in Autumn" (1950), 10, HRHRC.

78. Harold Nicolson to Vita Sackville-West (December 9, 1942), *Letters and Diaries,* vol. 2, ed. Nigel Nicolson (New York: Atheneum, 1967), 265.

79. Bowen, quoted in Glendinning, *Elizabeth Bowen,* 133.

80. Stephen Spender, *The Thirties and After* (New York: Random House, 1967), 68.

81. Elizabeth Bowen to Noreen Colley (Mrs. Gilbert Butler) (September 24, 1940), quoted in Glendinning, *Elizabeth Bowen,* 128; Preface to *Ivy Gripped the Steps,* x.

82. Charles Ritchie, *The Siren Years: Undiplomatic Diaries, 1937–1945* (July 20, 1944) (London: Macmillan, 1974), 176.

83. Lehmann, *In My Own Time,* 321.

84. Evelyn Waugh, *Put Out More Flags* (1942; reprint, Boston: Little, Brown, 1970), 136.

85. Bowen to Woolf (July 1, 1940), University of Sussex; reprinted in *The Mulberry Tree,* 214–216.

86. John A. Murphy, *Ireland in the Twentieth-Century* (Dublin: Gill and Macmillan, 1975), 101.

87. Trevor C. Salmon, *Unneutral Ireland: An Ambivalent and Unique Security Policy* (Oxford: Clarendon, 1989), 151–53.

88. Salmon, *Unneutral Ireland,* 145, 146, 137.

89. Terence Brown, *Ireland: A Social and Cultural History, 1922–1979* (London: Fontana, 1981), 175.

90. Peter Connolly, *Literature and the Changing Ireland* (Totowa, N.J.: Barnes and Noble, 1982), 173, 175.

91. Connolly, *Horizon* 5 (January, 1942): 7.

92. Bowen to Woolf (July 1, 1940), in *The Mulberry Tree*, 214–16; (January 5, 1941), 218

93. In *In Time of War: Ireland, Ulster and the Price of Neutrality: 1939–1945* (Philadelphia: University of Pennsylvania Press, 1983), Robert Fisk quotes extensively from Bowen's report, which can be found under the file at the Public Records Office (PRO) entitled FO 800/310, Mrs. Cameron. Hereafter this report is cited in the text as PRO. Apart from mentioning the fact that Bowen did engage in this work, literary scholars have not discussed the contents of the report in any detail. R. F. Foster (*Modern Ireland*) notes that in Ireland there existed a form of "pro-British neutrality . . . secret intelligence and strategic liaisons were made with Britain and the United States, not often realized at the time or since" (560).

94. *Irish Times*, March 24, 1975, 9; Mollie Panter-Downes, *London War Notes*, ed. William Shawn (New York: Farrar, Straus and Giroux, 1971), 115–16.

95. Bowen to William Plomer (September 24, [1940]), Durham University Library.

96. Lee notes Bowen's Burkean belief in an "enlightened imperialism," which I believe governs her philosophy here (*Elizabeth Bowen*, 23).

97. See Carpenter, *Brideshead Generation*, 338.

98. Lehmann, *In My Own Time*, 324.

99. Elizabeth Bowen, "Eire," *New Statesman and Nation* 22 (April, 1941): 383. In what can be seen as her own partial attempt to come to terms with the Gaelic name for southern Ireland, Bowen omitted the accent above the *E*.

100. Bernard Share, *The Emergency: Neutral Ireland, 1939–1945* (Dublin: Gill and Macmillan, 1978), 139. Share has written of Bowen's role as being one of "sounding out opinion." According to him, one of the problems "besetting spies in Ireland was that there was very little to spy on" (139).

101. Foster, *Modern Ireland*, 561.

102. Connolly, *Literature and the Changing Ireland*, 115–16.

103. Murphy, *Ireland*, 100.

104. See Fisk, *In Time of War*, 366.

105. Connolly, *Literature and the Changing Ireland*, 93.

106. Financial Records for Elizabeth Bowen, Curtis Brown Statement, HRHRC. The record for 1944–45 showed that the Ministry of Information paid her 115 pounds and 10 shillings for her work.

107. Bowen to Woolf (February 18, 1941), *The Mulberry Tree*, 219–20.

108. Cranborne to Halifax (November 25, 1940), PRO FO 800/310.

109. Hodgson, *Few Eggs* (May 16, 1945), 474.

110. Brittain, *Wartime Chronicle* (May 8, 1945), 265.

111. Lehmann, *In My Own Time*, 391.

112. Elizabeth Bowen to Charles Ritchie, quoted in Glendinning, *Elizabeth Bowen*, 155, 157

113. Powell, *Faces in My Time*, 181.

114. Waugh, *Diaries* (May 6, 1945), 627; (March 31, 1945), 623; (April 13, 1945), 625.

115. Waugh, *Diaries* (July 1, 1945), 628.

116. "There are additional ways in which *Brideshead Revisited* constitutes a compensatory fantasy of no-war" (Fussell, *Wartime,* 223). Humphrey Carpenter notes that *Unquiet Grave* and *Brideshead Revisited* share some characteristics in their "evocation of lushness in wartime austerity, a lament for lost loves, and a fear of what was to come in peacetime" (*Brideshead Generation,* 375).

Chapter 7

1. Woolf to Bowen, *Letters,* vol. 5 (May 1, 1934), 298.
2. Woolf to Vanessa Bell, *Letters,* vol. 5 (May 4 [May 3, 1934]) 299–300.
3. Woolf, *Diary,* vol. 4 (April 30, 1934), 210–11.
4. Seán O'Faoláin to Elizabeth Bowen (April 22, 1937), HRHRC.
5. Elizabeth Bowen, "Grace," Review of *Unforgotten Years,* by Logan Pearsall Smith (1938), reprinted in Elizabeth Bowen, *Collected Impressions* (London: Longmans, Green, 1950), 130.
6. John Lehmann, *I Am My Brother* (New York: Reynal, 1960), 32; J. B. Priestley (September 29, *1940*), in *Postscripts,* 1940 (London: Heinemann, 1940), 81. John Hayward, *Prose Literature since 1939* (London: Longmans, Green, 1947) discusses the popularity of autobiography: "The crystallized past [is] so much more transpicuous than the turbulent present." Hayward lists the following contemporaneous authors of autobiography: Lord Berner, Sir John Buchan, Cyril Connolly, Sean O'Casey, William Plomer, Sir Herbert Read, Siegfried Sassoon, Sir Osbert Sitwell (Ommanney), Enid Starkie, Desmond Welch (24, 25).
7. Edmund Burke, *Reflections on the Revolution in France* (1790; reprint, New York: Anchor Books, 1973), 153.
8. As Samuel Hynes has pointed out in *The Auden Generation: Literature and Politics in England in the 1930s* (London: Bodley Head, 1976), other writers turned to autobiography in this time of turmoil. He discusses Cyril Connolly, Christopher Isherwood, and Edward Upward, but he does not mention Bowen (322).
9. Sir Osbert Sitwell, Introduction to *Left Hand, Right Hand!* vol. 1 (London: Macmillan, 1949), v.
10. Woolf, *Diary,* vol. 5 (June 29, 1939), 222.
11. Brittain, *Wartime Chronicle* (November 30, 1939), 36–37.
12. Howard Moss wrote in his obituary on Elizabeth Bowen that, of all the arts, architecture meant the most to her ("Obituary," *New York Times Book Review,* [April 8, 1973], 2–3).
13. See Elizabeth Bowen, "Weeping Earl," Review of *The Great O'Neill,* by Seán O'Faoláin, reprinted in *Collected Impressions,* on the "extra-Europeanism of Ireland, the lack of common memories based on Roman Rule, that has been and still may be found repugnant" (170). Terence Brown recognizes "a recurrent intellectual motif in the writings of Irish Ireland's thinkers [that] is the provision of historical accounts of Ireland's European uniqueness" (*Ireland,* 68).
14. Elizabeth Bowen, "The Big House" (1940), reprinted in *The Mulberry Tree,* 27. Hereafter this essay will be referred to in the text as "Big House."

15. Elizabeth Bowen, "This Unhappy Autumn," Review of *Overtures to Death*, by C. Day Lewis, *Now and Then* 61 (Winter 1938): 32; "Out of a Book" (1946), reprinted in *The Mulberry Tree*, 53.

16. Bowen, "Autobiography," in *Seven Winters*, 70. In the same essay she refers to autobiography as "artist's work" (75); "Anthony Trollope—A New Judgement" (1945), in *The Mulberry Tree*, 244. The narrator attributes Trollope's wartime appeal to his ability to "hold up a mirror" to the past (245).

17. Burke, *Reflections*, 45, 184.

18. Bowen to Woolf (July 1, 1940), University of Sussex, 1; also reprinted in *The Mulberry Tree*, 214–16.

19. Virginia Woolf, "The Leaning Tower," in *The Moment and Other Essays*, 158, 140.

20. Bowen to Woolf (July 1, 1940).

21. Bowen to Woolf (July 1, 1940).

22. Woolf, *Diary*, vol. 5, (February 11, 1940), 266–67.

23. Elizabeth Bowen, "Uncle Silas," Introduction to *Uncle Silas*, by Sheridan Le Fanu (1948), reprinted in *The Mulberry Tree*, 101. Le Fanu (1814–73) was an Irish Gothic writer whom Seamus Deane has described as feeling "increasingly excluded from Ireland by the triumphs of O'Connell, by Emancipation, the Tithe War of the early thirties, the Famine, the rise of Fenianism" (*A Short History*, 100). Hermione Lee calls this review "Elizabeth Bowen's outstanding critical essay" (*The Mulberry Tree*, 94). In general, Lee has written the best studies of Bowen's autobiographical works; see especially her introduction to the Virago edition of *Bowen's Court and Seven Winters* (London: Virago Press, 1984).

24. L. P. Hartley, Review of *Bowen's Court*, in *Sketch* 197 (July, 1942): 78. Edward Sackville-West wrote in "Interim Epitaph": "One can overdo the pathos apparent in the spectacle of this sensitive, brilliantly intelligent woman, the last of a once-teeming race, writing alone in that remote, half-empty house, while the leaves fall across the rain outside the tall windows. The picture is tempting, and Miss Bowen does a good deal towards evoking it. But the truth, one feels, lies elsewhere" (*New Statesman*, July 25, 1942, 63).

25. Bowen, "The Bend Back," reprinted in *The Mulberry Tree*, 57.

26. Elizabeth Bowen, "The Moores," review of *The Moores of Moore Hall*, by Joseph Hone, *New Statesman*, November, 25, 1939, 759–60; reprinted in *The Mulberry Tree*, 151.

27. Bowen, "Britain in Autumn" (1950), 9–10, HRHRC. Graham Greene copied this verse, which Stephen Spender wrote in 1938, into his commonplace book of the time: "We who live under the shadow of a war,/ What can we do that matters?" ("While Waiting for a War," *Granta* 17 [Autumn 1985]: 13).

28. Bowen, "Horse Shoe," *Seven Winters*, 24; "Brass Plates," in *Seven Winters*, 33; "The Bend Back," 56.

29. Although Bowen originally titled her essay about Sarah Barry, the loyal housekeeper of Bowen's Court, "Tipperary Woman," in revising it for a larger audience she called it "The Most Unforgettable Character I've Met."

30. See Glendinning, *Elizabeth Bowen*, 180.

31. The Bellman, "Meet Elizabeth Bowen," interview in the *Bell* 4 (September, 1942): 425, 426.

32. Fussell, "Writing in Wartime: The Uses of Innocence," in *Thank God for the Atom Bomb*, 67–68. He writes, "And I would propose further that his presence and mission were not unknown to the Canadian William Stephenson (the celebrated 'man called intrepid'), who managed the New York office of the bureau mock-innocently designated 'British Security Co-Ordination'" (68). In describing the publishing scene at Harcourt Brace, Fussell writes that "one informant has declared the atmosphere [there] was that of 'an unofficial pro-allied propaganda organization'" (72).

33. Hayward to Morley (June, 1942), King's College Library, Cambridge.

34. Hayward to Morley (September, 1939); (June, 1942).

35. Virginia Woolf, *Three Guineas*, 54–55.

36. Michael Kenneally, "The Autobiographical Imagination and Irish Literary Autobiographies," in *Critical Approaches to Anglo-Irish Literature*, ed. Michael Allen and Angela Wilcox (Gerrards Cross, Buckinghamshire: Colin Smythe, 1989). Kenneally notes that the Irish autobiographical style "stems from an inordinate concern with place, not so much in the sense of private memories associated with the location which is endemic to the genre, but with the sense of historical and mythical place. In Anglo-Irish autobiographies, this concern manifests itself in a stress on familial connections with the land"—in works by such writers as George Moore, William Butler Yeats, and Elizabeth Bowen (126).

37. Bowen, "Autobiographical Note," 5, HRHRC.

38. William Butler Yeats, "Coole and Ballylee, 1931," in *The Poems: A New Edition*, 244.

39. As late as 1952, Bowen believed that the Ascendancy could "be maintained" "only by character" (Elizabeth Bowen, review of *The Anglo-Irish*, by Brian Fitzgerald, the *Observer*, [November 16, 1952], reprinted in *The Mulberry Tree*, 175). In his review of *Bowen's Court* D. A. Binchy wrote that the "tragedy of the Anglo-Irish is that in England they were regarded as Irish because they had ceased to be English, and at home they were still regarded as English because they had not become Irish" (*Bell* 4 [August 1942]: 370).

40. Bowen, "The Moores," 151.

41. T. R. Henn in "The Big House" sees these houses as having given "singularly little to the literary and artistic production of the last hundred years." He dates the decline of the Anglo-Irish as beginning with the Act of Union in 1800 (*Last Essays*, 218). In discussing the appeal of these houses, Humphrey Carpenter wrote, "In his unfinished novel, *Work Suspended*, written in 1939, Waugh suggests that his generation's enthusiasm for the architecture of the country house was a substitute for more common kinds of aesthetic emotion" (*Brideshead Generation*, 295).

42. Elizabeth Bowen, "Confessions," in *The Saturday Book*, ed. Leonard Russell (London: Hutchinson, 1949), 109.

43. Kenneally isolates the "anecdotal approach to the narrative" common to Irish autobiographies. He also points out that the "Irish literary tradition [has

a] marked propensity for hyperbole, the fantastic, the episodic narrative, for invective and vituperation and linguistic self-indulgence, for all manner of word play and verbal high jinks" ("Autobiographical Imagination," 127, 129).

44. It is noteworthy that Bowen pinpoints this occurrence as happening so much later than modern historians of the Anglo-Irish do.

45. Woolf, *Three Guineas*, 189.

46. Bowen's comments bear out Seamus Deane's belief that, after the union, the Anglo-Irish "security had been bought by the Ascendancy at the expense of integrity." He views Catholic Emancipation (won in 1829) as the ultimate "price paid for union" (Deane, *A Short History*, 68, 91).

47. Richard Gill, *Happy Rural Seat: The English Country House and the Literary Imagination* (New Haven, Conn.: Yale University Press, 1972), 184. Antoinette Quinn perceives that Bowen wrote *Bowen's Court* as "an act of self-definition as well as ancestral piety ... [which] was also significant in that it involved coming to terms with her Anglo-Irishness at a time when Anglo-Ireland itself was undergoing a severe identity crisis" ("Elizabeth Bowen's Irish Stories: 1939–1945," in *Studies in Anglo-Irish Literature*, ed. Heinz Kosok [Bonn: Bouvier, 1982], 315).

48. Lee, Introduction to *The Mulberry Tree*, 4.

49. Burke, *Reflections*, 46.

50. Elizabeth Bowen, "Hamilton Rowan," review of *The Desire to Please*, by Harold Nicolson (1943), reprinted in *Collected Impressions*, 166. James Gindin refers to Bowen's use of history and generations as a concern "with the changes in and transmissions of ethical values from one generation to another" ("Ethical Structures in John Galsworthy, Elizabeth Bowen, and Iris Murdoch," *Forms of Modern British Fiction*, ed. Alan Warren Friedman [Austin: University of Texas Press, 1975], 30).

51. Elizabeth Bowen, "Origins," in *Pictures and Conversations*, 26–27.

52. Bowen to Woolf (January 5, 1941), University of Sussex library, reprinted in *The Mulberry Tree*, 217–18.

53. R. F. Foster, *Modern Ireland*, 194.

54. Elizabeth Bowen, "Doubtful Subject," review of *Irish Life in the Seventeenth Century*, by Edward MacLysaght; *The Sword of Light*, by Desmond Ryan; and *Irish Cavalcade*, by M. J. MacManus (1939) in *Collected Impressions*, 173. In *Elizabeth Bowen*, Hermione Lee explains that *Bowen's Court* is not written from a "self-indulgent perspective" but, rather, forms a "rational account of Irish politics from a localized Anglo-Irish viewpoint." Lee identifies the central mood of the book as one that "defines the historical nature of loss" (18, 157).

Chapter 8

1. Elizabeth Bowen to Alan Cameron ([April] 28 [1923]), reprinted in *The Mulberry Tree*, 196.

2. Elizabeth Bowen, "The Short Story in England" (1945), 5, 4, 7, HRHRC.

3. Bowen, Preface to *Ivy Gripped the Steps*, viii. For discussion of Bowen's

excellence as a short story writer, see *Elizabeth Bowen's Irish Stories*, ed. Victoria Glendinning (Dublin: Poolbeg Press, 1978), 7. Hermione Lee notes that, in the short stories, Bowen's "careful effects, her mannered emphases, her exact detailing of atmosphere, and the disconcerting suggestiveness produced by these techniques are most accurately and resonantly employed" (*Elizabeth Bowen*, 129). Patricia Craig and Mary Cadogan speak of the stories in *The Demon Lover* as having a "tension, the immediate, dislocating tension of war, [which] has been suppressed or interrupted by another, more personal, obsessional stress or access of feeling" (*Women and Children First: The Fiction of Two World Wars* [London: Gollancz, 1978], 201). See also Margaret Church's essay, "Social Consciousness in the Works of Elizabeth Bowen, Iris Murdoch, and Mary Lavin," *College Literature* 7 (Spring 1980): 158–63.

4. Bowen, BBC broadcast, Interview with John Bowen, William Craig, and W. N. Ewer (September 11, 1959), 9, HRHRC.

5. Bowen, "Autobiographical Note," 4, HRHRC.

6. Glendinning, *Elizabeth Bowen*, 149.

7. Bowen, Preface to *Ivy*, x.

8. Reed, *The Novel since 1939*, 21.

9. Bowen published ten short stories after the war: "Gone Away" (1946), "I Died of Love" (1946), "The Light in the Dark" (1950), "So Much Depends" (1951), "Hand in Glove" (1952), "Emergency in the Gothic Wing" (1954), "The Claimant" (1955), "A Day in the Dark" (1955), "Candles in the Window" (1958), and "Happiness" (1959). In addition, the HRHRC collections include a number of other undated and unpublished stories and fragments. For a complete listing, see Sellery and Harris, *Elizabeth Bowen*, under E: Unpublished Writings.

10. Bowen, review of *In My Good Books*, by V. S. Pritchett, 158.

11. Elizabeth Bowen, Preface to *A Day in the Dark and Other Stories* (London: Jonathan Cape, 1965), 7; "Rx for a Story" (1958), reprinted in *Opinions and Perspectives from the New York Times Book Review*, ed. Francis Brown (Boston: Houghton Mifflin, 1964), 234.

12. Elizabeth Bowen, Preface to *The Faber Book of Modern Short Stories* (1936) in *Collected Impressions*, 38.

13. Bowen to Plomer (August 17 [n.y.]), Durham University Library.

14. Elizabeth Bowen, "The Poetic Element in Fiction" (December 22, 1950), 8, HRHRC. V. S. Pritchett referred to Bowen as a "dispossessed poet" ("The Future of Fiction" in *New Writing and Daylight* 7 [1946]: 75). Bowen once said that her favorite comment about her work was that she was a "muffled poet" ("Miss Bowen on Miss Bowen," 33). In the preface to a new edition of *Encounters* in 1949, she described herself in those early years as a *poet manquée* (*Encounters* [reprint; 1949, London: Ace Books, 1961], 9). Stephen Spender corroborates her desire in his review of *Look at All Those Roses* where he claims that her subject is "poetry." For Spender, Bowen's focus on "imaginative sympathy" diverts her from paying the attention he felt necessary to facts about the characters and their incomes ("Books and the War: The Short Story Today," *Penguin New Writing* 5 [April, 1941]: 140, 142).

15. Elizabeth Bowen, Preface to *Faber Book of Modern Short Stories*, 43.

Bowen also engaged in other critical work on the short stories in the 1930s, such as her review of *The Best Short Stories of 1936: English and American,* ed. Edward O'Brien, in *New Statesman,* December 5, 1936, 938–39. After I wrote this section I discovered a review of *Look at All Those Roses* by Desmond Hawkins, which appeared in the *New Statesman* on February 8, 1941. He points to the connection between the short story and poetry, particularly the lyric, and speculates on the meaning behind these links: "The short story in the same period is perhaps more numerously and variously successful than it has ever been. . . . I don't profess to know the reason, but my guess would be that contemporary literature—when it is not merely ideological—is dominated by its poets; and the short story is as near poetry as fiction can get. It is capable of a comparably great compression; and its total gesture, its meaning, is not rendered solely in terms of narrated drama or of explicit ideas, but in the elusive quality of 'tone.' . . . What the modern short story has achieved is a prose equivalent to that sort of lyric poem [Blake's poem 'I told my Love']." Hawkins calls Bowen's collection "an impressive achievement" and points to her "blending [of] a tenderly malicious wit with an unexpected intimation of remote horror (incidentally, not unlike Auden) in some of her stories from the thirties such as 'Attractive Modern Homes'" (*New Statesman,* February 8, 1941, 144–45). Clare Hanson writes that the short story "mediates between the lyric poem and the novel" ("The Free Story," *Short Story and Short Fictions* [New York: Macmillan, 1985], 9).

16. Elizabeth Bowen, "Why Do I Write?" reprinted in *The Mulberry Tree,* 228.

17. Elizabeth Bowen, "Notes for Lectures at Vassar College on Short Story," notebook 1 (March 24, 1960), 29; (February 11, 1960), 4, HRHRC.

18. Elizabeth Bowen, quoting Flaubert, in "The Flaubert Omnibus" (1947), reprinted in *Collected Impressions,* 34; interview with Charles Monaghan, "Elizabeth Bowen," 6.

19. Bowen, Preface to *Stories by Elizabeth Bowen,* 180.

20. Bowen, Preface to *Ivy,* ix.

21. Sebastian Knowles writes that, "for writers during the war itself, the ghosts result from the appalling proximity of the other world" (*A Purgatorial Flame,* 30).

22. Elizabeth Bowen, Preface to *A Day in the Dark and Other Stories,* 9.

23. Eudora Welty, "Seventy-nine Stories to Read Again," review of *The Collected Stories of Elizabeth Bowen, New York Times Book Review,* February 8, 1981, 22.

24. Elizabeth Bowen, Preface to *Ivy,* xii; Introduction to *The Second Ghost Book,* ed. Lady Cynthia Asquith (1952), reprinted in *Seven Winters,* 208.

25. Bowen, Preface to *Ivy,* xii; Review of *In My Good Books,* by V. S. Pritchett, 158.

26. Wallace Stevens, "Imagination as Value," in *The Necessary Angel* (New York: Alfred A. Knopf, 1951), 153.

27. See Daniel V. Fraustino, "Elizabeth Bowen's 'The Demon Lover': Psychosis or Seduction?" *Studies in Short Fiction* 17 (Fall 1980): 483–87; and

Douglas A. Hughes, "Cracks in the Psyche: Elizabeth Bowen's 'Demon Lover,'" *Studies in Short Fiction* 10 (Fall 1973): 411–13. Hughes's article, the more useful of the two, examines the potential ambiguity of the story: Is the lover a demon, or is Mrs. Drover a lover of demons?

28. See Hughes, "Cracks in the Psyche," 411. He argues that the war is the demon but then deflates his own argument by stating that Mrs. Drover is "obviously mentally disturbed" (413).

29. Elizabeth Bowen, "The Demon Lover," in *Collected Stories*, 661. Hereafter this collection is referred to as *CS*.

30. Sandra M. Gilbert and Susan Gubar argue that "The Demon Lover" "analyzes male willfulness by describing a woman's futile efforts to flee the terrifying advances of the dead lover with whom she had plighted a 'sinister troth' and who has returned from the grave to assert his claim on her" (*No Man's Land: The Place of the Woman Writer in the Twentieth Century* [New Haven, Conn.: Yale University Press, 1988], 112–13).

31. Wallace Stevens, "The Noble Rider and the Sound of Words," in *The Necessary Angel*, 36.

32. Elizabeth Bowen, Review of stories by Maksim Gorky (1939), reprinted in *Collected Impressions*, 153.

33. Bowen, Preface to *Ivy*, viii.

34. Elizabeth Bowen, "The Poetic Element in Fiction," 7, HRHRC.

35. Bowen, "Notes for Lectures," notebook 2, (undated), HRHRC. In "'There is No Elsewhere': Elizabeth Bowen's Perception of War," Jeslyn Medoff discusses Bowen's choice of subject for her wartime stories (*Modern Fiction Studies* 30 [Spring 1984]: 73–81).

36. Tom Harrisson, in an article entitled "War Books," follows the same impulse. He claims that since "the war has taken the whole stage in every country and in every life . . . it is harder to write large" (*Horizon* 4 [December, 1941]: 416–37).

37. Bowen, Preface to *Ivy*, xiv.

38. Bowen, Preface to *Ivy*, viii, xii, viii.

39. Bowen, "Anthony Trollope," 242.

40. Bowen to Woolf (August 26 [1935]), Henry W. and Albert A. Berg Collection, New York Public Library, Astor, Lenox and Tilden Foundations; also reprinted in *The Mulberry Tree*, 212–14. As Eudora Welty has noted in reviewing *The Collected Stories of Elizabeth Bowen*, Bowen's "awareness of place, of *where she was*, seemed to approach the seismic" ("Seventy-nine Stories to Read Again," 3).

41. Elizabeth Bowen, "London, 1940," reprinted in *The Mulberry Tree*, 24, 9. This essay was also reprinted in *Collected Impressions*. An expanded version of this essay entitled "Britain in Autumn," dated April 24, 1950, can be found at HRHRC.

42. Bowen, Preface to *Ivy*, ix. Cyril Connolly selected this story for *Horizon Stories* (London: Faber and Faber, 1947), 112.

43. Elizabeth Bowen, "In the Square," in *Collected Stories*, 609.

44. Bowen to Woolf (January 5, 1941), University of Sussex, also reprinted in *The Mulberry Tree*, 216–18.
45. Bowen, Preface to *Ivy*, viii.
46. Mollie Panter-Downes (January 4, 1941), in *London War-Notes*, 128.
47. See Calder, *The People's War*, 400. George Orwell, in his column of August 4, 1944, in the *Tribune*, discusses the ramifications of the return of some of the railings that began later in the war: "So the lawful denizens of the squares can make use of their treasured keys again and the children of the poor can be kept out" (*As I Please*, vol. 3 [1943–45] [London: Secker and Warburg, 1968], 200).
48. Rosamond Lehmann, "The Future of the Novel?" *Britain Today* 122 (June, 1946): 8.
49. Charles Ritchie, *The Siren Years: Undiplomatic Diaries* (February 10, 1941) (London: Macmillan, 1974), 88; (September 2, 1941), 115–16.
50. Elizabeth Bowen to Charles Ritchie, quoted in Glendinning, *Elizabeth Bowen*, 139.
51. Ritchie, *Siren Years* (November 19, 1941), 124.
52. Elizabeth Bowen, Preface to *Stories by Elizabeth Bowen*, 129–30.
53. H. Rider Haggard, *She: A History of Adventure* (1886; reprint, London: MacDonald, 1954), 143, 149.
54. Elizabeth Bowen, "Mysterious Kôr" in *Collected Stories*, 738.
55. Bowen, Preface to *A Day in the Dark*, 9.
56. Ritchie, *Siren Years* (August 12, 1944), 176; see also Glendinning, *Elizabeth Bowen*, 128.
57. Elizabeth Bowen, "The Happy Autumn Fields" (1944), in *Collected Stories*, 681, 672. In *Elizabeth Bowen*, Hermione Lee believes, I think wrongly, that this story provides the "only idyllic account" in Bowen's wartime stories (136). For another discussion of the story, see Brad Hooper, "Elizabeth Bowen's 'The Happy Autumn Fields': A Dream or Not," *Studies in Short Fiction* 21 (Spring 1984): 151–53.
58. Bowen, Preface to *Ivy*, xi.
59. Bowen to Woolf (January 5, 1941), University of Sussex library; reprinted in *The Mulberry Tree*, 216–17.
60. Bowen, Interview with the *Bell*, 425.
61. Elizabeth Bowen, in her preface to *A Day in the Dark and Other Stories* (1965) notes that, of the twenty stories in the volume, nine are from wartime (7).
62. Bowen, "Miss Bowen on Miss Bowen," 33; "Notes for Lectures," notebook 1, 35, HRHRC. In her article "Elizabeth Bowen's Irish Stories," Antoinette Quinn argues that World War II "provoked her [Bowen's] most sustained response to the tensions of her Anglo-Irish heritage" (315). In her introduction to *Elizabeth Bowen's Irish Stories* (from which she omits Bowen's first Irish story, "The Back Drawing-Room") Glendinning notes that it is surprising that there are so few Irish stories and that they "came so late" in Bowen's career. She postulates that Bowen's "vision of Ireland . . . [was] sharpened in middle life, perhaps because only then could she see it objectively" (5, 6).
63. V. S. Pritchett, "Elizabeth Bowen," *New Statesman*, March 9, 1973, 350.

64. Seán O'Faoláin, *The Short Story* (New York: Devin-Adair, 1951), 209.
65. Bowen, Preface to *Faber Book of Modern Short Stories*, reprinted in *Collected Impressions*, 40.
66. Quinn, "Elizabeth Bowen's Irish Stories," 317.
67. Bowen, "Eire," 31, 32.
68. Louise Bogan, review of *Look at All Those Roses*, *Nation*, October 25, 1941, 406.
69. Elizabeth Bowen, "Ireland" (written after the war), 7, HRHRC.
70. Bowen, "Sunday Afternoon" (1941), in *Collected Stories*, 616. "Sunday Afternoon" was published in both England and Ireland. It appeared in *Life and Letters Today* 30 (July, 1941): 45–55; and in the *Bell* 5 (October, 1942): 19–27. This issue of the *Bell* was advertised in the previous issue: "There is no lack of good short stories in Ireland. To prove it the October issue will be a special Short Story Number, with stories by Elizabeth Bowen, Elizabeth O'Connor, Maura Laverty, Frank O'Connor, D. S. G. Sullivan and. . . ."
71. Bowen, "Ireland," 7, HRHRC.
72. Quinn, "Elizabeth Bowen's Irish Stories," 317.
73. W. H. Auden, *Collected Poems* (New York: Random House, 1945), 98. Samuel Hynes suggests that the poem shows us that "no private world would be secure against the pressure of events"; see *The Auden Generation* (London: The Bodley Head, 1976), 133–34.
74. Bowen, "Eire," 33.
75. Elizabeth Bowen, "Summer Night" (1941), in *Collected Stories*, 599.
76. Elizabeth Bowen, review of *The Portable D. H. Lawrence*, ed. Diana Trilling (1947), reprinted in *Collected Impressions*, 158.
77. One in a series of characters named Emma, she seems an inversion or a contradiction of all that the Austen's Emma embodied—as though the world had been turned upside down.
78. Quinn infers that Queenie's "deafness symptomizes the malady of neutrality" ("Elizabeth Bowen's Irish Stories," 317).
79. "Clock," published in *Cornhill* 961 (January, 1944): 36–53; "Ivy" published in *Horizon* 12 (September, 1945): 23–29.
80. Bowen, Preface to *Ivy*, xii.
81. Elizabeth Bowen, "The Inherited Clock" (1944), in *Collected Stories*, 631.
82. According to Howard Moss, who wrote in an obituary that Bowen was a "master of English prose," every short story class should study the end of the introductory paragraph of "Ivy Gripped the Steps" ("Obituary," 3–4).
83. Bowen, Preface to *Stories By Elizabeth Bowen*, 129.
84. Bowen, "Ivy Gripped the Steps," 711, 686.
85. Bowen, Preface to *Ivy*, xii, ix. "The Cheery Soul," published in December, 1942, and "Green Holly," published in December, 1944, both examine the affronts of the war on the Christmas season, which Bowen evoked so poignantly in *Bowen's Court*.
86. *New Yorker*, October 11, 1941, 58–59.
87. Henry Reed, review of the *Demon Lover*, in *New Statesman*, November

3, 1945, 302. Hermione Lee talks briefly of the connection between Bowen's "secret official work" and her "wartime fiction" when she discusses "Careless Talk" and "Green Holly" as "two wryly comical stories" (*Elizabeth Bowen*, 166).

88. E. R. Chamberlain, *Life in Wartime Britain* (London: B. T. Batsford, 1972), 162, 163. One of the more imaginative posters in the campaign contained the following legend: "Do you know Mr. Secrecy Hush Hush, Mr. Knowall, Miss Leaky Mouth, Miss Teacup Whisper, Mr. Pride in Prophecy, Mr. Glumpot?" (161).

89. Chamberlain, *Life in Wartime Britain*, 162.

90. Paul Fussell writes that "the bus . . . can be thought of as the Second World War's emblematic vehicle" (*Wartime*, 69).

91. Elizabeth Bowen, "The Beginning of this Day," 2, HRHRC.

92. Bowen, "Songs My Father Sang Me" (1944), in *Collected Stories*, 657.

93. Bowen, "I Hear You Say So" (1945), in *Collected Stories*.

94. Reprinted in Lewis, *A People's War*, 186.

95. Panter-Downes (May 12, 1945), *London War-Notes*, 12.

96. Elizabeth Bowen to A. Scholley, Esq., Westminster Bank (November 6, 1944), HRHRC

97. Elizabeth Bowen to Mrs. Spencer Curtis Brown (November 6, 1944); (January 16, 1945), HRHRC. Bowen wrote to Mrs. Curtis Brown on July 24, 1944, about the bomb blasts in Clarence Terrace.

98. Henry Reed pronounced that "no living writer has . . . produced a finer collection of stories than this," in his review of *The Demon Lover* (103); Sellery and Harris, *Elizabeth Bowen*, 58.

99. Glendinning, *Elizabeth Bowen*, 149.

100. Elizabeth Bowen to Mrs. Sewell Haggard at Curtis Brown Ltd., Bowen's literary agent in New York (February 19, 1945), HRHRC.

Chapter 9

1. Elizabeth Bowen, quoted in V. S. Pritchett, "Elizabeth Bowen," 350; "On Writing *The Heat of the Day*," *Now and Then* 77 (Autumn 1949): 11.

2. Bowen to Sir William Rothenstein (June 27, 1939), Houghton Library, Harvard University.

3. Elizabeth Bowen, "Material for Broadsheet" (n.d., but presumably published just after *The Shelbourne Hotel*), HRHRC. For an analysis of the connection between public and private in *The Heat of the Day*, see Edwin J. Kenney, Jr., *Elizabeth Bowen* (Lewisburg, Penn.: Bucknell University Press, 1975), 74.

4. Elizabeth Bowen, *English Novelists* (Glasgow: William Collins, 1942), 14. See also Dominique Gauthier: "precarité de cet équilibre [between society and man] exacerbée par le climat de la guerre" (*L'image du réel dans les romans d'Elizabeth Bowen* [Paris: Dider Erudidian, 1985], 108).

5. Bowen, "Miss Bowen on Miss Bowen," 33.

6. Elizabeth Bowen, "The Cost of Letters," in *Ideas and Places*, ed. Cyril Connolly (London: Weidenfeld and Nicolson, 1953), 83.

7. Bowen, "Autobiographical Note" (October 11, 1948), HRHRC.

8. Elizabeth Taylor to Elizabeth Bowen (February 24, 1949), HRHRC. In "The Future of the Novel," Rosamond Lehmann wrote that "the war proved that people's private lives do very much go on, with an inner intensity to match the external violence" (*Britain To-day* 109 [June, 1946], 8).

9. Rosamond Lehmann to Elizabeth Bowen (March 4, 1949), 1; (February 14, 1949), 4, HRHRC.

10. Charles Ritchie to the author (April 18, 1988).

11. Michael Howard, *Jonathan Cape, Publisher* (London: Jonathan Cape, 1971), 240. See J. B. Priestley, *Literature and Modern Man* (New York: Harper and Brothers, 1960), 370. For a further discussion of the relation between the war and the novel, see P. H. Newby, *The Novel, 1945–1950* (London: Longmans, 1951). In *The Novel Now* (New York: W. W. Norton, 1967) Anthony Burgess argued that "comparatively few good novels" resulted from the Second World War because the war "only stimulated the desire to keep records" (48). See also Alan Munton, *English Fiction of the Second World War* (London: Faber and Faber, 1989).

12. See "Why Not War Writers" (manifesto signed by Arthur Calder-Marshall, Cyril Connolly, Bonamy Dobrée, Tom Harrisson, Arthur Koestler, Alun Lewis, George Orwell, and Stephen Spender), *Horizon* 4 (October, 1941): 236–39.

13. See Lee, *Elizabeth Bowen*, for an excellent discussion of *The Heat of the Day*. She notes that Bowen connects the personal and the historical through "loaded imagery, with which the novel is as tense as any short story" (181). See also Walter Allen's review of *The Heat of the Day* where he argues that Bowen exhibits "the unity of method and single-mindedness of purpose which hitherto she has maintained only in short stories" (*New Statesman*, February 26, 1949, 208).

14. Bowen, "Stories by Elizabeth Bowen," in *Seven Winters*, 181.

15. Elizabeth Bowen, *The Death of the Heart*, 320. Lee sees the "idea of a civilization that has earned, and deserves, its own destruction" as central to *The Heat of the Day* (*Elizabeth Bowen*, 157).

16. Elizabeth Bowen to William Plomer (Thursday [194-]), Durham University Library.

17. Bowen, "Meet Elizabeth Bowen," 425.

18. See Glendinning, *Elizabeth Bowen*, 152.

19. Andrew Boyle, *The Climate of Treason: Five Who Spied for Russia* (London: Hutchinson, 1979), 155. I disagree with Lee, who believes that *The Heat of the Day* portrays "a woman's view of the male 'Intelligence' world" (*Elizabeth Bowen*, 175).

20. Frank Kermode, *History and Value* (Oxford: Clarendon Press, 1988), 80.

21. Peter Quennell, *Customs and Characters: Contemporary Portraits*, 9.

22. Elizabeth Bowen to Charles Ritchie, quoted in Glendinning, *Elizabeth Bowen*, 149.

23. Lehmann to Bowen (March 4, 1949), 2, HRHRC. Other critics have described a similar difficulty with him. P. H. Newby in *The Novel, 1945–1950* writes, "It is hard to believe in him or the form which his treason takes" (20).

In the words of L. P. Hartley, he is "a force rather than a human being." He wondered if Bowen ever fully explained the important distinction between "passive and active disloyalty" (review of *The Heat of the Day*, *Time and Tide* 30 [March, 1949]: 230, 229). Elizabeth Hardwick in "Elizabeth Bowen's Fiction" questioned why Bowen had not made Robert anti-Semitic, concluding that she was "too cautious" to mention the topic. The book as a whole was disappointing to her: "as a political novel, or a commentary on the English middle class, or a character novel, except for the engaging treatment of Stella Rodney, it is too impalpable to be held in the mind" (*Partisan Review* 16 [November, 1949], 1118).

24. Bowen, "Meet Elizabeth Bowen," 423–24.

25. Bowen, quoted in Charles Ritchie (March 3, 1942), *Siren Years*, 137; "Miss Bowen on Miss Bowen," 33.

26. Benedict Kiely, *Modern Irish Fiction: A Critique* (Dublin: Golden Eagle, 1950), 152–53. He identifies Robert's parallels with the character of Lois in *The Last September*, who can only appreciate her country on an intellectual basis.

27. In her "Autobiographical Note," Bowen wrote that at one point she thought of dedicating *The Heat of the Day* to her Irish housekeeper at Clarence Terrace, who played a crucial role in the completion of the book—"but for her it could never have been written" (5).

28. Ritchie, *Siren Years*, 132.

29. Bowen to Plomer (September 9, 1952), Durham University Library.

30. Allan E. Austin, *Elizabeth Bowen*, rev. ed. (Boston: Twayne, 1989), 54.

31. Elizabeth Bowen, "People," in *Pictures and Conversations*, 58.

32. John Hayward to Frank Morley (September 7, 1942), King's College Library, Cambridge.

33. Bowen, *Heat of the Day*, 93, 26. Hereafter this edition will be referred to in the text as *HD*.

34. Ritchie to the author (April 18, 1988).

35. Harriet Blodgett, *Patterns of Reality: Elizabeth Bowen's Novels* (The Hague: Mouton, 1975), 160–63.

36. See Lee, *Elizabeth Bowen*, for a further discussion of the Gothic style in Bowen's fiction (178–79). John Hildebilde also notes that in Bowen's work: "any house built after 1900 is more than likely not quite up to the mark" (*Five Irish Writers*, 108).

37. Bowen's depiction of Robert has the vehemence of her "Yeatsian hatred of the middle class." See F. S. L. Lyons, *Culture and Anarchy in Ireland, 1890–1939*, 78.

38. Ritchie, *Siren Years*, 120.

39. John Atkins attributes the divorce of house and owner in *The Heat of the Day* to the war (*Six Novelists Look at Society* [London: Calder, 1977], 50).

40. Edward Stokes places the "ex-gentry" in *The Heat of the Day* on "the side of the angels" ("Elizabeth Bowen—Pre-Assumptions or Moral Angle?" *Journal of Australasian Universities Language and Literature Association* 11 [September, 1959]: 45).

41. In *Happy Rural Seat*, Richard Gill discusses the "spiritual crisis" that Bowen develops between Holme Dene and Mt. Morris (187). He also argues

that Bowen's understanding of the Big House as a "symbol of community" was strengthened by writing *Bowen's Court* and *The Heat of the Day* (57–58).

42. See John Coates's discussion of Victor as a World War I veteran in "The Rewards and Problems of Rootedness in Elizabeth Bowen's *The Heat of the Day*" (*Renascence* 39 [Summer 1987]: 488–90).

43. Note that in *To the North* Bowen named a dog Roderick (169).

44. William Heath identifies useful distinctions in the way in which Bowen presents war in *The Last September* and *The Heat of the Day*. He views Bowen's portrayal of the "war in Ireland, like the one outside Troy, as an apathetic, mythical one" in the earlier novel, whereas in *The Heat of the Day* World War II "threatens integrity and attacks the individual's heart" (*Elizabeth Bowen: An Introduction to Her Novels* [Madison: University of Wisconsin Press, 1961], 118).

45. Antoinette Quinn discusses the "symbolic healing" that the plot of *The Heat of the Day* projects—that is, "that an English soldier *can* inherit the big house" ("Elizabeth Bowen's Irish Stories," 320).

46. Nicolson, *Letters and Diaries*, vol. 2, 252.

47. Woolf, *Three Guineas*, 184.

48. Jocelyn Brooke argues that the very "thinness" of the language gives "the effect of some neurotic impediment, a kind of stammer" (*Elizabeth Bowen* [London: Longmans, Green, for the British Council, 1952], 26). See also Barbara Bellow Watson, who observes that "Bowen has devised a form capable of enclosing grotesque aberration within an extraordinarily realistic narrative" ("Variations on an Enigma: Elizabeth Bowen's War Novel," *Elizabeth Bowen*, ed. Harold Bloom [New York: Chelsea House, 1987], 82).

49. For a discussion of Robert's death in the novel, see Angela G. Dorenkamp, "Fall or Leap: Bowen's *The Heat of the Day*," *Critique* 10 (1968): 13–21.

50. For an analysis of Stella as Bowen's "most vivid character," see Vida Marković, *The Changing Face: Disintegration of Personality in the Twentieth-Century British Novel 1900–1945* (Carbondale: Southern Illinois University Press, 1970), 113.

51. Critics have both applauded and been disturbed by Bowen's unorthodox decisions, which startled particularly those readers who had come to expect quiet, domestic fiction from Bowen. John McCormick attacked the novel as one of the least successful novels of wartime by commenting that, "it is as though someone had moved a Jamesian interior into a windswept field" (*Catastrophe and Imagination* [London: Longmans, Green, 1957], 229). Walter Sullivan decided that the novel involved Bowen in what she was least suited for: "discussion of ideologies, questions of political right and wrong" ("A Sense of Place: Elizabeth Bowen and the Landscape of the Heart," *Sewanee Review* 84 [1976]: 148). In his review of *The Heat of the Day* Brendan Gill wrote that Bowen "has taken a big, if unsteady, step forward.... as an artist she is risking more than she has ever risked before"; her vision was "wider and deeper than it has ever been before" (*New Yorker*, February 19, 1949, 88–89). Lee determines that the novel is not Bowen's best; it is "highly strained, and there is evidence of a struggle" in the mannerisms of "double-negatives, inversions, the breaking up of the natural sentence order, [and] passive constructions" (*Elizabeth Bowen*, 164–65).

52. Daniel George, Reader's report on *The Heat of the Day*, quoted in Howard, *Jonathan Cape*, 181.

53. Elizabeth Bowen, "Elizabeth Bowen and Jocelyn Brooke," BBC broadcast, (October 3, 1950), 11, 12, HRHRC.

54. Paul Fussell, "Killing, in Verse and Prose," in *Thank God for the Atom Bomb*, 131.

55. Coates, "Rewards and Problems of Rootedness," 484.

56. Elizabeth Bowen, review of *The People's War*, by Angus Calder (1969), reprinted in *The Mulberry Tree*, 182. Penny Summerfield argues that "social mixing among women war workers . . . has been exaggerated" ("The Levelling of Class," in *War and Social Change*, ed. Harold L. Smith, 194).

57. Elizabeth Bowen, "Advice" (1960), reprinted in *Seven Winters*, 89.

58. Elizabeth Bowen, review of "Royal Academy" (1936), reprinted in *Collected Impressions*, 210.

59. In fact, "illegitimacy rose from 4.4 per cent of all live births in 1939 to 9.1 per cent in 1945, the main change being that fewer extramarital conceptions were legitimated by marriage than before, and there was a four-fold increase in the number of divorce petitions filed for adultery between 1939 and 1945." See Penny Summerfield, "Women, War and Social Change: Women in Britain in World War I," 111.

60. The birth of her baby was not an isolated occurrence; in fact nearly 880,000 births were reported in the British Isles in 1944. See Longmate, *How We Lived Then*, 167.

61. Ritchie, *Siren Years*, 166.

62. Elizabeth Bowen, "Disloyalties" (1950), reprinted in *Seven Winters*, 64.

63. Dorenkamp discusses the swans as a symbol of art in the context of Bowen's view of the Second World War as a "failure of art" ("Fall or Leap," 20). See Coates, "Rewards and Problems of Rootedness," on this recurrence (501).

64. In ending her novel with the crescendo of D day, Bowen makes clear her belief in the haunting effects of the "apocalyptic" nature of the war and its indelible and recurring imprint on modern consciousness. See Watson, "Variations on Enigma," 131–51.

Chapter 10

1. Bowen, review of *The People's War*, by Angus Calder, *The Mulberry Tree*, 182.

2. Bowen to Plomer (September 24, 1945), Durham University Library.

3. Edmund Wilson, "Notes on London at the End of the War," in *Europe without Baedeker* (New York: Farrar, Straus and Giroux, 1947), 14.

4. Elizabeth Bowen, "Thoughts in New York" (1950), 1, HRHRC.

5. *The Home Front: The Best of "Good Housekeeping," 1939–1945*, comp. Brian Braithwaite, Noelle Walsh, and Glyn Davies (London: Edbury Press, 1987), 96.

6. Elizabeth Bowen to Sonia Chapter (April 18, 1946), HRHRC.

7. Anthony Powell, *Faces in My Time*, 196.

8. Elizabeth Bowen, "I Hear You Say So" (1945), in *Collected Stories*, 757.

9. Evelyn Waugh, quoted in Carpenter, *Brideshead Generation*, 447

10. William Plomer, *The Autobiography of William Plomer* (London: Jonathan Cape, 1975), 397; Elizabeth Bowen, Interview with John Hutchens, 3.

11. Bowen, "Opening up the House," 3, HRHRC.

12. Bowen to Plomer (September 24, 1945), 5b, Durham University Library.

13. Bowen to Plomer (January 11 [1940s]); (September 24, 1945), 5a–b, Durham University Library.

14. Elizabeth Bowen, "Folkestone, July 1945," reprinted in *Collected Impressions*, 228–30.

15. Bowen to Alice Runnells James (February 16, 1953), Houghton Library, Harvard University.

16. Eudora Welty to Elizabeth Bowen (1951), 6, HRHRC.

17. Waugh, *Diaries* (November 9, 1946), 661.

18. John Lehmann, *The Ample Proposition* (London: Eyre and Spottiswoode, 1966), 250.

19. Elizabeth Bowen, "How I Write," 8, HRHRC.

20. Elizabeth Bowen, Interview with Monaghan, "Elizabeth Bowen," 6.

21. Elizabeth Bowen, "Christmas at Bowen's Court," *Flair* 1 (December, 1950): 21.

22. Elizabeth Bowen, "Autobiographical Note," for *Mademoiselle*, August 17, 1953, 1, HRHRC; Preface to *A Day in the Dark and Other Stories*, 9.

23. Elizabeth Bowen, "Coming to London" (1956), in *The Mulberry Tree*, 86. James C. Beckett defines Anglo-Irish ambivalence as "ambiguity of outlook, arising from the need to be at once Irish and English, and leading sometimes to a detachment, sometimes to a fierce aggressiveness that may, on occasion, mark an underlying sense of insecurity" (*The Anglo-Irish Tradition*, 144). Lee concludes that the Anglo-Irish contradictions in Bowen produced "theatrical bravado and alienation, pride of poverty, and sense of deracination, repining and self-parody" (see her introduction to *Bowen's Court and Seven Winters*, xiv).

24. Elizabeth Bowen, "Hand in Glove" (1952), in *Collected Stories*, 767.

25. Elizabeth Bowen to L. P. Hartley (July 14, 1948), 3, The John Rylands University Library of Manchester; "Confessions" in *The Saturday Book*, ed. Leonard Russell (London: Hutchinson, 1949), 108.

26. Bowen, "Why Do I Write?" (1948), in *The Mulberry Tree*, 227.

27. Elizabeth Bowen, *A World of Love* (1955; reprint, Harmondsworth, Middlesex: Penguin, 1983); also see Brown, *Ireland*, 212.

28. Rosamond Lehmann, "The Future of the Novel?" *Britain Today* 122 (1946): 8.

29. Elizabeth Bowen, *The Little Girls* (1964; reprint, Harmondsworth, Middlesex: Penguin, 1985). Hereafter this novel will be cited in the text as *LG*. "Autobiographical Note," 1, HRHRC.

30. Elizabeth Bowen, "The Bend Back" (1950), reprinted in *The Mulberry Tree*, 55. Lee connects this essay with Bowen's "political antipathy for the modern world, a Burkean conservatism which is most apparent when she is writing

about the history of the Anglo-Irish or the wartime and post-war climate of feeling in England" (Preface to *The Mulberry Tree*, 4).

31. Elizabeth Bowen, "The Cult of Nostalgia," *Listener*, 46 (August, 1951): 225.

32. Elizabeth Bowen, *A Time in Rome* (New York: Alfred A. Knopf, 1960), 203.

33. Elizabeth Bowen, "First Writing," *Mademoiselle*, January, 1951, 118; Bowen to Plomer (May 6, 1958), Durham University Library.

34. Elizabeth Bowen, "How to Be Yourself—But Not Eccentric," *Vogue*, July, 1956, 55; "Ireland," 7, HRHRC.

35. Bowen, "Miss Bowen on Miss Bowen," 33.

36. Bowen to May Sarton, quoted in Glendinning, *Elizabeth Bowen*, 200.

37. Bowen to Hartley (September 15, 1954), The John Rylands University Library of Manchester. In his review Hartley accurately described the dense novel as "verbally difficult" and "relentless in its demands on one's attention" (review of *A World of Love*, *Spectator* 194 [March, 1955]: 293).

38. Bowen, "Ireland," 12, HRHRC. Lee compares *Friends and Relations* and *A World of Love*, calling them Bowen's "most mannered" works but remarking upon the "shadowiness" of *A World of Love* in comparison to *Friends and Relations* (*Elizabeth Bowen*, 191, 195). Some critics believe that Bowen's narrowed focus reflects her demise as a novelist after the Second World War. May Sarton speculates that maybe the war "reduced what had seemed inexhaustibly creative" in her judgment that no postwar novel "comes up to *The House in Paris* or *The Death of the Heart*" (*A World of Light: Portraits and Celebrations* [New York: W. W. Norton, 1976], 206). In his obituary on Bowen, however, Howard Moss argued that he would recommend the fifth chapter of *A World of Love* "to anyone writing a novel" (*New York Times Book Review*, April 8, 1973, 3).

39. Raymond Mortimer to Elizabeth Bowen (February 14, 1955), HRHRC.

40. Gerard Hopkins to Elizabeth Bowen (March 30, [1955]), HRHRC. Walter Allen views the novel as portraying the "disintegration of language" (*The Modern Novel in Britain and the United States* [New York: E. P. Dutton, 1964], 195).

41. Stephen Spender to Elizabeth Bowen (n.d.), HRHRC.

42. Rosamond Lehmann to Elizabeth Bowen (March 20, 1955), HRHRC.

43. Glendinning believes that the house is "based on a deserted farmhouse near Bowen's Court" (*Elizabeth Bowen*, 197).

44. Deane, *Short History*, 187–88, 207. Richard Gill has written that *A World of Love* "suggests the inadequacies of a class . . . by embodying its collapse" ("The Country House in a Time of Troubles," in *Elizabeth Bowen*, ed. Harold Bloom, 60).

45. Bowen, "Ireland Makes Irish," 217.

46. See Richard Rupp, "The Post-War Fiction of Elizabeth Bowen," *Xavier University Studies* 4 (1965): 55–67. He asserts that "what Elizabeth Bowen believes in is dead, if not after one war, then certainly after another. There remains only memory, nostalgia for an ordered society long since vanished" (66).

47. Anthony Powell wrote that Maud was one of the most terrifying children in all of Bowen's work (review of *A World of Love, Punch,* March 9, 1955, 327).

48. Elizabeth Bowen, Preface to *The Second Ghost Book,* ed. Lady Cynthia Asquith (London: James Barrie, 1952), reprinted in *Seven Winters,* 208.

49. See Glendinning, *Elizabeth Bowen,* 204.

50. Bowen to Plomer (May 6, 1958), Durham University Library.

51. Bowen to Hartley (December 18, 1954) The John Rylands University Library of Manchester.

52. Charles Ritchie, *Diplomatic Passport* (March 23, 1957), 157.

53. Elizabeth Bowen, "Enemies of Charm in Women, in Men," *Vogue,* September, 1959, 158, 159.

54. Elizabeth Bowen, "An Enormous Channel of Expectation," *Vogue,* July, 1953, 55.

55. Bowen, "Ireland Makes Irish," 180.

56. Elizabeth Bowen, "Home for Christmas," *Mademoiselle,* December, 1955, 57.

57. Bowen, "Ireland Makes Irish," 217.

58. Glendinning, *Elizabeth Bowen,* 154.

59. Bowen, "Ireland Makes Irish," 217.

60. Elizabeth Bowen, "Bowen's Court," *Holiday,* December, 1958, 192.

61. Elizabeth Bowen, "The Light in the Dark" (published in *Vogue* [1950]), reprinted in *The World in Vogue,* ed. Bryan Holme (New York: Viking, 1963), 292.

62. Bowen, "Bowen's Court," 192, 190, 87, 86.

63. Bowen, "Confessions," 109.

64. Bowen, Afterword to *Bowen's Court* (1964), 458.

65. In his foreword to Bowen's *Pictures and Conversations* Spencer Curtis Brown wrote of the guilt Bowen felt toward her ancestry in selling Bowen's Court (xxxvi).

66. Bowen, Afterword to *Bowen's Court* (1964), 459.

67. Bowen, Afterword to *Bowen's Court* (1964), 459.

68. Bowen, Afterword to *Bowen's Court* (1964), 455.

69. Elizabeth Bowen, *Eva Trout, or Changing Scenes* (1968; reprint, New York: Avon Books, 1978). Hereafter this edition will be referred to in the text as *ET.*

70. Elizabeth Bowen, "Notes" to *The Little Girls;* she also wrote that the book was about the "involuntary element in behaviour" (HRHRC).

71. Bowen to Plomer (June 18, 1963), Durham University Library.

72. See Harry Strickhausen, "Elizabeth Bowen and Reality," *Sewanee Review* 73 (Winter 1965): 163.

73. Bowen quoted in Glendinning, *Elizabeth Bowen,* 218.

74. Elizabeth Bowen, "Time" (1956), in *Seven Winters,* 268; Bowen to Plomer (June 18, 1963), Durham University Library.

75. Glendinning associates the children's book entitled *The Good Tiger,* which Bowen wrote in these years, with the more terrifying aspects of children she emphasized in her last fiction (*Elizabeth Bowen,* 226).

76. For example, Dinah asks Clare if she is a lesbian, with more candor than Bowen usually allowed her characters. Lee speaks of Bowen's last two novels as "incorporat[ing] the idea of a future without any verbal 'style.'" Bowen became "increasingly concerned with the concept of a breakdown in language" (*Elizabeth Bowen*, 206, 205). I think that Bowen was preempting potential accusations that her language might be out-of-date; in her attempt to change with the times she relied on what she perceived to be current.

77. Bowen to Plomer (June 18, 1963), Durham University Library.

78. Elizabeth Bowen, "Language" (n.d.), 2, 3, HRHRC.

79. Lee portrays the novel as providing an "unfocussed and bizarre conclusion to her *opus*" (*Elizabeth Bowen*, 206). John Hildebidle calls *Eva Trout* "sadly, by far the worst of Elizabeth Bowen's novels" (*Five Irish Writers*, 5). Margaret Drabble voiced familiar questions in her review of *Eva Trout:* "what after all, is she up to? Is she merely the highly elegant, dazzlingly intelligent star of the psychological thriller class, or is she a serious contender for a place in the Great Tradition?" (Review of *Eva Trout*, *Listener* 81 [February, 1969]: 214).

80. Harriet Chessmann underlines the connection between Eva and Eve in Genesis as the prototypical woman ("Women and Language in the Fiction of Elizabeth Bowen," *Twentieth Century Literature* 29 (Spring 1983): 82.

81. Burke, *Reflections*, 170.

82. Burke, *Reflections*, 207–8.

83. Lee describes Bowen's postwar essays and the late novels as emphasizing the "cauterization of feeling in modern civilization" (Preface to *The Mulberry Tree*, 5).

84. Gindin, "Ethical Structures," 32.

85. Seamus Deane suggests that the ending of the novel has an "abruptness" because it depicts a world where "the likelihood of emotional and cultural amputation is bitterly strong" (*Short History*, 206).

86. Elizabeth Bowen, "Places" (first published posthumously, 1975), in *Pictures and Conversations*, 46.

87. Elizabeth Bowen, last television appearance, quoted in Janet Egleson Dunleavy, "Elizabeth Bowen," in *Dictionary of Literary Biography*, 38.

88. Elizabeth Bowen, "Notes to Publisher," *Pictures and Conversations*, 61.

89. Bowen to William Plomer (May 6, 1958), Durham University Library.

90. Ritchie, *Diplomatic Passport* (January 19, 1957), 126.

91. Elizabeth Bowen, "Sources of Influence" (1953), reprinted in *Seven Winters*, 81.

92. Elizabeth Bowen, "The Roving Eye" (originally published as "The Search for a Story to Tell" [1952]), reprinted in *The Mulberry Tree*, 65.

93. Virginia Woolf, *A Room of One's Own* (1929; reprint, New York: Harcourt Brace Jovanovich, 1981), 108.

Bibliography

Bibliographies

Finneran, Richard. *Anglo-Irish Literature: A Review of Research.* New York: Modern Language Association, 1976.
Harmon, Maurice. *Select Bibliography for the Study of Anglo-Irish Literature.* Port Credit, Ont.: Meany, 1977.
Sellery, J'nan M., and William O. Harris. *Elizabeth Bowen: A Bibliography.* Austin: Humanities Research Center, University of Texas at Austin, 1981.
Stanton, Robert. *A Bibliography of Modern British Authors.* Troy: Whitson, 1978.

Manuscript Collections

Elizabeth Bowen letters to Alice Runnells James and William Rothenstein, Houghton Library, Harvard University.
Elizabeth Bowen letters to Edward Sackville-West and Virginia Woolf, Henry A. and Albert W. Berg Collection, the New York Public Library, Astor, Lenox and Tilden Foundations.
Elizabeth Bowen letters to L. P. Hartley, The John Rylands University Library of Manchester.
Elizabeth Bowen letters to William Plomer, Plomer mss., Durham University Library.
Elizabeth Bowen papers, Harry Ransom Humanities Research Center, University of Texas at Austin.
The Foreign Office Papers (FO 800/310), Public Records Office, Kew, London.
John Hayward letters to Frank Morley, King's College Library, Cambridge.

Works By Elizabeth Bowen

Ann Lee's and Other Stories. London: Sidgwick and Jackson, 1926.
Bowen's Court. New York: Alfred A. Knopf, 1942 (Reissued in 1964 with a revised Afterword).
Bowen's Court and Seven Winters. Ed. Hermione Lee. London: Virago Press, 1984.
"Candles in the Window." *Woman's Day* 22 (December, 1958): 32, 81–83.

"The Claimant." In *The Third Ghost Book*. Ed. Lady Cynthia Asquith. London: James Barrie, 1955.
Collected Impressions. New York: Longmans, Green, 1950.
The Collected Stories of Elizabeth Bowen. New York: Vintage Books, 1981.
A Day in the Dark and Other Stories. London: Jonathan Cape, 1965.
The Death of the Heart. 1938. Reprint. New York: Viking Penguin, 1984.
Early Stories. New York: Alfred A. Knopf, 1951 (reissue of *Encounters*, originally published in 1923, and *Ann Lee's*, originally published in 1926).
Elizabeth Bowen's Irish Stories. Ed. Victoria Glendinning. Dublin: Poolbeg Press, 1978.
"Emergency in the Gothic Wing." *Tatler* 214 (November 18, 1954): 18–19, 52.
Encounters. 1923. Reprint, with a revised Preface. London: Ace Books, 1949.
English Novelists. London: William Collins, 1942.
Eva Trout, or Changing Scenes. 1968. Reprint. New York: Avon Books, 1978.
Friends and Relations. 1931. Reprint. New York: Avon Books, 1980.
"Happiness." *Woman's Day* 23 (December, 1959): 58, 122–24.
The Heat of the Day. 1949. Reprint. Harmondsworth, Middlesex: Penguin, 1984.
The Hotel. 1927. Reprint. New York: Viking Penguin, 1984.
The House in Paris. 1935. Reprint. New York: Alfred A. Knopf, 1936.
Ivy Gripped the Steps and Other Stories. New York: Alfred A. Knopf, 1946.
The Last September. 1929. Reprint. New York: Avon Books, 1979.
"The Light in the Dark." In *The World in Vogue*. Ed. Bryan Holme. New York: Viking, 1963, 291–92.
The Little Girls. 1964. Reprint. New York: Viking Penguin, 1985.
Look at All Those Roses. London: Gollancz, 1941.
The Mulberry Tree: Writings of Elizabeth Bowen. Ed. Hermione Lee. London: Virago Press, 1986.
Pictures and Conversations. London: Allen Lane, 1975.
Seven Winters and Afterthoughts. New York: Alfred A. Knopf, 1962. (*Seven Winters* was originally published in 1942.)
"She Gave Him." *Consequences: A complete story in the manner of the old parlour game in nine chapters each by a different author*. Boston: Houghton Mifflin, 1933.
The Shelbourne Hotel. New York: Alfred A. Knopf, 1951. (English edition published as *The Shelbourne: A Centre in Dublin Life for More Than a Century* [London: George C. Harrap, 1951].)
A Time in Rome. New York: Alfred A. Knopf, 1960.
To the North. 1932. Reprint. Harmondsworth, Middlesex: Penguin, 1987.
A World of Love. 1955. Reprint. Harmondsworth, Middlesex: Penguin, 1983.

Articles By Elizabeth Bowen

"Advance in Formation." *Spectator* 42 (January, 1941): 65.
"Anthony Trollope—A New Judgement." 1945. Reprinted in *The Mulberry Tree*. Ed. Hermione Lee (London: Virago Press, 1986).
"Ascendancy." Review of *The Anglo-Irish* by Brian Fitzgerald. *Observer*, November 16, 1952, 8.

"Autobiography as an Art." *Saturday Review of Literature*, March 17, 1951, 9–10.
"Books in General." Review of *Mr. Beluncle* by V. S. Pritchett. *New Statesman*, October 20, 1951, 438–39.
"Bowen's Court." *Holiday*, December, 1958, 86–87, 190–93.
"By the Unapproachable Sea." *Christian Science Monitor Magazine*, February 5, 1944, 10.
"Christmas at Bowen's Court." *Flair*, December 1, 1950, 20–21.
"Confessions." In *The Saturday Book*. Ed. Leonard Russell. London: Hutchinson, 1949.
"Contemporary." Review of *In My Good Books* by V. S. Pritchett. *New Statesman*, May 23, 1942, 340.
"The Cult of Nostalgia." *Listener* 46 (August, 1951): 225–26.
"Ecstasy of the Eye." *Vogue*, December, 1968, 189–90.
"Eire." *New Statesman and Nation* 21 (April, 1941): 383.
"Elizabeth Bowen of Cork and London." *New York Herald Tribune Book Review*, October 8, 1950, 9.
"Enemies of Charm in Women, in Men." *Vogue*, September, 1959, 158–59.
"An Enormous Channel of Expectations." *Vogue*, July, 1953, 54–55.
"First Writing." *Mademoiselle*, January, 1951, 57, 117–20.
"For the Feminine Shopper." *Holiday*, April, 1956, 90, 129, 131–32.
"How to Be Yourself—But Not Eccentric." *Vogue*, July, 1956, 54–55.
"Ireland." *House and Garden*, June, 1954, 92, 158.
"Ireland Makes Irish." *Vogue*, August, 1946, 180–81, 214–17.
"Home for Christmas." *Mademoiselle*, December, 1955, 56–57, 120–22.
"Life in the Irish Counties." Review of *The Fire in the Dust* by Francis MacManus. *New York Herald Tribune Book Review*, February 11, 1951, 7.
"Manners." Review of *Can I Help You?* by Viola Tree. *New Statesman*, November 6, 1937, 727–28.
"Meet Elizabeth Bowen." Interview with the *Bell* 4 (September, 1942): 420–26.
"Mental Annuity." *Vogue*, September, 1955, 108–9.
"Miss Bowen on Miss Bowen." *New York Times Book Review*, March 6, 1949, 33.
"The Moores." Review of *The Moores of Moore Hall* by Joseph Hone. *New Statesman*, November 25, 1939. Reprinted in *The Mulberry Tree*. Ed. Hermione Lee (London: Virago Press, 1986).
"The Next Book." *Now and Then* 77 (Autumn 1948): 11–12.
"On Writing *The Heat of the Day*." *Now and Then* 79 (Autumn 1949): 11.
Review of *Between the Acts* by Virginia Woolf. *New Statesman and Nation* 22 (July, 1941): 63–64.
"Rx for a Story Worth Telling." In *Opinions and Perspectives from "The New York Times Book Review."* Ed. Francis Brown. Boston: Houghton Mifflin, 1964.
"Short Stories." Review of *Collected Short Stories* by Stella Benson and *Best Short Stories of 1936: English and American*, ed. Edward J. O'Brien. *New Statesman*, December 5, 1936, 938, 940.
"The Short Story in England." *Britain Today* 109 (May, 1945): 11–16.
"Strength of Mind—Do Conventions Matter?" *Listener* 26 (December, 1941): 823–24.

"Strength of Mind—Do Women Think Like Men?" *Listener* 26 (October, 1941): 593–94.

"They Were All Guests in Ireland." Review of *The Stranger in Ireland* by Constantia Maxwell and *The Deserters* by Honor Tracy. *Tatler and Bystander,* June 30, 1954, 740, 754.

"This Freedom." Review of *Our Freedom and Its Results*. Ed. Ray Strachey. *New Statesman,* October 31, 1936, 678.

"This Unhappy Autumn." Review of *Overtures to Death* by C. Day Lewis. *Now and Then* 61 (Winter 1938): 32–33.

"Truths about Ireland." Review of *Ireland—Atlantic Gateway* by Jim Phelan. *Spectator* 167 (September 5, 1941): 240.

"What We Need in Writing." *Spectator* 157 (November 20, 1936): 901–2.

Why Do I Write? An Exchange of Views between Elizabeth Bowen, Graham Greene, and V. S. Pritchett. London: Percival Marshall, 1948. Reprinted in part in *The Mulberry Tree.* Ed. Hermione Lee (London: Virago Press, 1986).

Other Works

Allen, Michael, and Angela Wilcox, eds. *Critical Approaches to Anglo-Irish Literature.* Gerards Cross, Buckinghamshire: Colin Smythe, 1989.

Allen, Walter. *The Modern Novel in Britain and the United States.* New York: E. P. Dutton, 1964.

———. "A Literary Aftermath." In *Promise of Greatness: The War of 1914–1918.* Ed. George A. Panichas, 504–15. London: Cassell, 1968.

———. Review of *The Heat of the Day. New Statesman,* February 26, 1949, 208–9.

Annan, Noel. "The Mood of the Twenties." *Listener* 45 (February, 1951): 221.

Arnold, Matthew. "Irish Catholicism and British Liberalism." In *Mixed Essays,* 98–142. New York: Macmillan, 1883.

Atkins, John. *Six Novelists Look at Society.* London: Calder, 1977.

Auden, W. H. *The Collected Poetry of W. H. Auden.* New York: Random House, 1945.

Austin, Allan E. *Elizabeth Bowen.* New York: Twayne, 1971. Rev. ed. Boston: Twayne, 1989.

Baker, Carlos. "Death of a Ghost." Review of *A World of Love. Nation,* February 5, 1955, 123.

Bates, Judith. "Undertones of Horror in Elizabeth Bowen's *Look at All Those Roses* and *The Cat Jumps.*" *Journal of the Short Story in English (Cahiers de la Nouvelle)* 8 (Spring 1987): 81–91.

Bayley, John. *The Short Story: Henry James to Elizabeth Bowen.* Sussex: Harvester Press, 1988.

Beauman, Nicola. *A Very Great Profession: The Woman's Novel, 1914–1939.* London: Virago Press, 1983.

Beck, Martha Ann. "Vassar Student Talks about Elizabeth Bowen." *Mademoiselle,* July, 1960, 88–89.

Beckett, James C. *The Anglo-Irish Tradition.* Ithaca: Cornell University Press, 1976.

---. *The Making of Modern Ireland, 1603–1923*. New York: Alfred A. Knopf, 1966.
Beddoe, Deidre. *Back to Home and Duty: Women between the Wars, 1918–1939*. London: Pandora, 1989.
Bence-Jones, Mark. *Twilight of the Ascendancy*. London: Constable, 1987.
Bergonzi, Bernard. *Heroes' Twilight: A Study of the Literature of the Great War*. London: Macmillan, 1980.
---. *Reading the Thirties: Texts and Contexts*. London: Macmillan, 1978.
---. Review of *Eva Trout*. *New York Review of Books*, January 2, 1969, 40–41.
Binchy, D. A. Review of *Bowen's Court*. *Bell* 4 (August, 1942): 368–71.
Blodgett, Harriet. *Patterns of Reality: Elizabeth Bowen's Novels*. The Hague: Mouton, 1975.
Bloom, Harold, ed. *Elizabeth Bowen*. New York: Chelsea House, 1987.
Blythe, Ronald, ed. *Components of the Scene: Stories, Poems, and Essays of the Second World War*. Harmondsworth, Middlesex: Penguin, 1966.
Bogan, Louise. *Selected Criticism: Prose and Poetry*. New York: Noonday Press, 1955.
---. Review of *Look at All Those Roses*. *Nation*, October 25, 1941, 405–6.
Booth, Wayne. *The Rhetoric of Fiction*. Chicago: University of Chicago Press, 1961.
Bowra, C. M. *Memories, 1898–1939*. Cambridge: Harvard University Press, 1967.
Boyle, Andrew. *The Climate of Treason: Five Who Spied for Russia*. London: Hutchinson, 1979.
Braithwaite, Brian, ed. *The Home Front: The Best of "Good Housekeeping," 1939–1945*. London: Edbury Press, 1987.
Braybon, Gail. *Women Workers in the First World War*. Totowa, N.J.: Barnes and Noble, 1981.
Brierre, Annie. "Littérature Anglo-Irlandaise." *La Revue des deux Mondes* 140 (January, 1968): 84–91.
Brittain, Vera. *Diary, 1939–1945: Wartime Chronicle*. Ed. Alan Bishop and Y. Aleksandra Bennett. London: Gollancz, 1989.
---. *England's Hour*. New York: Macmillan, 1941.
---. *Honourable Estate*. London: Gollancz, 1936.
---. *Testament of Youth*. 1933. Reprint. New York: Wideview Books, 1978.
Brooke, Jocelyn. *Elizabeth Bowen*. London: Longmans, Green (for the British Council), 1952.
Brothers, Barbara. "Pattern and Void: Bowen's Irish Landscapes and *The Heat of the Day*." *Mosaic* 12 (Spring 1979): 129–38.
Brown, Ernest Francis, ed. *Opinions and Perspectives from "The New York Times Book Review."* Boston: Houghton Mifflin, 1964.
Brown, Terence. *Ireland: A Social and Cultural History, 1922–1979*. London: Fontana, 1981.
Bufkin, E. C. "Elizabeth Bowen: A Portrait." *Review* 2 (1980): 297–306.
Burgess, Anthony. *Ninety-Nine Novels: The Best in English since 1939*. London: Allison and Busby, 1984.

———. *The Novel Now*. New York: W. W. Norton, 1967.
———. "Treasures and Fetters." Review of *The Little Girls*. *Spectator* 212 (February, 1964): 254.
Burke, Edmund. *Reflections on the Revolution in France*. 1790. Reprint. New York: Anchor Press, 1973.
Cadogan, Mary, and Patricia Craig. *Women and Children First: The Fiction of Two World Wars*. London: Gollancz, 1978.
Cahalan, James M. *The Irish Novel: A Critical History*. Boston: Twayne, 1988.
Calder, Angus. *The People's War: Britain, 1939–1945*. New York: Pantheon Books, 1969.
Carpenter, Humphrey. *The Brideshead Generation*. Boston: Houghton Mifflin, 1990.
Carroll, Joseph T. *Ireland in the War Years*. Newton-Abbott, United Kingdom: David and Charles, 1975.
Cecil, Lord David. "Chronicler of the Heart: The British Writer, Elizabeth Bowen." *Vogue,* November, 1953, 118–19.
———. Review of *The Heat of the Day*. *Now and Then* 31 (Autumn 1957): 31.
Chamberlain, E. R. *Life in Wartime Britain*. London: B. T. Batsford, 1972.
Chessman, Harriet S. "Women and Language in the Fiction of Elizabeth Bowen." *Twentieth Century Literature* 29 (Spring 1983): 69–85.
Church, Margaret. "The Irish Writer, Elizabeth Bowen, 'Her Table Spread': Allusion and Anti-Roman." *Folio* 11 (1978): 17–20.
———. "Social Consciousness in the Works of Elizabeth Bowen, Iris Murdoch, and Mary Lavin." *College Literature* 7 (Spring 1980): 158–63.
"The Climate of Treason." Review of *The Heat of the Day*. *Times Literary Supplement,* March 5, 1949, 152.
Cloyne, George. "Is It Irish to Be Modest?" Review of *Seven Winters and Afterthoughts*. *New York Herald Tribune Books,* June 10, 1962, 16.
Coates, John D. "In Praise of Civility: Conservative Values in Elizabeth Bowen's *The Death of the Heart*." *Renascence* 37 (Summer 1985): 248–65.
———. "The Rewards and Problems of Rootedness in Elizabeth Bowen's *The Heat of the Day*." *Renascence* 39 (Summer 1987): 484–501.
Cobb, Richard. "Survivors of the Home Front." Review of *The Other Garden* by Francis Wyndham. *Times Literary Supplement,* October 2–8, 1987, 1073.
Coles, Robert. *Irony in the Mind's Life: Essays on Novels by James Agee, Elizabeth Bowen, and George Eliot*. Charlottesville: University Press of Virginia, 1973.
Colum, Mary M. "Do We Learn from History?" Review of *Bowen's Court*. *Saturday Review of Literature,* September 5, 1942, 3–4, 17–18.
Condell, Diana, and Jean Liddiard. *Working for Victory? Images of Women in the First World War, 1914–1918*. London: Routledge and Kegan Paul, 1987.
Connolly, Cyril. *The Condemned Playground*. New York: Macmillan, 1946.
———. *Cyril Connolly: Journal and Memoir*. Ed. David Pryce-Jones. London: William Collins, 1983.
———. *Ideas and Places*. London: Weidenfeld and Nicolson, 1953.
———. *The Selected Essays of Cyril Connolly*. Ed. Peter Quennell. New York: Stanley Moss / Persea Books, 1984.

———, ed. *The Golden Horizon*. London: Weidenfeld and Nicolson, 1953.
———, ed. *Horizon Stories*. London: Faber and Faber, 1943.
———. "Elizabeth Bowen: A Poet Working in Prose." *Sunday Times of London*, February 25, 1973, 12.
———. "Comment." *Horizon* 5 (January, 1942): 3–11.
Connolly, Peter, ed. *Literature and the Changing Ireland*. Totowa, N.J.: Barnes and Noble, 1982.
Conrad, Peter. "Tons of Fear." Review of *A Pacifist's War* by Francis Partridge. *New Statesman*, July 28, 1978, 124.
Cooper, Duff [Viscount Norwich]. *Old Men Forget*. London: Rupert Hart-Davis, 1953.
Cooper, Helen, Adrienne Munich, and Susan Squier, eds. *Arms and the Woman: War, Gender, and Literary Representation*. Chapel Hill: University of North Carolina Press, 1989.
Corn, Alfred. "An Anglo-Irish Novelist." In *The Metamorphoses of Metaphor: Essays in Poetry and Fiction*. New York: Viking Penguin, 1987.
Craig, David, and Michael Egan. *Extreme Situations: Literature and Crisis from the Great War to the Atom Bomb*. London: Macmillan, 1979.
Craig, Patricia. *Elizabeth Bowen*. New York: Viking Penguin, 1986.
Cronin, John. *The Anglo-Irish Novel*. Belfast, Ireland: Apple Tree Press, 1990.
Cruickshank, Charles. *Deception in World War II*. New York: Oxford University Press, 1979.
Cunningham, Valentine. *British Writers of the Thirties*. New York: Oxford University Press, 1988.
———. *The Present Age in British Literature*. Bloomington: Indiana University Press, 1958.
Curtis, L. P. "The Anglo-Irish Predicament." *Twentieth Century Studies* 4 (November, 1970): 37–63.
Daiches, David. "The Novels of Elizabeth Bowen." *English Journal* 38 (1949): 305–13.
Dangerfield, George. *The Strange Death of Liberal England*. New York: Harrison Smith and Robert Haas, 1935.
Davenport, Basil. "Bowenettes." Review of *Look at All Those Roses*. *Saturday Review of Literature*, August 2, 1941, 13.
Davenport, Gary T. "Elizabeth Bowen and the Big House." *Southern Humanities Review* 8 (1974): 27–34.
Davidson, H. R. Ellis. *Myths and Symbols in Pagan Europe: Early Scandinavian and Celtic Rituals*. Syracuse, N.Y.: Syracuse University Press, 1988.
Davis, Robert M. "Contributions to Night and Day by Elizabeth Bowen, Graham Greene, and Anthony Powell." *Studies in the Novel* 3 (Winter 1971): 401–4.
Deane, Seamus. *A Short History of Irish Literature*. London: Hutchinson, 1986.
de Vries, Peter. "Touch and Go (with a low bow to Elizabeth Bowen)." *New Yorker*, January 26, 1952, 30–32.
Donnelly, Brian. "The Big House in the Recent Novel." *Studies* (Dublin) 64 (1975): 133–42.

Donovan, Katie. *Irish Women Writers*. Dublin, Ireland, Raven Arts, 1988.
Dorenkamp, Angela G. "Fall or Leap: Bowen's *The Heat of the Day*." *Critique* 10 (1968): 13–21.
Drabble, Margaret. Review of *Eva Trout, or Changing Scenes*. *Listener* 81 (February, 1969): 214–16.
Dunleavy, Janet Egleson. "Elizabeth Bowen." In *Dictionary of Literary Biography: British Novelists, 1930–1959*. 15th ed. Ed. Bernard Oldsey, 34–46. Detroit: Gale, 1983.
———. "The Subtle Satire of Elizabeth Bowen and Mary Lavin." *Tulsa Studies in Women's Literature* 2 (Spring 1983): 69–82.
Dyhouse, Carol. *Girls Growing Up in Late Victorian and Edwardian England*. London: Routledge and Kegan Paul, 1981.
Eliot, T. S. *Collected Poems, 1909–1962*. New York: Harcourt Brace Jovanovich, 1970.
Elshtain, Jean Bethke. "Women as Mirror: Toward a Theory of Women, War, and Feminism." *Humanities in Society* 5 (Winter–Spring 1982): 32–44.
Eva Trout, or Changing Scenes. Review. *Times Literary Supplement*, January 30, 1969, 101.
Evans, B. Ifor. *English Literature between the Wars*. London: Methuen, 1948.
Farson, Negley. *Bomber's Moon*. London: Gollancz, 1941.
Ferguson, John, ed. *War and the Creative Artist: An Anthology*. London: Macmillan, 1972.
Fisk, Robert. *In Time of War: Ireland, Ulster and the Price of Neutrality, 1939–1945*. Philadelphia: University of Pennsylvania Press, 1983.
Fitzpatrick, David. *Politics and Irish Life, 1913–1921*. Dublin: Gill and Macmillan, 1977.
Foster, John Wilson. "The Geography of Irish Fiction." In *The Irish Novel in Our Time*. Ed. Patrick Rafroidi and Maurice Harmon, 89–102. Villeneuve-d'Ascq, France: Publications de L'Université de Lille, 1975–76.
Foster, R. F. *Modern Ireland, 1600–1972*. London: Allen Lane/Penguin, 1988.
Fougasse [Bird, Cyril Kenneth]. *The Changing Face of Britain*. London: Methuen, 1940.
———. *Family Group*. London: Methuen, 1944.
Fraustino, Daniel V. "Elizabeth Bowen's 'The Demon Lover': Psychosis or Seduction?" *Studies in Short Fiction* 17 (Fall 1980): 483–87.
Frierson, William C. *The English Novel in Transition, 1885–1940*. Norman: University of Oklahoma Press, 1942.
Fussell, Paul. *The Great War and Modern Memory*. New York: Oxford University Press, 1975.
———. *Thank God for the Atom Bomb and Other Essays*. New York: Summit Books, 1988.
———. *Wartime: Understanding and Behavior in the Second World War*. New York: Oxford University Press, 1989.
Gallagher, S. F., ed. *Women in Irish Legend, Life, and Literature*. Gerrards Cross, Buckinghamshire: Colin Smythe, 1983.
Gallant, Mavis. *Paris Notebooks*. Toronto: Macmillan, 1986.

Gardner, Brian, ed. *The Terrible Rain: The War Poets, 1939–1945* London: Methuen, 1966.
Gauthier, Dominique. *L'image du réel dans les romans d'Elizabeth Bowen*. Paris: Didier Erudidian, 1985.
Gilbert, Sandra M., and Susan Gubar. *No Man's Land: The Place of the Woman Writer in the Twentieth Century*. New Haven, Conn.: Yale University Press, 1988.
Gill, Brendan. Review of *The Heat of the Day*. *New Yorker*, February 19, 1949, 88–89.
Gill, Richard. *Happy Rural Seat: The English Country House and the Literary Imagination*. New Haven, Conn.: Yale University Press, 1972.
———. "The Country House in a Time of Troubles." In *Elizabeth Bowen*. Ed. Harold Bloom, 51–61. New York: Chelsea House, 1987.
Gindin, James. "Ethical Structures in John Galsworthy, Elizabeth Bowen, and Iris Murdoch." In *Forms of Modern British Fiction*. Ed. Alan Warren Friedman, 15–41. Austin: University of Texas Press, 1975.
———. "The Fable Begins to Break Down." *Wisconsin Studies in Contemporary Literature* 8 (1967): 1–18.
Glendinning, Victoria. *Elizabeth Bowen: Portrait of a Writer*. 1977. Reprint. New York: Viking Penguin, 1985.
Goldsmith, Margaret. *Women at War*. London: Lindsay Brummond, 1943.
Graves, Robert, and Alan Hodge. *The Long Week-End: A Social History of Great Britain, 1918–1939*. New York: W. W. Norton, 1963.
Green, George. "Elizabeth Bowen: Imagination as Therapy." *Perspective* 14 (Spring 1965): 42–52.
Green, Henry. *Pack My Bag*. London: Hogarth Press, 1940.
Greene, Graham. *Collected Essays*. New York: Viking, 1966.
———. "While Waiting for a War." *Granta* 17 (Autumn 1985): 11–29.
Haggard, H. Rider. *She: A History of Adventure*. 1886. Reprint. London: MacDonald, 1954.
Halifax, Earl of. *Fulness of Days*. London: Collins, 1957.
Halio, Jay L. "A Sense of the Present." *Southern Review* 2 (Autumn 1966): 952–65.
Hall, James. *The Lunatic Giant in the Drawing Room: The British and American Novel since 1930*. Bloomington: Indiana University Press, 1968.
Hanson, Clare. *Short Stories and Short Fictions, 1880–1980*. London: Macmillan, 1985.
Hardwick, Elizabeth. "Elizabeth Bowen's Fiction." *Partisan Review* 16 (November, 1949): 1114–21.
Harkness, Bruce. "The Fiction of Elizabeth Bowen." *English Journal* 44 (1955): 499–506.
Harries, Meirion, and Susie Harries. *The War Artists: British Official War Art of the Twentieth Century*. London: Michael Joseph, 1983.
Harrisson, Tom. "War Books." *Horizon* 4 (December, 1941): 416–37.
Hartley, L. P. Review of *Bowen's Court*. *Sketch* 197 (July, 1942): 78.
———. Review of *The Heat of the Day*. *Time and Tide* 30 (March, 1949): 229–30.

———. Review of *Look at All Those Roses*. *Sketch* 193 (January, 1941): 118.
———. Review of *A World of Love*. *Spectator* 194 (March, 1955): 293–94.
———. "Three Wars." In *Promise of Greatness: The War of 1914–1918*. Ed. George A. Panichas, 250–58. London: Cassell, 1968.
Hawkins, Desmond. Review of *Look at All Those Roses*. *New Statesman*, February 8, 1941, 144–45.
Hawtree, Christopher, ed. *Night and Day*. London: Chatto and Windus, 1985.
Hayward, John. *Prose Literature since 1939*. London: Longmans, Green, 1947.
———. Review of *The Heat of the Day*. *Observer*, February 20, 1949, 3.
Heath, William. *Elizabeth Bowen: An Introduction to Her Novels*. Madison: University of Wisconsin Press, 1961.
Heinemann, Alison. "The Indoor Landscapes in Bowen's *The Death of the Heart*." *Critique: Studies in Modern Fiction* 10 (1968): 5–12.
Henn, Thomas Rice. In *Last Essays: Mainly on Anglo-Irish Literature*. New York: Barnes and Noble, 1976.
———. "The Weasel's Tooth." In *Last Essays*.
———. "Yeats and the Poetry of War." In *Last Essays*.
Hewison, Robert. *Under Siege: Literary Life in London, 1939–1945*. New York: Oxford University Press, 1977.
Hicks, Granville. "Literature in This Global War." *College English* 4 (May, 1943): 453–59.
Higgins, Ian, ed. *The Second World War in Literature*. Edinburgh: Scottish Academic Press, 1986.
Higonnet, Margaret Randolph, Jane Jensen, Sonya Michel, and Margaret Collins Weitz, eds. *Behind the Lines: Gender and the Two World Wars*. New Haven, Conn.: Yale University Press, 1987.
Hildebidle, John. *Five Irish Writers: The Errand of Keeping Alive*. Cambridge: Harvard University Press, 1989.
Hill, Derek, and Vivian Mercier. "Letters from Ireland." *Horizon* 13 (April, 1946): 268–85.
Hodgson, Vere. *Few Eggs and No Oranges*. London: Dennis Dobson, 1976.
Hooper, Brad. "Elizabeth Bowen's 'The Happy Autumn Fields': A Dream or Not?" *Studies in Short Fiction* 21 (Spring 1984): 151–53.
Howard, Michael S. *Jonathan Cape, Publisher*. London: Jonathan Cape, 1971.
Hughes, Douglas A. "Cracks in the Psyche: Elizabeth Bowen's 'Demon Lover.'" *Studies in Short Fiction* 10 (Fall 1973): 411–13.
Huston, Nancy. "The Matrix of War: Mothers and Heroes." In *The Female Body in Western Culture*. Ed. Susan Rubin Suleiman, 119–36. Cambridge: Harvard University Press, 1986.
Hutchens, John K. Interview with Elizabeth Bowen. *New York Herald Tribune Book Review*, March 26, 1950, 3.
Hynes, Samuel. *The Auden Generation: Literature and Politics in England in the 1930s*. London: Bodley Head, 1976.
———. *A War Imagined: The First World War and English Culture*. London: Bodley Head, 1990.

"Irish 'Wave of Panic' over Churchill's War Ports Bid, but Feeling Was Pro-British." *Irish Times,* March 24, 1975, 9.
Isherwood, Christopher. *Lions and Shadows: An Education in the Twenties.* London: Methuen, 1953.
Jarrett, Mary. "Ambiguous Ghosts: The Short Stories of Elizabeth Bowen." *Journal of the Short Story in English (Cahiers de la Nouvelle)* 8 (Spring 1987): 71–79.
Johnstone, J. K. "World War I and the Novels of Virginia Woolf." In *Promise of Greatness: The War of 1914–1918* Ed. George A. Panichas, 528–40. London: Cassell, 1968.
Jones, Edward T. *L. P. Hartley.* Boston: Twayne Publishers, 1978.
Karl, Frederick R. *A Reader's Guide to the Contemporary English Novel.* New York: Noonday Press, 1962.
Kee, Robert. *Ireland: A History.* Boston: Little, Brown, 1980.
Kenneally, Michael, ed. *Cultural Contexts and Literary Idioms in Contemporary Irish Literature.* Gerrards Cross, Buckinghamshire: Colin Smythe, 1988.
———. "The Autobiographical Imagination and Irish Literary Autobiographies." In *Critical Approaches to Anglo-Irish Literature.* Ed. Michael Allen and Angela Wilcox, 111–31. Gerrards Cross, Buckinghamshire: Colin Smythe, 1989.
Kenney, Edwin J., Jr. *Elizabeth Bowen.* Lewisburg, Penn.: Bucknell University Press, 1975.
Kermode, Frank. *History and Value.* Oxford: Clarendon Press, 1988.
Kiely, Benedict. *Modern Irish Fiction: A Critique.* Dublin: Golden Eagle Books, 1950.
———. "Elizabeth Bowen." *Irish Monthly* 78 (1950): 175–81.
———. "The Great Gazebo." *Eire* 2 (1967): 72–86.
Klein, Holger, ed. *The First World War in Fiction.* New York: Harper and Row, 1977.
Klein, Holger, John Flower, and Eric Homberger, ed. *The Second World War in Fiction.* London: Macmillan Studies in Twentieth-Century Literature, 1984.
Knowles, Sebastian D. G. *A Purgatorial Flame: Seven British Writers in the Second World War.* Philadelphia: University of Pennsylvania Press, 1990.
Laigle, Deidre. "Images of the Big House in Elizabeth Bowen: *The Last September.*" *Cahiers du Centres d'Etudes Irlandaises* (Université de Haute Bretagne) 9 (1984): 61–80.
Lancaster, Osbert. *More Pocket Cartoons.* London: John Murray, 1943.
Lassner, Phyllis. *Elizabeth Bowen.* Houndsmills, Basingstoke: Macmillan Education, 1990.
———. "The Past is a Burning Pattern: *The Last September.*" *Eire* 21 (Spring 1986): 40–54.
———. "Reimagining the Arts of War: Language and History in Elizabeth Bowen's *The Heat of the Day* and Rose Macaulay's *The World My Wilderness.*" *Perspectives in Contemporary Literature* 14 (1988): 30–38.
The Last September. Review. *New York Times Book Review,* February 3, 1929, 9.

Lee, Hermione. *Elizabeth Bowen: An Estimation.* London and Totowa, N.J.: Vision / Barnes and Noble, 1981.
Lee, J. J. *Ireland, 1912–1985: Politics and Society.* Cambridge: Cambridge University Press, 1989.
Leed, Eric. *No Man's Land: Combat and Identity in World War One.* New York: Cambridge University Press, 1979.
Le Fanu, Sheridan. *In a Glass Darkly: Stories by Sheridan le Fanu.* Ed. V. S. Pritchett. London: John Lehmann, 1947.
Lehmann, John. *The Ample Proposition.* London: Eyre and Spottiswoode, 1966.
———. *I Am My Brother.* New York: Reynal, 1960.
———. *In My Own Time: Memoirs of a Literary Life.* 1955. Reprint. Boston: Little, Brown, 1969.
———. *Thrown to the Woolfs.* London: Weidenfeld and Nicolson, 1978.
———, ed. *Coming to London.* London: Phoenix House, 1957.
———, ed. *New Writing and Daylight.* London: Hogarth Press, 1942–46.
———, ed. *The Penguin New Writing.* Harmondsworth, Middlesex: Penguin, 1941–44.
———, and Roy Fuller, eds. *The Penguin New Writing: An Anthology, 1940–1950.* Harmondsworth, Middlesex: Penguin, 1985.
Lehmann, Rosamond. *The Swan in the Evening: Fragments of Autobiography.* London: Collins, 1967.
———. "Elizabeth Bowen." *Times* (London), February 28, 1973, 18.
———. "The Future of the Novel?" *Britain Today* 122 (June, 1946): 5–11.
Lewis, Peter. *A People's War.* London: Thames Methuen, 1986.
Longmate, Norman. *How We Lived Then: A History of Everyday Life during the Second World War.* London: Hutchinson, 1971.
Ludwig, J. B. "The New World of Elizabeth Bowen." Review of *A World of Love. New Republic,* January 31, 1955, 18–19.
Lyons, F. S. L. *Culture and Anarchy in Ireland, 1890–1939.* Oxford: Clarendon Press, 1979.
———. *Ireland since the Famine.* Glasgow: William Collins, 1973.
———. "The Twilight of the Big House." *Ariel* 1 (July, 1970): 110–22.
Macaulay, Rose. *Noncombatants and Others.* London: Hodder and Stoughton, 1916.
McCormack, W. J. *Ascendancy and Tradition in Anglo-Irish Literary History, 1789–1939.* Oxford: Clarendon Press, 1985.
McCormick, John. *Catastrophe and Imagination: An Interpretation of the Recent English and American Novel.* London: Longmans, Green, 1957.
Macdonald, Sharon, Pat Holden, and Shirley Ardener, eds. *Images of Women in Peace and War: Cross-Cultural and Historical Perspectives.* Houndsmill, Basingstoke: Macmillan Education, 1987.
McDowell, Alfred. "*The Death of the Heart* and the Human Dilemma." *Modern Language Studies* 8 (1979): 5–16.
McGowan, Martha. "The Enclosed Garden in Elizabeth Bowen's *A World of Love.*" *Eire* 16 (Spring 1981): 55–70.

McHugh, Roger, and Maurice Harmon. *Short History of Anglo-Irish Literature*. Dublin: Wolfhound Press, 1982.
Mack, Joanna, and Steve Humphries. *The Making of Modern London, 1939–1945*. London: Sidgwick and Jackson, 1985.
Maclaren-Ross, Julian. *Memoirs of the Forties*. London: Alan Ross, 1965.
———. "A World of Women." *Punch*, March 23, 1955, 366–67.
MacNeice, Louis. *The Collected Poems of Louis MacNeice*. Ed. E. R. Dodds. New York: Oxford University Press, 1962.
Marcus, Jane, ed. *Virginia Woolf: A Feminist Slant*. Lincoln: University of Nebraska Press, 1983.
———. "The Asylums of Antaeus, Women, War and Madness: Is There a Feminist Fetishism?" In *The Difference Within: Feminism and Critical Theory*. Ed. Elizabeth Meese and Alice Parker, 49–83. Philadelphia: John Benjamins, 1989.
Marković, Vida E. *The Changing Face: Disintegration of Personality in the Twentieth-Century British Novel, 1900–1950*. Carbondale: Southern Illinois Press, 1970.
Marwick, Arthur. *The Home Front: The British and the Second World War*. London: Thames and Hudson, 1976.
———. *Total War and Social Change*. London: Macmillan, 1988.
———. *Women at War*. London: Fontana Paperbacks, 1977.
Matthews, T. S. "Review of Bowen's *The Last September*." *Bookman* 69 (March, 1929): 340–42.
Meade, Norah. "The Anglo-Irish Mind." Review of *The Last September*. *Nation*, May 15, 1929, 589–90.
Medoff, Jeslyn. "'There is No Elsewhere': Elizabeth Bowen's Perception of War." *Modern Fiction Studies* 30 (Spring 1984): 73–81.
Meese, Elizabeth, and Alice Parker, eds. *The Difference Within: Feminism and Critical Theory*. Philadelphia: John Benjamins, 1989.
Mellors, John. "Dreams in War—Second Thoughts on Elizabeth Bowen." *London Magazine* 19 (1979): 64–69.
Mitchell, Edward. "Themes in Elizabeth Bowen's Short Stories." *Critique: Studies in Modern Fiction* 8 (Spring–Summer 1966): 41–54.
Monaghan, Charles. "Portrait of a Woman Reading: Elizabeth Bowen." *Chicago Tribune Book World*, November 10, 1968, 6.
Moore, Reginald, and Woodrow Wyatt, eds. *Stories of the Forties*. London: Nicholson and Watson, 1945.
Mowatt, Charles Loch. *Britain between the Wars, 1918–1940*. London: University of Chicago Press, 1955.
Moynahan, Julian. "Elizabeth Bowen, Anglo-Irish Post-Mortem." *Raritan* 10 (Fall 1989): 68–88.
Morris, Alice S. "Miss Bowen Illuminates the Landscape of War." Review of *The Heat of the Day*. *New York Times Book Review*, February 20, 1949, 1, 25.
Moss, Howard. "Elizabeth Bowen." *New York Times Book Review*, April 8, 1973, 2–3.

———. "Review of Victoria Glendinning's *Elizabeth Bowen*." *New Yorker*, February 5, 1979, 121–28.
Munton, Alan. *English Fiction of the Second World War*. London: Faber and Faber, 1989.
Murphy, John A. *Ireland in the Twentieth Century*. Dublin: Gill and Macmillan, 1975.
Newby, P. H. *The Novel: 1945–1950*. London: Longmans, Green, 1951.
Nicolson, Harold. *Harold Nicolson, The War Years, 1939–1945, Diaries and Letters*. Vol. 2. Ed. Nigel Nicolson. New York: Atheneum, 1967.
Noble, Joan Russell, ed. *Recollections of Virginia Woolf*. London: Peter Owen, 1972.
North, Michael. *Henry Green and the Writing of His Generation*. Charlottesville: University Press of Virginia, 1984.
Nowlan, K. B., and T. Desmond Williams, eds. *Ireland in the War Years and After*. Dublin: Gill and Macmillan, 1969.
O'Faoláin, Seán. *The Irish: A Character Study*. New York: Devin-Adair, 1949.
———. *An Irish Journey*. London: Longmans, Green, 1941.
———. *The Short Story*. New York: Devin-Adair, 1951.
———. *The Vanishing Hero: Studies in Novelists of the Twenties*. Boston: Little, Brown, 1956.
———. "A Reading and Remembrance of Elizabeth Bowen." *London Review of Books*, March 4–17, 1982, 15–16.
———. "New Novels." Review of *The Heat of the Day*. *Listener* 41 (February, 1949): 331.
Onions, John. *English Fiction and Drama of the First World War, 1918–1939*. London: Macmillan, 1990.
Orwell, George. *As I Please*. Vol. 3. London: Secker and Warburg, 1968.
———. *Inside the Whale and Other Essays*. London: Gollancz, 1940.
———. *The War Commentaries*. Ed. W. J. West. New York: Pantheon Books, 1985.
O'Toole, Bridget. "Three Writers of the Big House: Elizabeth Bowen, Molly Keane, and Jennifer Johnston." In *Across a Roaring Hill: The Protestant Imagination in Modern Ireland*. Ed. Gerald Dawe and Edna Longley, 124–38. Belfast: Blackstaff Press, 1985.
Page, Martin, ed. *"Kiss Me Goodnight...": The Songs and Ballads of World War II*. London: Granada, 1975.
Panichas, George A., ed. *Promise of Greatness: The War of 1914–1918*. London: Cassell, 1968.
Panter-Downes, Mollie. *London War Notes*. Ed. William Shawn. New York: Farrar, Straus and Giroux, 1971.
———. *One Fine Day*. London: Virago Press, 1985.
Parfitt, George. *Fiction of the First World War: A Study*. London: Faber and Faber, 1988.
Parrish, Paul. "Loss of Eden: Four Novels of Elizabeth Bowen." *Critique: Studies in Modern Fiction* 15 (1973): 86–100.

Partridge, A. C. *Language and Society in Anglo-Irish Literature.* Totowa, N.J.: Barnes and Noble, 1984.

———. "Language and Identity in the Shorter Fiction of Elizabeth Bowen." In *Irish Writers and Society at Large.* Ed. Masaru Sekine, 169–80. London and Totowa, N. J.: Vision/ Barnes and Noble, 1985.

Pierson, Ruth Roach. "'Did Your Mother Wear Army Boots?': Feminist Theory and Women's Relation to War, Peace and Revolutions." In *Images of Women in Peace and War: Cross-Cultural and Historical Perspectives.* Ed. Sharon Macdonald, Pat Holden, and Shirley Ardener, 205–27. Houndsmill, Basingstoke: Macmillan Education, 1987.

Plomer, William. *The Autobiography of William Plomer.* London: Jonathan Cape, 1975.

Powell, Anthony. *To Keep the Ball Rolling: The Memoirs of Anthony Powell.* Vol. 3: *Faces in My Time.* London: Heinemann, 1980.

———. Review of *A World of Love. Punch,* March 9, 1955, 327.

Prescott, Orville. *In My Opinion: An Inquiry into the Contemporary Novel.* New York: Bobbs-Merrill, 1952.

———. Review of *Ivy Gripped the Steps. Yale Review* 35 (Summer 1946): 766.

Priestley, J. B. *Literature and Western Man.* New York: Harper and Brothers, 1960.

———. *Postscripts, 1940.* London: Heinemann, 1940.

Pritchett, V. S. *A Cab at the Door and Midnight Oil.* Harmondsworth, Middlesex: Penguin, 1986.

———. *In My Good Books.* London: Chatto and Windus, 1943.

———. *The Novel since 1939.* London: Longmans, Green, 1946.

———. "Bowen's Inner Lives." *Vogue,* March, 1981, 328–62.

———. "Elizabeth Bowen." *New Statesman,* March 9, 1973, 350.

———. "The Future of Fiction?" *New Writing and Daylight* 7 (1946): 75–81.

Pryce-Jones, David, ed. *Evelyn Waugh and His World.* London: Weidenfeld and Nicolson, 1973.

Quennell, Peter. "The Bowen's Court Way." In *Customs and Characters: Contemporary Portraits,* 86–107. London: Weidenfeld and Nicolson, 1982.

Quinn, Antoinette. "Elizabeth Bowen's Irish Stories: 1939–1945." In *Studies in Anglo-Irish Fiction.* Ed. Heinz Kosok, 314–21. Bonn: Bouvier, 1982.

Reed, Henry. Review of *The Demon Lover. New Statesman,* November 3, 1945, 302–3.

Rees, Goronwy. *A Chapter of Accidents.* London: Chatto and Windus, 1972.

Reilly, Catharine W. *Chaos of the Night.* London: Virago Press, 1984.

Ritchie, Charles. *Diplomatic Passport.* Toronto: Macmillan of Canada, 1981.

———. *The Siren Years.* London: Macmillan, 1974.

Robinson, Lennox. *The Big House.* London: Macmillan, 1926.

Rolo, C. J. Review of *A World of Love. Atlantic,* February, 1955, 84.

Rule, Jane. *Lesbian Images.* New York: Doubleday, 1975.

Rutherford, Andrew. *The Literature of War: Five Studies of Heroic Virtue.* New York: Barnes and Noble, 1978.

Rupp, Richard. "The Post-War Fiction of Elizabeth Bowen." *Xavier University Studies* 4 (1965): 55–67.
Rutherford, Andrew. *Five Studies in Heroic Virtue*. New York: Barnes and Noble, 1978.
Sackville-West, Edward. *Inclinations*. London: Secker and Warburg, 1949.
———. "Interim Epitaph." Review of *Bowen's Court*. *New Statesman,* July 25, 1942, 62–63.
Salmon, Trevor C. *Unneutral Ireland: An Ambivalent and Unique Security Policy*. Oxford: Clarendon, 1989.
Sarton, May. *A World of Light: Portraits and Celebrations*. New York: W. W. Norton, 1976.
Saul, George B. "The Short Stories of Elizabeth Bowen." *Arizona Quarterly* 21 (Spring 1965): 53–59.
Scanlan, Margaret. *Traces of Another Time: History and Politics in Postwar British Fiction*. Princeton: Princeton University Press, 1990.
———. "Rumors of War: Elizabeth Bowen's *The Last September* and J. G. Farrell's *Troubles*." *Eire* 20 (Summer 1985): 70–89.
Schorer, Mark. "With Intellectual Iron." Review of republication of *The Last September*. *New Republic,* November 3, 1953, 18–19.
Sears, Sallie. "Theater of War: Virginia Woolf's *Between the Acts*." In *Virginia Woolf: A Feminist Slant*. Ed. Jane Marcus, 212–35. Lincoln: University of Nebraska Press, 1983.
Seward, Barbara. "Elizabeth Bowen's World of Impoverished Love." *College English* 18 (October, 1956): 30–37.
Share, Bernard. *The Emergency: Neutral Ireland, 1939–1945*. Dublin: Gill and Macmillan, 1978.
Sharp, Sister M. Corona. "The House as Setting and Symbol in Three Elizabeth Bowen Novels." *Xavier University Studies* 2 (December, 1963): 93–103.
Shelden, Michael. *Friends of Promise: Cyril Connolly and the World of Horizon*. London: Hamish Hamilton, 1989.
Silver, Brenda R. "*Three Guineas* Before and After: Further Answers to Correspondents." In *Virginia Woolf: A Feminist Slant*. Ed. Jane Marcus, 254–76. Lincoln: University of Nebraska Press, 1983.
Sitwell, Osbert. *Left Hand, Right Hand! Vol. 1: The Cruel Month*. 1945. Reprint. London: Macmillan, 1949.
———. *Left Hand, Right Hand! Vol. 2: The Scarlet Tree*. 1946. Reprint. New York: Quartet Books, 1977.
Smith, Harold L. "The Effect of the War on the Status of Women." In *War and Social Change*. Ed. Harold L. Smith, 208–29. Manchester: Manchester University Press, 1986.
———, ed. *War and Social Change*. Manchester: Manchester University Press, 1986.
Somerville, Edith, and Martin Ross. *The Big House of Inver*. London: Heinemann, 1925.
Spender, Stephen. *The Thirties and After*. New York: Random House, 1967.
———. *World within World*. New York: Harcourt, Brace, and Company, 1948.

———. "Books and the War: The Short Story Today." *Penguin New Writing* 5 (April, 1941): 131–42.
———. "Books and the War: Time, Violence, and Macbeth." *Penguin New Writing* 3 (February, 1941): 115–26.
———. "Books and the War: Tragedy and Some Modern Poetry." *Penguin New Writing* 4 (March, 1941): 138–50.
Stanford, Derek. *Inside the Thirties*. London: Sidgwick and Jackson, 1977.
Stevens, Wallace. *The Necessary Angel*. New York: Alfred Knopf, 1951.
Stevenson, Randall. *The British Novel since the Thirties*. Athens: University of Georgia Press, 1986.
Stokes, Edward. "Elizabeth Bowen—Pre-Assumptions or Moral Angle?" *Journal of Australasian Universities Language and Literature Association* 11 (September, 1959): 35–47.
Strachey, John. *Digging for Mrs. Miller: Some Experiences of An Air-Raid Warden*. New York: Random House, 1941.
Strange, Joan. *Despatches from the Home Front: The War Diaries of Joan Strange, 1939–1945*. Ed. Chris McCooey. Eastbourne, E. Sussex: Monarch Publications, 1989.
Strickenhausen, Harry. "Elizabeth Bowen and Reality." *Sewanee Review* 73 (Winter 1965): 158–65.
Strong, L. A. G. "Elizabeth Bowen." *Personal Remarks*. New York: Liveright, 1953.
Suleiman, Susan Rubin, ed. *The Female Body in Western Culture*. Cambridge: Harvard University Press, 1986.
Sullivan, Walter. "A Sense of Place: Elizabeth Bowen and the Landscape of the Heart." *Sewanee Review* 84 (1976): 142–49.
Summerfield, Penny. *Women Workers in the Second World War*. London: Croom Helm, 1984.
———. "The 'Levelling of Class.'" In *War and Social Change*. Ed. Harold L. Smith, 179–207. Manchester: Manchester University Press, 1986.
———. "Women, War and Social Change: Women in Britain in World War II." In *Total War and Social Change*. Ed. Arthur Marwick, 95–118. London: Macmillan, 1988.
Summers, Anne. *Angels and Citizens: British Women as Military Nurses, 1854–1914*. London: Routledge and Kegan Paul, 1988.
Swinden, Patrick. *The English Novel of History and Society, 1940–1980*. London: Macmillan, 1984.
Taylor, Elizabeth. Review of *Eva Trout, or Changing Scenes*. *New Statesman*, January 24, 1969, 119.
Tomalin, Claire. "A Woman of the World." Review of *Elizabeth Bowen: Portrait of a Writer*, by Victoria Glendinning. *Sunday Times* (London), October 9, 1977, 40
Toynbee, Philip. "Elizabeth Bowen." *Observer*, February 25, 1973, 36.
Tracy, Robert. "Laying the Ghost: Elizabeth Bowen's *A World of Love*." Paper given at the Modern Language Association Meeting, December, 1988.

Trevor, William. "Between Holyhead and Dun Laoghaire." *Times Literary Supplement,* February 6, 1981, 4062, 4131.
Trilling, Diana. Review of *The Heat of the Day. Nation,* February 26, 1949, 254–56.
———. Review of *Ivy Gripped the Steps. Nation,* April 20, 1946, 484–86.
Tylee, Claire M. *The Great War and Women's Consciousness: Images of Militarism and Womanhood in Women's Writings, 1914–1964.* London: Macmillan, 1990.
Van Duyn, Mona. "Pattern and Pilgrimage: A Reading of *The Death of the Heart.*" *Critique: Studies in Modern Fiction* 4 (Spring–Summer 1961): 52–66.
Wagner, Geoffrey. "Elizabeth Bowen and the Artificial Novel." *Essays in Criticism* 13 (April, 1963): 155–63.
Watson, Barbara Bellow. "Variations on an Enigma: Elizabeth Bowen's War Novel." *Southern Humanities Review* 15 (Spring 1981): 131–51; reprinted in *Elizabeth Bowen,* ed. Harold Bloom (New York: Chelsea House, 1987).
Waugh, Evelyn. *Put Out More Flags.* 1942. Reprint. Boston: Little, Brown, 1970.
———. *The Diaries of Evelyn Waugh.* Ed. Michael Davie. Boston: Little, Brown, 1976.
Weatherhead, A. Kingsley. "Elizabeth Bowen: Writer in Residence." *CEA Critic* 50 (Winter 1987–Summer 1988): 35–44.
Wedgewood, Dame Veronica. Supplementary letter about the obituary of Elizabeth Bowen. *Times* (London), February 27, 1973, 16.
Weekes, Ann Owen. *Irish Women Writers: An Uncharted Tradition.* Lexington: University Press of Kentucky, 1990.
Welty, Eudora. "Seventy-nine Stories to Read Again." Review of *The Collected Stories of Elizabeth Bowen. New York Times Book Review,* February 8, 1981, 3, 22.
White, Terence de Vere. *The Anglo-Irish.* London: Gollancz, 1972.
Williams, Raymond. *The Long Revolution.* London: Chatto and Windus, 1961.
———. "Realism and the Contemporary Novel." *Partisan Review* 26 (Spring 1959): 200–213.
Wilson, Angus. "Evil in the English Novel." *Listener* 44 (1950): 279–80.
Wilson, Edmund. "Notes on London at the End of the War." In *Europe without Baedecker,* 3–37. New York: Farrar, Straus and Giroux, 1947.
Wilson, Elizabeth. *Only Halfway to Paradise: Women in Postwar Britain, 1945–1968.* London: Tavistock, 1980.
Wilson, Trevor. *The Myriad Faces of War.* London: Macmillan, 1987.
Wohl, Robert. *The Generation of 1914.* Cambridge: Harvard University Press, 1979.
Wolle, Francis. "Novels of the Two World Wars." *Western Humanities Review* 4 (Summer 1951): 279–90.
Woolf, Leonard. *The Journey Not the Arrival Matters: Autobiography of the Years 1939–1969.* London: Hogarth Press, 1969.
Woolf, Virginia. *Between the Acts.* 1941. Reprint. New York: Harcourt Brace Jovanovich, 1969.
———. *The Diary of Virginia Woolf.* Vol. 4 (1931–35). Ed. Anne Oliver Bell. New York: Harcourt Brace Jovanovich, 1982.

———. *The Diary of Virginia Woolf.* Vol. 5 (1936–41). Ed. Anne Oliver Bell. London: Hogarth Press, 1984.
———. *The Letters of Virginia Woolf.* Vol. 4 (1931–35). Ed. Nigel Nicolson and Joanne Trautman. New York: Harcourt Brace Jovanovich, 1979.
———. *The Moment and Other Essays.* Ed. Leonard Woolf. New York: Harcourt Brace Jovanovich, 1948.
———. *A Room of One's Own.* 1929. Reprint. New York: Harcourt Brace Jovanovich, 1981.
———. *Three Guineas.* 1938. Reprint. London: Hogarth Press, 1952.
———. "The Leaning Tower." In *The Moment and Other Essays.* Ed. Leonard Woolf, 128–54. New York: Harcourt Brace, 1948.
———. "Thoughts on Peace during an Air Raid." In *The Death of the Moth and Other Essays,* 154–57. London: Hogarth Press, 1942.
A World of Love. Review. *Times* (London), March 3, 1955, 11.
A World of Love. Review. *Times Literary Supplement,* March 4, 1955, 132.
Wright, Gordon. *The Ordeal of Total War, 1939–1945.* New York: Harper, 1968.
Wyndam, Francis. "Twenty-Five Years of the Novel." In *The Craft of Letters.* Ed. John Lehmann, 44–59. London: Cresset Press, 1956.
Yeats, William Butler. *The Poems: A New Edition.* Ed. Richard J. Finneran. New York: Macmillan, 1983.
Young, Vernon. "Hell on Earth." Review of *The Heat of the Day. Hudson Review* 11 (Summer 1949): 311–18.
Younger, Carlton. *Ireland's Civil War.* New York: Taplinger, 1969.
Zwerdling, Alex. *Virginia Woolf and the Real World.* Berkeley: University of California Press, 1986.

Unpublished Doctoral Dissertations

Davenport, Gary Tolleson. "Four Irish Writers in Time of Civil War: Liam O'Flaherty, Frank O'Connor, Sean O'Faolain, and Elizabeth Bowen." University of South Carolina, 1971.
Kirkpatrick, Larry James. "Elizabeth Bowen and Company: A Comparative Essay in Literary Judgment." Duke University, 1965.
Lassner, Phyllis. "The Myth of the Ancestral Home: A Study of the Novels of Elizabeth Bowen." Wayne State University, 1983.
McDowell, Alfred B. "Identity and the Past: Major Themes in the Fiction of Elizabeth Bowen." Bowling Green State University, 1972.
Rupp, Richard. "The Achievement of Elizabeth Bowen." Indiana University, 1963.
Stern, Joan Oberwager. "A Study of Problems in Values and the Means by Which They Are Presented in the Novels of Elizabeth Bowen." New York University, 1974.
Wheeler, Ann Marie. "Shape and Shapelessness: The Symbolic Function of Setting in the Novels of Elizabeth Bowen." Vanderbilt University, 1984.

Index

Allen, Walter, 10, 221n.13, 226n.40
Arnold, Matthew, 8
Asquith, Cynthia, 35, 178
Auden, W. H., 88, 89, 110, 144, 215n.15
Austen, Jane, 1, 69, 113

Bate, Walter Jackson, 86
Bates, H. E., 88
Bell (Dublin), 101, 113, 140, 155, 156, 219n.70
Bergonzi, Bernard, 20, 201n.21
Betjeman, John, 88, 98, 100–101
Big House (Anglo-Irish residence), ix, x, 6, 8, 42, 47–59, 61, 62, 72, 73, 75, 78, 107–28, 142, 160, 161, 173, 175, 180–81, 204n.9, 222n.41. *See also* Bowen's Court
Blunden, Edmund, 20
Blythe, Ronald, 10, 89
Bogan, Louise, 142
Books and reading in World War II, 86–90, 114, 169–70, 207n.18
Bowen, Elizabeth: childhood and upbringing, x ff; education, xiii; home see Bowen's Court; husband see Cameron, Alan; marriage, 31; teaching at Vassar, 131, 134, 179; teaching at University of Wisconsin, 179; work for BBC, 13; work during World War II, 95–96; work for Ministry of Information, x, 8, 98–104, 124, 140, 141, 142, 146, 155, 156, 171, 210n.93, 210n.100, 210n.106, 219n.87
Bowen, Elizabeth, short stories of, 31–45, 129–51, 214n.3, 215n.9, 218n.62
Bowen, Elizabeth, works of: *Afterthought: Pieces about Writing,* 174; *Ann Lee's and Other Stories,* 29, 33; "Anthony Trollope—A New Judgement," 109, 212n.16; "Attractive Modern Homes," 78, 215n.15; "Aunt Tatty," 15–16; "Autobiography," 212n.16; "The Back Drawing-Room," 42–43; "The Beginning of this Day," 148; "The Bend Back," 112; "The Big House," 113; *Bowen's Court,* 9, 54, 58, 59, 75, 107–28, 130, 161, 173, 174, 181, 187, 212n.24, 213n.39, 214n.47, 214n.54, 222n.41; "Candles in the Window," 215n.9; "Careless Talk," 148, 219n.87; *Castle Anna,* 113; "The Cat Jumps," 79; *The Cat Jumps and Other Stories,* 64; "Charity," 29; "The Cheery Soul," 132, 148, 219n.85; "The Claimant," 178, 215n.9; "Coming Home," 32; "The Cult of Nostalgia," 174; "Daffodils," 34; "A Day in the Dark," 215n.9; *A Day in the Dark and Other Stories,* 141; *The Death of the Heart,*

249

16, 26–27, 64, 66, 67, 71, 79, 80–81, 122, 127, 130, 153, 155, 166, 168, 189, 226n.38; "The Demon Lover," 10, 51, 132, 133, 134, 177, 216n.27, 217n.30; *The Demon Lover,* 130, 135, 178, 214n.3; "The Disinherited," 26, 69, 72–73, 76, 78; "Downe House," xiii; "Eire," 141; "Emergency in the Gothic Wing," 178, 215n.9; *Encounters,* 31, 34, 43, 215n.14; "Enemies of Charm in Women, in Men," 179; *Eva Trout, or Changing Scenes,* 182, 184–89, 228n.79; "Everything's Frightfully Interesting," 148; "Firelight in the Flat," 15; "First Writing," 175; "Folkestone," 171; "Foothold," 36; *Friends and Relations,* 13, 16, 63, 67, 68, 69, 78, 155, 226n.38; "Gone Away," 215n.9; "Green Holly," 132, 148, 219n.85, n.87; "Hand in Glove," 172, 215n.9; "Happiness," 215n.9; "The Happy Autumn Fields," 132, 139, 140, 141, 218n.57; *The Heat of the Day,* xii, 3, 5, 7, 9, 11, 13, 14, 18, 21, 27, 37, 48, 52, 67, 72, 76, 80, 97, 109, 129, 130, 151, 153–68, 169, 170, 176, 184, 187, 188, 189, 203n.1, 221n.13, 222n.27, 222n.41, 223n.44, 223n.45; "Home for Christmas," 180; *The Hotel,* 9, 13, 14, 23–26, 27, 29, 30, 33, 35, 39–42, 44–45, 48, 68, 141; *The House in Paris,* 5, 9, 13, 21–22, 27, 29, 62, 64, 67, 70, 71, 73–78, 125, 135, 174, 189, 226n.38; "How to Be Yourself, But Not Eccentric," 64, 175; "Human Habitation," 42; "I Died of Love," 215n.9; "I Hear You Say So," 150, 170; "The Inherited Clock," 132, 146, 176; "In the Square," 135–38; "Ireland Makes Irish," 180; "Ivy Gripped the Steps," 29, 132, 146–47, 176, 183, 219n.82; *Ivy Gripped the Steps,* 130, 134; "Joining Charles," 37, 43; *Joining Charles and Other Stories,* 34;

"The Last Bus," 148; "The Last Night in the Old Home," 27–28, 79; *The Last September,* xvi, 9, 13, 15, 21, 33, 45, 47–59, 61, 64, 66, 68, 75, 80, 110, 119, 120, 125, 135, 153, 163, 173, 175, 176, 203n.1, 223n.44; "The Light in the Dark," 180, 215n.9; *The Little Girls,* 174, 182–84, 185; "London, 1940," 217n.41; *Look at All Those Roses,* 130, 144, 215n.15; "A Love Story: 1939," 141, 142; "Maria," 71; "The Most Unforgettable Character I've Met," 212n.29; "Mrs. Windemere," 34; "Mysterious Kor," 10, 132, 139; "The New House," 43–44; "The Next Book," 154; "Oh, Madam...," 91, 134, 138–39, 166; *The Move-In,* 190; "Opening up the House," 170; "The Parrot," 38–39, 43; *Pictures and Conversations,* 189, 190; "Pink May," 10, 132; "A Queer Heart," 79; "Recent Photograph," 35; "Requiescat," 37; "The Same Way Home," 79; *Seven Winters* (also *Seven Winters and Afterthoughts*), 9, 112, 174; *The Shelbourne Hotel,* 14, 47, 173; "The Short Story in England," 151; "So Much Depends," 215n.9; "Songs My Father Sang Me," 150; "Summer Night," 69, 141, 142, 143–46, 186; "Sunday Afternoon," 141, 142–43, 144, 146, 177, 186, 206n.37, 219n.70; "Tears, Idle Tears," 28; "Telling," 35–36; *A Time in Rome,* 173; "Tipperary Woman," 113, 212n.29; *To the North,* 5, 13, 15, 22–23, 41, 63, 67–73, 75, 111, 184; "The Tommy Crans," 28–29; "Uncle Silas," 212n.23; "Unwelcome Idea," 141, 142; "A Walk in the Woods," 78; "Weeping Earl," 211n.13; "Women's Place in the Affairs of Men," xvi; "The Working Party," 36; *A World of Love,* 30, 173, 175–78, 180, 183, 185, 186, 188, 189, 226n.38, 226n.44; *A Year I Remember*—1918, 13, 14, 18, 20

Index

Bowen's court, xi, 8, 32, 62–63, 66, 98, 170, 171, 172, 180–81, 183, 186, 226n.43, 227n.65. *See also Bowen's Court*
Bowra, C. M., 32
Brittain, Vera, 20, 94, 108, 201n.21
Brown, Spencer Curtis, 190
Browning, Robert, 189
Buchan, William, 137
Burgess, Anthony, 221n.11
Burgess, Guy, 155
Burke, Edmund, xii, 61, 62, 108, 110, 121, 159, 170, 181, 185, 203n.1, 210n.96, 225n.30

Cameron, Alan, xiv, 31, 32, 42, 170, 171
Cecil, David, 32, 180
Chekhov, Anton, 131
Children and childlessness, 28–29, 61, 71, 161, 181, 182, 186, 189, 227n.47, 227n.75
Churchill, Winston, 100, 148, 170, 171
Cobb, Richard, 9,
Coles, Robert, 196n.26
Connolly, Cyril, xiv, 6, 7, 8, 11, 61, 64, 83, 86, 88–89, 90, 92, 99, 154, 171, 180, 211n.6, 211n.8
Cornhill, 63, 88
Cranborne, Lord, 100, 103, 104
Criterion, 88
Cromwell, Oliver, 112
cummings, e. e., 66

Deane, Seamus, xii, 176, 214n.46, 228n.85
Delafield, E. M., 4
de la Roche, Mazo, 88
de Valera, Eamon, 98, 99–100
de Vries, Peter, x
Dickens, Charles, 188
Dillon, James, 101
Drabble, Margaret, 228n.79

Easter Rising, 1916, 53
Eliot, T. S., 11, 64, 95, 113, 114

Empson, William, 88
English Story, 130

Faber Book of Modern Stories, The, 131
Feminism, Bowen's attitudes toward, ix, xv–xvi, 3, 197n.35
Flaubert, Gustave, 131
Forster, E. M., 173
Foster, R. F., xii, 62, 126, 210n.93
Fougasse (Cyril Kenneth Byrd), 148
Fussell, Paul, 7, 8, 86, 113, 165, 200n.3, 207n.19, 207n.34, 208n.38, 211n.116, 213n.32, 220n.90

Galsworthy, John, 88
George, Daniel, 165
Ghosts and supernaturalism, ix, x, 36, 130, 132, 139, 177, 178
Gilbert, Sandra, 21, 217n.30
Gill, Brendan, 223n.51
Glendinning, Victoria, xi, 196n.26, 214n.3, 218n.62, 226n.43, 227n.75
Goldsmith, Margaret, 4
Gollancz, Victor, 144
Graves, Robert, 20, 87
Green, Henry, 89, 108
Greene, Graham, 2, 11, 63, 64, 89, 91, 98, 131, 212n.27

Haggard, H. Rider, 218n.53
Halifax, Earl of, 100, 104
Hardwick, Elizabeth, 196n.26, 221n.23
Hardy, Thomas, ix
Hartley, L. P., 7, 8, 14, 64, 112, 172, 175, 179, 221n.23, 226n.37
Hayward, John, 11, 113, 114, 157, 211n.6
Hodgson, Vere, 83–84, 85, 90, 91, 92, 104
Holtby, Winifred, 4
Hone, Joseph, 112
Hopkins, Gerard, 176
Horizon, 88–89, 99, 130, 207n.31, 207n.34, 208n.38

Huxley, Aldous, 131
Hynes, Samuel, 211n.8, 219n.73

Irish Civil War, xiii, 6, 9, 125, 173
Isherwood, Christopher, 18, 85, 91, 211n.8

James, Alice Runnells, 32
James, Henry, xv, 87, 188
Jameson, Storm, 4
Joyce, James, 131–32

Kermode, Frank, 155
Kipling, Rudyard, 88, 131
Knopf, Alfred and Blanche, 180, 181

Lawrence, D. H., 131, 144, 145, 188
Lee, Hermione, 120, 196n.26, 197n.2, 203n.1 (2), 210n.96, 212n.23, 214n.54, 214n.3, 218n.57, 219n.87, 221n.13, 221n.15, 221n.19, 222n.36, 223n.51, 225n.23, 225n.30, 226n.38
Lee, Laurie, 98
Le Fanu, Sheridan, 111, 212n.23
Lehmann, John, xiv, 11, 64, 83, 84, 85, 86, 87, 89, 90, 91, 92, 93, 94, 98, 101, 104, 108, 171
Lehmann, Rosamond, xiv, 4, 64, 154, 155, 156, 173, 176, 221n.8
Lewis, C. Day, 89, 98, 110
London Mercury, 88
Lyons, F. S. L., xii

Macaulay, Rose, 4, 31, 201n.21
Maclaren-Ross, Julian, 88, 89
MacNeice, Louis, 88, 89, 108
Maugham, Somerset, 131
Maupassant, Guy de, 131
Mayor, F. M., 4
Mitchelstown Castle, xiii, 16, 119
Mitford, Nancy, 87, 170
Moore, George, 213n.36
Moore, Henry, 90
Morley, Frank, 113
Mortimer, Raymond, 176

Moss, Howard, xii, 196n.26, 211n.12, 219n.82, 226n.38
Murdoch, Iris, 171, 196n.26

New Statesman and Nation, 63
New Verse, 88
New Writing and Daylight, 130
New Yorker, 136
Nicolson, Harold, 97, 122, 162
Night and Day 63
"Nightingale Sang in Berkeley Square, A," 150

O'Connor, Frank, 131
O'Faoláin, Seán, xiv, 43, 63, 101, 108, 131, 141
O'Flaherty, Liam, 131
Orczy, Baroness, 2
Orion, 130
Orwell, George, 88, 89, 218n.47

P.E.N., 172
Panter-Downes, Mollie, 136, 150
Penguin New Writing, 89, 101, 130, 208n.38
Plomer, William, 51, 64, 66, 100, 131, 156, 170, 171, 175, 179, 182, 190, 211n.6
Powell, Anthony, 64, 87, 104, 105, 170, 227n.47
Priestly, J. B., 87, 95, 108
Pritchett, V. S., xiv, 2, 64, 88, 89, 130, 131, 141, 215n.14
Property, Bowen's understanding of, 61–63, 72–73, 78–79. *See also* Burke, Edmund

Queen Elizabeth II, 179
Quennell, Peter, 31, 155

Race, Bowen's understanding of, ix, xii, 8, 62, 64, 74, 75, 112, 119, 159, 172, 177, 205n.5
Ransome, Arthur, 88
Read, Herbert, 88, 211n.6
Reed, Henry, 130, 148, 220n.98

Index 253

Rees, Goronwy, 11, 155
Richardson, Dorothy, 4
Ritchie, Charles, 97, 104, 137, 140, 154, 155, 156, 158, 159, 179, 184, 190
Rothenstein, Sir William, 153
Rutherford, Andrew, 20

Sackville-West, Edward, 212 n.24
Sackville-West, Vita, 97
Sarton, May, 226 n.38
Sartre, Jean-Paul, 89
Sassoon, Siegfried, 20, 211 n.6
Scott, Sir Walter, 1
Shakespeare, William, 23
Shaw, George Bernard, 9, 87
Shaw, Irwin, 134
Showalter, Elaine, 30
Sidgwick, Frank, 31
Sinn Féin, 56, 58
Sitwell, Osbert, 87, 108, 211 n.6
Spark, Muriel, 196 n.26
Spectator, 63
Spender, Stephen, xiv, 88, 89, 97, 110, 212 n.27, 215 n.14
Stephenson, William, 213 n.32
Stevens, Wallace, 132–33

Tables and chairs, permanence of, 140
Tatler, 63
Taylor, A. J. P., 136
Taylor, Elizabeth, 154
Thomas, Dylan, 88, 89
Trevelyan, G. M., 87
Trollope, Anthony, 87, 109–10
Troubles, The (Anglo-Irish war), x, 6, 9, 43, 47–59, 125, 128, 173
Twentieth-Century Verse, 88

Upward, Edward, 211 n.8

Walpole, Hugh, 88
Walsh, Joe, 102
Watson, Victor William, 88
Waugh, Evelyn, 11, 84, 85, 87, 88, 90, 91, 93, 98, 104–5, 170, 171, 180, 211 n.116, 213 n.41
Welles, H. G., 87
Welty, Eudora, 132, 171, 180, 217 n.40
West, Rebecca, 4
Wilde, Oscar, 9
Wilson, Edmund, 169
Women and World War I, 19–21, 27–28, 39–40
Women and World War II, 4, 96–97, 209 n.72, 209 n.75, 224 n.59
Woolf, Virginia, x, xiv, 1, 3, 4, 6, 9, 11, 31, 48, 63, 64, 67, 80, 83, 84, 85, 88, 90, 91, 94, 99, 100, 103, 107, 108, 110–11, 114, 115, 119, 124, 135, 140, 144, 164, 180, 191, 196 n.26, 201 n.21
Woolf, Virginia, works of: "The Artist and Politics," 67; *Between the Acts*, 80; "The Leaning Tower," 110–11; *Mrs. Dalloway*, 201 n.21; *A Room of One's Own*, 31, 191; "A Sketch of the Past," 108; *Three Guineas*, 3, 115, 119, 164; *The Waves*, 48
World War I, x, xiii, 6–12, 13–30, 36, 47, 67, 169, 173, 175
World War II, x, xiv, 1–12, 14, 17, 64, 81, 83–106, 120, 125, 129–68, 169–171, 221 n.11

Yeats, William Butler, 8, 9, 53, 66, 115, 213 n.36